WHEN
GENERATIONS
COLLIDE

WHEN GENERATIONS COLLIDE

Who They Are. Why They Clash.
How to Solve the Generational Puzzle at Work.

LYNNE C. LANCASTER and DAVID STILLMAN

HarperBusiness

An Imprint of HarperCollins*Publishers*

HarperCollins books may be purchased for educational, business, or sales promotional use. For information please write to: Special Markets Department, HarperCollins Publishers Inc., 10 East 53rd Street, New York, New York 10022.

When Generations Collide™ and ClashPoints™ are registered trademarks of BridgeWorks™ LLC.

Designed by William Ruoto

Library of Congress Cataloging-in-Publication Data

Lancaster, Lynne.
When generations collide : who they are. why they clash. how to solve the generational puzzle at work. / by Lynne Lancaster & David Stillman.
p.   cm.
Includes bibliographical references and index.
ISBN 0-06-662106-2 (alk. paper)
1. Diversity in the workplace—United States.   2. Age groups—United States.
3. Conflict of generations—United States.   4. Intergenerational relations—United States.   5. Supervision of employees.   I. Stillman, David.   II. Title.

HF5549.5.M5 L36   2002
658.3'0084—dc21   2001039221

02   03   04   05   06   RRD   10   9   8   7   6   5   4   3

We dedicate this book to our spouses, Allan and Sharon. Without your love, patience, and wisdom we could not achieve our dreams.
We also dedicate this book to each other. Without experiencing it ourselves, we never would have known what it takes for the generations to collide and click the way we have.

ACKNOWLEDGMENTS

It's Friday, May 5, 2000, and David is on a trip with his wife in New York City. His cell phone rings and it's Lynne, calling to tell him great news: "HarperCollins is interested in our book and wants to meet with you while you're there!" Needless to say, we are thrilled.

The appointment is set for three P.M., and by two-thirty David is dressed and ready to go. One slight problem. It is ninety-five degrees outside, and all traffic in Manhattan is at a standstill because it is the day of Cardinal O'Connor's memorial. Getting a cab is out of the question, so David takes off on a twenty-five-block jog. He finally arrives at HarperCollins, puffing and sweating profusely, but with a couple of minutes to spare. David announces himself and leans over to sign the visitor pad. When the security guard notices sweat streaming down and pooling on the sign-in sheet, he suggests that David hold on a minute before going up to meet the "big guys." He takes David into the back room, stands him in front of a construction-site-size fan, and throws the switch to power it to "high" to dry David off. Five minutes later, David emerges looking dry, professional, and ready for the meeting.

That meeting was the first of what has turned out to be a wonderful relationship with HarperCollins. Although we never got his name, we want to thank the security guard for looking out for us on that first day. He set the tone for all of our relationships at Harper-Collins, and they have looked out for us every step of the way.

To Edwin Tan, our editor. We couldn't have asked for a better match. Your grasp of our subject matter and your understanding of the writing process have made you an invaluable mentor, adviser, champion, and friend. We are in awe of your talents and are eternally grateful.

To Adrian Zackheim. You have been a big supporter of generational diversity, and we cannot thank you enough for making this project a reality. It has been an honor.

To Lisa Berkowitz. It is one thing to get the words down on paper, it is another to make sure they get out the door and into the stores. Your ability to understand audiences and how to reach them is not only immensely important, but an often unrecognized piece of the puzzle. We would never be where we are without you.

To Kate Kazeniac, Chin Yee, Sona Vogel, and the Harper sales force. Each of you has played a vital role in this mysterious journey. Thank you for getting excited about the project, giving it your all, and adding your special talents.

To our agent, Sandy Dijkstra. You have gone above and beyond the call of duty numerous times to help us with just the right piece of sage advice at the right moment. You have believed in this project from the get-go and have done an amazing job of keeping us on track. To you, and to Nicole Pitesa and the rest of the crew in your office, we say thank you for being such advocates for the generations, as well as advisers and friends.

To Leslie Keenan. If it weren't for you, we would never have been able to stay sane and, even more important, on schedule. Your insights into the way the mind and the heart work ought to be in a book of their own.

To Susan Page, Dorothy Wall, Roseanne Sullivan, John Gerber, and Bruce Benidt. Thank you for helping us shape the manuscript and for helping us see past our blind spots. Your ability to understand our mission and your sensitive reading of our book are greatly appreciated.

To Beth Leonard, Steve Rubin, and Debbie Orenstein. From nitpicky contract details to big-picture strategies, your counsel is not only needed, but truly cherished. Thanks for making the complex seem so simple.

To Chris Brettingen. One of our biggest goals with this book was to prove that it is not just anecdotal. The research study wasn't an easy one. Thank you for sticking with us and helping us achieve our goal.

To Dennis Anderson, Peter Capell, Terry Danahey, Mike Fiterman, Jan Haeg, Dave Lenzen, Curtis Nelson, Bill Reid, and Billy Weisman. Your companies were among the first to explore how generational differences impact the workplace, and you have always cared about the people side of the profit equation. You truly inspire us.

To David Grossman and the team at Grossman Design. Your ability to graphically represent who we want to be has turned our messages into art. You are all creative geniuses.

To Kris Evans-Bien. You are a networking goddess. Thank you for extending our network and playing such a key role in our success.

To Gary Lindberg. Your insight into training has given our topic true legs. You make a wonderful partner and have taught us so much.

To Tori Janaya. You were there at the beginning, put up with our evolving company, and helped us grow. We will never forget where we started, which means we could never forget all you did.

Last, but perhaps most important, to Deanna Walsh, our fearless and funny program coordinator. You make coming to work every day a dream come true. You bridge gaps in our own workplace and with countless clients. You make our work lives and our personal lives much richer for knowing you. We thank our lucky stars for everything that you are and everything that you do. And we're serious when we say you can't retire until we do!

To Lynne's family and friends. I was lucky enough to have the most wonderful role models growing up, most particularly my very strong and kind grandparents, who first taught me about bridging generation gaps, and my amazing parents, Pat and Herb Lancaster, who taught me about love and everything else. That I can speak, write, think, and laugh is due to them. Dad, we know you watch over us every day in spirit. And Mom, words cannot describe how grateful I am to you for being such an extraordinary person.

Harvey Mackay, after my father you've been my number one mentor. You taught me all sorts of unforgettable things about being successful, the most important of which is that success is really about being a good father, a good husband, a good citizen, and a good friend. "Thank you" doesn't really say it, but you know you have my undying gratitude.

Linda Ferraro and Greg Bailey in Harvey's office. You taught me more about books, publishing, and getting things done than I could have learned in a year of classes. You're both class acts, and Harvey is a lucky man.

To my friends Eunice Jensen and Linda McDonald. You both shared my love of the written word and made me believe I could be a writer. Thank you for every minute of idea-rich conversation and for your faith.

To my sisters, Betsy Foster and Jean Compton. You inspire me constantly with your common sense, kindness, and ability to see through to the heart of things. Thank you for always supporting your sister. You two are the best examples of unconditional love I have in my daily life. Knowing you are there makes me strong.

To Mark Compton and David Foster. You are the brothers I never had. Thank you for making my life so much richer. And Betsy and David, thank you for giving our family four wonderful Millennials to enjoy and discover. Aaron, Nathan, Hannah, and Daniel are truly gifts, and I treasure them.

Bradley and Dan Grosh, my stepsons. I wonder if this book would have ever been written without you. You two were the first Xers in my Boomer life, and you have always been more than willing to say what you think, speak from your heart, and call me on things when you disagreed. I can't tell you how glad I am that you're in my life.

To Allan. You see me for who I am, which is the greatest gift anyone could give another person or another generation. I would not be who I am without your love and guidance. Your wisdom is irreplaceable, as is your great, wonderful, loving heart. As the poem says, "When I read my first romantic story I started dreaming of you." I couldn't have hoped for a better husband or friend.

To David's family and friends. In Judaism there is an expression: *"L'dor va' dor."* It means "From generation to generation." I am so blessed to be able to embrace this phrase, as I come from such a wonderful lineage that has always passed on knowledge, values, and, most of all, endless love. I only wish my grandparents were here to see what they started.

To my parents, Tom and Liba Stillman. You two are the masters at bridging generation gaps. More than being my parents, you are truly my friends. Thank you for giving me your undivided attention and making me feel special always. Everything I am today I owe to you. You have taught me the most important lesson of all—how to love.

To Marty. Not a day goes by that I don't thank God for giving me such a wonderful brother. Our daily calls are like medicine to me, as you always know how to make me laugh and appreciate what's important in life. I am so proud of all of your accomplishments.

To my late brother, Howie. I know how much you dreamed of writing a book, and I share this journey with you. Thank you for being the angel on our shoulder and the daily reminder of just how precious life really is.

To my sisters-in-law, Amy and Debbie; my in-laws, Eunice and Brian; and my nephew, Jacob. Family is everything to me, because each of you proves that no matter what happens, your family will always be there. Thank you for always supporting me.

To my extended family and friends. From e-mails to lining up to buy books, your encouragement and belief in me never go unnoticed, and I wouldn't know what to do without it.

To Mitch Albom. It is very easy as a first-time author to get caught up in best-seller lists, media hits, and more. Thank you for reminding me to keep my eyes on the real prize—bridging generational gaps.

To Jeff Linzer. Thank you for being the unconditional ear I can bend and for making things clearer.

To Mike Fiterman. You are truly my mentor. I have learned so much from you and appreciate your willingness to learn from me. Our relationship is a model for how generational gaps should be bridged.

To Allan Grosh. Thank you for sharing your wisdom and time. So much of my success I owe to you. I learn from you every day, not just about how to run a business, but about how to be a good human being. You are a gift to me, and I treasure our relationship.

To Sharon Stillman. If there is one person who has allowed me to reach my dreams, it is you. And if there is one dream that has come true, it is finding you as my wife. You are my soul mate and best friend. I have loved the journey we have been on and look forward to where we are going. I hope you know how much I appreciate your ability to be a wonderful mother to our children and a true pillar in our relationship. One songwriter put it best: "I love you more today than yesterday, but not as much as tomorrow."

To Ellie and Jonah. I only pray I can prove my expertise in bridging gaps and be as wonderful a parent to you as my parents have been to me. Thank you for being my greatest teachers. You two give me hope that the generations to follow will truly make the world a better place, because one thing is for sure—you make my life worth living.

CONTENTS

FOREWORD

BY HARVEY MACKAY

People go around all their lives and ask, What should I buy? What should I sell? Wrong questions. The right questions are: *When* should I buy? *When* should I sell? In short, timing is everything. And *When Generations Collide* is exceedingly well timed.

With the U.S. economy in flux, there's never been a more important time to be supersavvy at recruiting and retaining the best and the brightest, because they are your greatest assets. Plus, companies that are heavy on Baby Boomers and old grizzlies need to be building bench strength now and for the future.

The information in this book is something every leader or manager needs to know, because at the heart of every company and at the root of everything are people. The generation gap is widening at work, and to be successful, you need to recruit, retain, manage, and motivate people. You need to relate to all generations and bridge the gaps.

I've known Lynne Lancaster professionally for fifteen years. She's served as a valuable resource to me for all five of my books, including *Swim with the Sharks without Being Eaten Alive.* I've spent a zillion hours with her because she's also my speech coach. Her wit, wisdom, and business sense have been invaluable to me. I've gotten to know David Stillman more recently and have been impressed by his smarts, his straight talk, and his perceptive read of people. He is one of the few Generation Xers I know who can relate to all generations at all levels of a company, from the boardroom to the mailroom. Their company, BridgeWorks, has taken off like a rocket. They've helped hundreds of organizations and associations understand the causes of generational clashes and bridge generation gaps to reduce turnover, control costs, improve sales, and boost morale.

Now they've put this valuable information in the book you are holding, subtitled *Who They Are, Why They Clash, and How to Bridge the Gaps at Work*. You'll learn about Traditionalists like myself, Baby Boomers like Lynne, and Generation Xers like David. Plus you'll get the scoop on the Millennials like my grandkids, whom I can't wait to encounter in the workforce.

When Generations Collide is sharp, well researched, funny, and practical. It's loaded with take-home tips and techniques that you can put to use immediately.

For example, many of us don't realize there are now forty-six million Generation Xers in the workforce. Those of us who were relieved to see our Generation X kids leave the nest are shocked to find them sitting across the desk from us. Management has been slow to figure out that its employee base is changing. And everything we didn't learn about managing them before is back to haunt us now.

What do we need to know about Xers? When asked in a recent survey to rank the ten most significant attributes they looked for in a job, Gen Xers ranked compensation seventh out of ten! More significant to them were recognition and praise, opportunities to learn, time spent with mentors, developing marketable skills, and fun at work.

What turns them off? *When Generations Collide* tells us Generation Xers don't like to hear about the past, especially *ours*. They also resent inflexibility in scheduling, being micromanaged, feeling pressured to conform, and being viewed as lazy or unambitious. In other words, a lot of the standard carrot-and-stick approaches to management that worked for the Baby Boomers are a bust with this crowd.

What can we do about it?

Lynne and David tell us to question the way we manage and reward people. Every generation very much wants to succeed. Ask them questions. Listen. Rethink your concept of motivation. Not everyone in the workplace is motivated by the same things anymore. To get the most out of each generation in the workforce, you have to be willing to be more flexible. When managers and companies learn to do this, it will be incredibly rewarding.

I would strongly recommend that you don't just read *When Generations Collide*. I recommend you study it! You'll definitely understand your employees, bosses, and co-workers better; but beyond the workplace, this book holds the key to understanding yourself, your family, and your friends better today and in the years to come.

After all, at the heart of everything are people.

INTRODUCTION

HOW THIS BOOK CAME TO BE

Whenever audiences attend one of our keynote speeches or workshops, one of the first questions we get asked is, "How did you two meet, and how did you end up in a business that focuses on generational differences?" They could see how much we enjoyed each other, they obviously found the eleven-year age difference interesting, but they couldn't quite figure out the nature of our business partnership. That should have been our first clue that intergenerational friendships are a lot less common than you might think.

When we met, Baby Boomer Lynne Lancaster was in her late thirties and had been working for over a decade as a corporate communications consultant and coach to senior executives and CEOs. Her client list was impressive and included work with author and CEO Harvey Mackay that resulted in five *New York Times* bestselling business books.

Generation Xer David Stillman was in his mid-twenties and was working as the creative director for an interactive multimedia company. Because David was doing pioneering work in the field of computer-based training, he had been asked to speak at a CEO conference about what companies should know to prepare for the learning environment of the future.

David's boss had some concerns that the CEOs might be a bit alarmed when presented with a keynote speaker the age of their grandchildren, and he politely suggested—okay, insisted—that David get some speech coaching. He also offered to foot the bill. After a conversation with Lynne, the appointment was made.

HOW THE ISSUES AROSE

At our first meeting, we drove each other nuts. As Lynne gave proven speaking tips and techniques that any Boomer would have been grateful to have, David was skeptical of the tried-and-true approach and pushed to do things his own way. Even though he was her youngest client ever, and she'd been coaching high-level presenters for over a decade, David felt free to question her credentials and challenge her methodology. (We won't even get started on David's ponytail and frayed jeans, other than to say that at one point Lynne furrowed her brow and said, "You do *own* a business suit, don't you?")

Lynne's attempts to get David to come up with a logical outline that began with A and transitioned smoothly to B, and so on, fell flat. Although the idea of the Aristotelian outline had worked superbly since the time of, well, Aristotle, David wanted to structure things his own way and didn't see why the audience wouldn't just go along with it. While Lynne was considering knocking him on the head, David was pulling out his hair at how rigid Lynne seemed and how quick she was to dismiss his suggestions just because he was new at this. Why couldn't he think and create outside the box, and why shouldn't this very senior audience be willing to go along with him? David felt as if he were being coached for the State of the Union address when what he wanted to do was get these executives to loosen up and play Jeopardy. (Of course, it didn't help our connection that Lynne was actually *dressed* for the State of the Union. At one point David furrowed his brow and asked, "Are you even *comfortable* in that?")

Over the course of several meetings, we clashed. At the time, neither one of us would have dreamed that five years later we would be partners in a successful business focused on the generations. (Or that David would become great friends with Lynne's Traditionalist husband, Allan. Or that Lynne and Allan would become godparents to David and Sharon's two children.) But over time, a mutual respect developed. We began to explore the values and beliefs that we shared about work and where they diverged. Gradually we realized that each of us had a compelling perspective and that if we'd had to fight so hard to find common ground, perhaps others were experiencing the same challenge at work.

We'll never forget the defining moment when David delivered his keynote address. Made up of part Boomer logic, persuasion, and protocol and part Gen X irreverence, flash, and fun, the speech proved irresistible to the audience. As David focused on establishing credibility for his points and himself, he acknowledged that Lynne had been right. The Traditionalists and Boomers in the audience started connecting with him better. And as Lynne looked around the room and saw CEOs, CFOs, and COOs having a ball playing an interactive game show that was way outside the realm of the typical presentations they attended, she acknowledged there was definitely more than one way to get from A to Z.

While we were bridging our own generation gap, we were also noticing the generational issues that existed in our respective lines of work. As Lynne continued to coach corporate leaders, she saw that their audience demographics were changing. Many of her clients were now faced with up to four generations in a single room and were becoming more and more unsure of their ability to get their messages across to all of them. The only way to do it was to explore who these generations were and design messages that would connect with them.

As the world of computer-based training expanded, David was colliding with top decision makers who were asking him to design training programs targeted to his peers. But whenever they described the "typical" Generation X audience, David couldn't believe how off the mark they were and how pervasive the stereotypes about his generation seemed to be. He realized that he needed to become an advocate for Gen X, translating their views of the workplace into language and techniques managers could use.

A BUSINESS IS BORN

One thing that came out loud and clear during our discussions was the level of resentment that existed between the generations. Loaded words like "respect," "loyalty," and "fairness" were being tossed around by all the generations, often in angry, accusing tones. For example, we heard Traditionalists complain about how the younger generations expected to be given so much so fast without having to pay their dues. We listened to Boomers complain how they had given years to a company only to be passed over or laid off in favor of younger employees who were more knowledgeable about technology and cost less money. We heard Generation Xers protest how tired they were of being treated like lazy slackers and ask why the other generations didn't seem to like them. We spoke with Millennials who told us they couldn't stand being put in the same category with Generation Xers and wanted to be judged on their own merits. The painful collision points went on and on, and there didn't seem to be too many points of connection. We knew we were on to something.

On January 1, 1997, we started a company called BridgeWorks, whose mission is

> *to bridge the gap between generations by helping people look*
> *beyond their own perspectives to understand the events, conditions,*
> *values, and behaviors that make each generation unique.*

Five years later, not only has our company grown, but so has our understanding of what makes the generations click and collide. We've come to see generational issues as the newest and hottest form of diversity on the business scene today, and we continue to be amazed by how many major business issues, like recruiting, retaining, managing, and motivating employees, are directly affected by generational collisions.

While it's easy to think that generational diversity consists mostly of listening to quaint anecdotes about how another generation did things twenty years ago, in reality it is a burning bottom-line issue for many organizations. We were determined to go beyond the anecdotes and prove its impact. Over the past five years, we have conducted countless small-scale surveys that show how generational differences are getting in the way of companies' success in recruiting employees and, ultimately, retaining and managing them. In 2000 and 2001, we conducted a larger-scale, Web-based survey that involved over four hundred respondents from a range of ethnic backgrounds, from a cross section of industries, and from all parts of the country. The Bridge-Works Generations Survey helped us prove whether many of our hypotheses had merit (some did, some didn't) and to quantify just how different the generations were in their beliefs and behaviors at work. Along with the surveys, we have led numerous focus groups and consulted with companies big and small in all different sectors of the economy. They have shared with us their stories of how generation gaps have caused costly mistakes and what it has taken to bridge them.

In this book, we offer numerous examples of what we call ClashPoints. Like those military "flashpoints" we all hear described on the national news, ClashPoints are those trouble spots where generational conflicts are most likely to explode. We talk about why they arise and what organizations and managers can do to defuse and even capitalize on them.

We based our structure for this book on the areas where we believe companies can derive the biggest "bang for the buck" by addressing intergenerational issues. While it's nice if people get along, it's absolutely essential that they are able to recruit, retain, motivate, and manage one another on a day-to-day basis.

Above and beyond all the tactical solutions included in this book, we believe that learning about generational differences will shed light not only on the individuals sitting across the conference table at work, but also on those individuals sitting across the dinner table at home. We hope you reap the rewards we have in getting to know what happens when the generations collide and what you can do to bridge the gaps.

WHO ARE THE GENERATIONS AND WHY DO THEY COLLIDE?

GENERATIONAL TURBULENCE

"You two do that for a *living?*" asked David's seatmate with a disapproving raise of the eyebrow.

Lynne observed David's reaction from across the aisle and hoped he wouldn't say something flippant. However, recognizing that this was a 3 ½-hour flight and we had just leveled off, David settled down and took a deep, cleansing breath.

The man's name was Paul. He was a craggy, sixty-five-year-old Traditionalist and the CEO of a national warehousing and distribution company. He liked the aisle seat, a vodka and tonic with no ice, and an extra pillow. He was probably wondering what two upstarts like us were doing in first class, but he was too polite to let on. Instead, he kept probing.

"So tell me, what exactly does a 'generational expert' do?" he asked with a patronizing but unmistakably curious tone.

Lynne jumped in: "We help employers and employees understand the differences among the generations, and we coach them in

THE WIDENING GENERATION GAP AT WORK

how to recruit, motivate, manage, and retain the generations more effectively."

As Paul pondered this information, we wondered if he, like so many successful leaders, had ever thought about "generational differences" as one of the fundamental reasons American companies are experiencing hiring challenges, skyrocketing turnover rates, increasing communication conundrums, and plummeting morale. Had he ever recognized that clashes among Traditionalists, Baby Boomers, Generation Xers, and Millennials at work could take a direct toll on his bottom line?

Paul fixed David with a thoughtful gaze. "When I was young, I didn't see eye to eye with my dad. Now my son's in the business and we butt heads all the time. Haven't there always been generational conflicts in the workplace?"

"Sure," David responded. "The generations have always clashed. But the generation gaps in the workplace today are wider than ever and of greater strategic importance. Think about it. Americans are living and working longer. The average life expectancy at birth in the year 1900 was forty-seven. Today it's closing in on eighty. Suddenly, four generations are facing off across the conference table instead of just one or two."

"Okay," Paul replied, "but what's the problem? As I see it, more generations mean more available workers."

"That's a good point," David responded. "But what most people overlook is that each generation brings its own set of values, beliefs, life experiences, and attitudes to the workplace, and *that* can be the problem. Take your generation, the Traditionalists. You grew up under the shadow of the Great Depression and felt lucky to have jobs. If we have learned one thing in our research, it is just how strong Traditionalists' beliefs are when it comes to patriotism, hard work, and respect for leaders, among other values they bring to the workplace."

Paul nodded.

"Now, compare that to my generation," David continued.

Paul eyed David's T-shirt and parachute pants "travel ensemble." "Hmm, and exactly what generation would that be?" he queried with a raised eyebrow.

"Generation X," David responded proudly. "We grew up seeing too many businesses downsize or merge, and we learned that the last thing we could trust was the permanence of the workplace. Let's face it, by the time we hit the job market, the employer-employee contract was already out the window and Social Security was headed down the toilet. And it sure didn't help that we've always been told we would never do as well as our parents had. As a result, we need to be recruited, rewarded, and managed differently from your generation if you hope to make us a contributing, loyal part of your workforce."

Paul turned back to Lynne. "I assume you're an Xer, too?"

"I must admit to actually being a Baby Boomer," she responded, blushing. David rolled his eyes and wanted to grab an airsickness bag.

"So, Boomer, what's your story?" Paul demanded.

"Well," answered Lynne, "My generation is different from yours and David's. When you've had to vie with eighty million peers every step of your career, you're bound to be competitive. We were raised by parents who convinced us we could make the world a better place; as a result, we tend to be idealists. We came to the workplace with a strong desire to put our own stamp on things."

"Yeah, I've definitely locked horns with a few of you in my workplace," Paul confirmed with a nod of his head.

Lynne continued: "You have to put the generations in an economic context. The long economic expansion of the 1990s created a situation of almost full employment in the United States. David's generation was promoted rapidly and was offered more financial and job growth opportunities than ever in history. Rather than paying their dues for a number of years, they've been able to demand that companies adapt to their ways of doing things. This has created both a culture clash and a resentment backlash as the generations collided around issues of fairness and opportunity.

"At the same time, low unemployment levels created major staffing problems. For example, one of our clients who owns a box factory in Catawba City, North Carolina, complained to us in 2000 that his town's unemployment rate had dropped to .8 percent! Imagine trying to recruit a workforce to operate a noisy plant that smells like diesel fumes and rotten eggs when the same workers can find jobs at an air-conditioned mall for the same money—and enjoy the scent of Mrs. Fields cookies!"

"Now hold on there," Paul interrupted. "Let's face it, as soon as our economy takes a nosedive, the younger generations are going to have to come begging for jobs."

"But that's only part of the picture," David countered. . . .

There's a talent war out there. Because Generation X is just a little over half the size of the Baby Boom, regardless of what happens with the economy, fewer workers will be available in the age group that's currently poised to move into the management ranks. At the same time, a large number of Boomers will become eligible to retire over the next few years, leaving a leadership gap in the upper echelons of organizations. Many Traditionalists will be able to afford to leave the work world at relatively young ages, and the bulk of the Millennials are still a decade or two away from filling management gaps. The result is that businesses will have to fight harder to recruit and retain the best and brightest employees.

"We help organizations understand how demographic shifts can affect their recruiting and succession planning, which gives them a distinct competitive advantage," Lynne explained, then offered some hard-core proof: "Consider this, Paul. In their recent 'war for talent' study, McKinsey and Company estimated that over the next thirty years, the *demand* for bright, talented thirty-five-to-forty-five-year-olds will increase by 25 percent, while the *supply* is predicted to decrease by 15 percent. We are facing tangible worker shortages that are expected to continue for some time. Companies have to start preparing for a mass exodus of know-how and experience that they're going to have to replace from a much smaller pool of talent that comes with a very different set of values and expectations."

"So we're headed for a sort of talent war *and* a culture clash," Paul summarized, waving at the flight attendant for another drink.

"Be glad you're not in the same boat as one of our Fortune 500 manufacturing clients," Lynne offered. "According to their head of human resources, the company's strategic plan calls for recruiting *thirty thousand* new people over the next ten years into a traditional company that's not exactly known for its high-tech bells and whistles. Companies like that are going to face huge hiring challenges!"

"Turnover rates are increasing, too," David added. Every industry is reporting higher turnover, the costs of which include tangible expenses like those of recruiting, hiring, and training new workers, as well as intangibles like reduced morale and decreased efficiency. Not to mention the brain drain that occurs when the most skilled employees walk out the door. What companies must realize is that culture clashes among the generations directly affect turnover. A culture that has been shaped by the values, standards, and policies of one generation isn't necessarily going to be compatible with the next generation that comes through the door. When generation gaps open up at work, employees who don't feel they "fit" decide to leave.

Lynne jumped in: "It's not just the Xers who feel out of place. Human resources managers tell us they are losing too many Traditionalists because they're feeling outmoded, and Boomers who are opting to become free agents. We often have to help companies find ways to get their valuable senior workers to stay. Organizations that can understand and bridge generation gaps have a real competitive edge in the retention game.

"Then there's also the fact that the accelerating pace of change over the past century has made it is increasingly difficult for the generations to find common ground. A few decades ago, three or four generations might have gathered together to listen to *The Shadow* on the radio. Now we hear a Traditionalist complaining there's nothing decent on television since *Murder, She Wrote* went off the air, a Boomer still lamenting the demise of *thirtysomething*, an Xer reminiscing about the tawdry goings-on at *Melrose Place,* and a Millennial waxing lyrical over *My So-Called Life.* As a result, it's no longer possible to assume that a multigenerational group of employees standing around the water cooler has the same life experiences and cultural touchstones in common. This can translate into communication challenges and a breakdown of the bonds that hold companies together.

"*The technological revolution has exacerbated the situation.* The advent of the Internet, supercomputers, and high-speed connections is driving massive change in the ways companies do business. This has put a greater divide between the generations who grew up with technology and the ones who are playing catch-up."

"Okay," Paul said decisively as he brought his seat into the locked and upright position in preparation for landing, "how do we make this problem go away?"

We both felt a little sorry that we had to tell him that it won't just "go away." While many hope that Traditionalists will eventually retire, that Boomers will relax and get a life, that Xers will quit challenging the status quo, and that Millennials won't present a whole new set of challenges when they arrive on the scene, the fact is that generational differences are here to stay.

While economic slowdowns are likely to make the job market tighter, it doesn't change the fact that different generations of employees won't become more alike with age. They will carry their "generational personalities" with them throughout their lives. In fact, when hard times hit, the generations are likely to entrench themselves even more deeply into the attitudes and behaviors that have been ingrained in them.

As the plane began a gentle descent, three generations quietly stowed their tray tables.

"Well," Paul said gruffly, breaking the silence. "I guess we have to stop trying to figure out which generation is right and which one is wrong, and instead figure out how to manage them appropriately."

He paused. "You know, this isn't really an obstacle—it's an opportunity, a tool in the arsenal that somebody like me can turn into a competitive advantage. As I see it, if we figure out the generations and make the adjustments needed to recruit, retain, and manage them, then it's just one more way to run our competitors into the ground, right?"

We both nodded, because we couldn't have said it better ourselves.

The plane touched down. Paul grabbed *Forbes* and *Fortune* from the seat pocket in front of him. David hid his *People* magazine under his coat. Lynne picked up her untouched copy of *American Demographics*. After all, it was way more fun to connect with the generations than to read about them, anyway.

Paul thrust out a hand holding his business card. "Let's stay in touch," he offered. "We might just have the need for another conversation."

We thanked Paul in unison, and he exited through the forward door with a wave. Just a few hours earlier, we weren't so sure Paul relished his seat between the two of us. Now we all felt like a million bucks. A good conversation resulting in a multigenerational connection—what more could you ask for?

2

FROM WORLD WAR II TO THE WORLD WIDE WEB

Not too long ago, David phoned Lynne, sounding really ticked off. When she asked him what was wrong, he admitted that he had just been reprimanded by one of our biggest clients. Lynne was amazed. Although the client company's leadership team consisted of high-level Baby Boomers and Traditionalists, and David was one of the youngest consultants they had ever hired, they had an excellent rapport with David and liked his work.

"I don't get it," Lynne said. "What on earth could you have done to have earned yourself a reprimand?"

And David explained that in order to kick off a new project, he had typed up a memo outlining the process, put the names of all the recipients at the top of the page, and sent it out to everyone. Fine, so he'd thought—until a few days later, when he received a very curt voice mail from a vice president.

"Uh, David, I received your memo and you neglected to *alpha-betize* the list of recipients at the top of the page. If this project is

TRADITIONALISTS, BABY BOOMERS, GENERATION XERS, AND MILLENNIALS AT WORK

going to succeed, you're going to have to pay attention to details! I'm sure this won't happen again." Click.

David was stupefied. Spelling and grammar in a formal memo he could understand, but alphabetizing? He didn't get it. So he immediately called Lynne, hoping that as a Baby Boomer she could explain this confusing outburst.

The first words out of her mouth were, "David! I can't believe you didn't alphabetize the list of recipients at the top of the page!"

After she calmed down, she explained that the client team in this large, multinational company was a competitive group of high-achieving Boomers and Traditionalists who had had to fight and claw their way into the positions they held, and to them it was extremely significant where the names appeared at the top of the memo.

A few days later, just as Lynne was feeling really good about having explained a bit of intergenerational business etiquette to a Generation Xer, she received a voice mail from our extreme Generation X video producer. It sounded exactly like this:

"Uh, dude, I'm a little concerned about the middle montage, it's looking radically raw. . . . Not to worry, we're doin' it digital, we can slice and dice and mix and match, it's gonna look stellar, but hook me with the 411 if you have any questions or I'll just assume you'll call me at three bells." Click.

To David, the expression on Lynne's face when she listened to this message was priceless. He relished every time he had to replay it so he could actually translate some of the words for her. Meanwhile, all she could say was, "How much money are we *paying* this loser!"

So now David was feeling really good about having decoded Generation X language for a Baby Boomer, until he found himself a couple of weeks later driving a fifteen-year-old Millennial baby-sitter home. She asked him where he and Sharon had gone for dinner that evening. With two children under the age of four at home, he and Sharon don't get out much, but that night they had gone to Café Brenda, one of those healthy, hip, and trendy restaurants in the warehouse district of Minneapolis where every other dish is served with pine nuts or arugula.

"Well," he announced just a little pompously, "we actually ate at Café Brenda."

"Oh, I love that place, it's so *fat*."

"Really?" David replied. "That surprises me, because they pride themselves on *low-fat* cooking!"

She then explained very slowly and patiently to David that she had said "phat," which to the Millennials means "cool," at which point he realized he definitely was not.

What just happened here? Clearly the Traditionalists at our client company just assumed David, a Generation Xer, understood their rules of etiquette. Lynne, a Boomer, just assumed that "Video Dude" would know how to speak her language. And David, our oh-so-hip-and-cool Generation Xer, just assumed he knew how to connect with any Millennial!

Kaboom! Three generational collisions at their finest.

ACROSS THE GENERATIONAL DIVIDE

These types of generational misunderstandings happen all the time on the *personal* level, and they can be extremely painful. But think for a moment about how costly they can be at the *institutional* level when companies have to set policies, develop procedures, and create everything from corporate cultures to compensation and benefit plans. And think how challenging these collisions can be for managers who are charged with recruiting, retaining, managing, and motivating up to four generations in the workplace at once.

From the public to the private sector, from the large, multinational corporation to the corner mom-and-pop shop, a conflict of earth-shattering proportions is unfolding right before our eyes. The American business scene is being rocked by a series of generational collisions at every turn.

The ramifications of these generational collisions at work include everything from reduced profitability to the loss of valuable employees, higher payroll costs, poor customer service, derailed careers, wasted human potential, and even potentially serious health problems caused by stress. Corporate cultures are being shaken to the very core as the cost of human capital spirals ever upward.

For years people have analyzed factors like age, life stage, gender, race, ethnicity, socioeconomic status, religion, educational background, thinking styles, Myers-Briggs profiles, and even signs of the zodiac to find ways to understand each other better. Yet somehow we've failed to recognize the form of diversity that affects every human being on a daily basis—*generational differences.*

AGELESS THINKING

For the first time in our history, we have four separate and distinct generations working shoulder-to-shoulder and face-to-face in a stressful, competitive workplace.

The Traditionalists, born between the turn of the last century and the end of World War II (1900–1945), combine two generations who tend to believe and behave similarly and who number about seventy-five million people. The Baby Boomers (1946–1964) are the largest population ever born in this country and number about eighty million. The Generation Xers (1965–1980) are a smaller but very influential population at forty-six million. And the Millennials (1981–1999) represent the next great demographic boom at seventy-six million.

While many generational experts have laid out age ranges to define the members of the generations, we believe these are just guidelines. There really is no magic birth date that makes you a part of a particular generation. Generational personalities go much deeper. To understand who the generations really are and what makes them tick, one needs to adopt an "ageless thinking" attitude and look at how each generation shares a common history. The events and conditions each of us experiences during our formative years determine who we are and how we see the world. As a result of these events and conditions, each generation has adopted its own "generational personality."

Icons can be people, places, or things that become reference points for a generation. For example, Martin Luther King Jr., Selma, Alabama, and the image of an empty bus are all icons of the Selma bus boycott of 1965. Icons can also be actual events, such as the assassination of a president, D-Day, or the explosion of the *Challenger* space shuttle.

Conditions are the forces at work in the environment as each generation comes of age. The cold war was a condition that permeated the youth of many Boomers, while Millennials born after 1989 will never know a world in which there were two different cities called East and West Berlin. Economic upheavals are conditions that profoundly affect the wealth and health of our citizens and permanently shape our way of looking at the world. Those who lived through the Great Depression, or who were raised by parents who did, were changed forever by the fear of not being able to put food on the table. Large-scale upheavals in the family, such as major changes in the divorce rate, the marriage rate, or the number of single-parent families, can all play a role in shaping the generations' identities.

As these icons and conditions play out in the lives of each of the generations, they shape the attitudes, values, and work styles that the generations bring with them when they come to work every day. These differences create the generation gaps that companies of all sizes across all industries are struggling to bridge.

Too many employers and employees ignore these differences because they assume that since we all experience the same life stages, we are bound to see them the same way. Don't we all have to be born, be educated, find work, find partners, create families, age, retire, and eventually die? And don't we perform these functions pretty similarly?

The answer is yes, and no. Yes, we all have certain *life stages* in common, but no, the different generations do not approach them the same way. According to the BridgeWorks Generations Survey, for example, the majority of Boomers plan never to retire. They intend to keep working in some form or another for as long as they can be productive. The majority of Traditionalists, on the other hand, view retirement as a well-earned reward and look forward to the days when they never have to punch the time clock again. In this case, retirement is a life stage the generations have in common, but the way each generation approaches it is going to look very different. Can you imagine what retirement will look like to an Xer or a Millennial?

BEWARE OF AV TECHS IN SUPPORT STOCKINGS

After a long, hard week on the road, we stepped into the heavily paneled lodge in northern Minnesota to give one last presentation before heading for home. David had somehow contracted food poisoning along the way and was looking green and shaken as he stood under an imposing moose head. Lynne, who was now seven time zones from where she had begun her day, was staring dazedly at a lamp made from a caribou hoof. It was very late; our speech was scheduled for early the next morning, and only the audiovisual check stood between us and our waiting hotel rooms. Both of us were thinking exactly the same thing: *Please, God, just give us a techno-savvy Xer with an attitude who'll knock this AV setup together in about ten minutes and get us out of here.* When you do a lot of speaking, it's amazing how dependent you get on the people

who run the cable and make the lights, sound, laptops and pro-
jectors all come alive. We'd gotten pretty good at spotting the
winners . . . or so we thought.

From around the corner we heard the AV cart rattling
over the rough pine floors, our cue to swing into action. The
cart hove into view followed by our . . . AV guy? It was Edna.
Gray hair, thick glasses, corrective shoes, support hose, and a
print cotton dress. Our hearts sank. She looked nice enough,
but not like anybody who could adjust a mixer. Our hopes of
getting this over with any time soon looked dim. But Edna
fixed us with a friendly gaze and said, "You two look pooped.
Let's make this quick and get you off to your rooms. Are you
using a VCR or running MPEG video right off the laptop?"

"Are we . . . huh?" David murmured, stunned, like a deer
caught in headlights.

Edna peered at us pityingly over her glasses, then whipped
her cart around and headed for the conference hall. "Let's go,
dears. Don't worry, we'll get you all figured out."

And she did. Edna was the fastest, most efficient, well-
organized, and professional AV person we encountered that
year, bar none. And she did it without once calling for backup,
swearing, or making us feel like idiots.

But of course we did feel like idiots. Because at the
moment of our first glimpse of Edna, we had both assumed
based on her generation and her looks that she wouldn't be
able to do the job.

Now if *we* find ourselves stereotyping a member of another
generation, when we spend all day every day thinking about the
topic, we can only wonder what's going on out there in the rest of
the business world. How often are all the generations being stereo-

typed, and what can we do to put a new face on the way the generations see each other?

We've all been exposed to too many media images of the annoyingly precocious Millennial kid, or the tattooed Generation X slacker, or the guilt-ridden, workaholic Boomer, or the lifeless retired Traditionalist leaning back on the porch swing. The media puts negative images into our minds, and these affect how we view each of the generations. And we *do* look at each other negatively. In our BridgeWorks Survey, when we asked the generations to respond to the statement "My generation is viewed positively by the other generations," 30 percent of Baby Boomers and 24 percent of Traditionalists answered, "No." The problem was even greater for Generation X. Over 60 percent of Xers said they feel they aren't seen in a positive light.

Stereotypes also arise from resentment. Xers resent Traditionalists for being resistant to change and unwilling to hand over the reins. Boomers resent Xers for finding it so easy to change jobs whenever they feel like it and for demanding balance in their lives the Boomers would never have thought to ask for. Traditionalists resent Millennials for their entitlement mentality when Traditionalists had to work for everything they've gotten. Millennials resent the Boomers for leaving the planet a mess when they were supposed to be the ones to clean it up. And on it goes. The resentment becomes worse at work, where the generations are competing for the same turf and fairness is on the line.

The only way we'll ever build bridges is to stop stereotyping and get to know who these generations really are and why they are that way. As we describe the generations below, please take this as an opportunity not to stereotype the generations, but to learn something about them you might not have known before.

WHO ARE THE PLAYERS?

The advent of the new millennium made many of us pause and look back before launching ourselves into a new century. Books such as Tom Brokaw's *The Greatest Generation* have reminded us of some of the amazing contributions of the matriarchs and patriarchs of many of our families. More fun-loving books like *Growing Up Brady* have taken a look at the clothing, hairstyles, and phrases of a particular generation's growing-up years. Our goal here isn't to bog you down with so much detail that your high school history textbook starts to sound fascinating, but to give you a snapshot of some of the people, places, things, and events that influenced the generations in their formative years.

TRADITIONALISTS (BORN 1900–1945)

The Traditionalists (about seventy-five million strong) were influenced by a host of people, some heroic, some villainous, some entertaining, and some patriotic. These were *people* like Joe DiMaggio, Joe Louis, Joe McCarthy, Dr. Spock, Alfred Hitchcock, the Rat Pack, Franklin Delano Roosevelt, Duke Ellington, Ella Fitzgerald, Charles Lindbergh, Edward R. Murrow, John Wayne, Bob Hope, Elizabeth Taylor, Betty Grable, Betty Crocker, and a host of others.

Places were far-flung as our country found itself taking on an international role for the first time. They ranged from Sarajevo to Pearl Harbor, Normandy, Hiroshima, Korea, the Bay of Pigs, Midway, and Iwo Jima. Back home, places stretched from bread lines to Victory gardens, from the front porch to the church pew to a cozy spot at the kitchen table with the family tuned in to *The Maxwell House Radio Hour.*

Things were often scarce for Traditionalists as they were growing up. Between two world wars and the Great Depression, this generation had plenty of opportunities to learn to do without. The need to "save for a rainy day" was tangible, and "Waste not, want not" was more than a slogan, it was a commandment. No wonder Traditionalists later disapproved of the Boomers' eagerness to pay two dollars for a bottle of fancy water! Symbols carried great weight. From swastikas to Sputnik and from flappers to flattops, this was a generation that drove their roadsters to drive-ins, smoked cigarettes and sucked down ice-cold Coca-Colas, and stacked a few 45s on the record player and did the twist.

Defining *events* such as World War I, the Roaring Twenties, the Great Depression, the New Deal, World War II, the Korean War, and the GI Bill changed millions of lives and shaped the God-fearing, hardworking, patriotic character of this amazing generation.

The generational personality of the Traditionalists, who lived through these events and conditions, could best be described by a single word: *loyal.* This is a generation that learned at an early age that by putting aside the needs and wants of the individual and working together toward common goals, they could accomplish amazing things. Traditionalists learned to partner with large institutions in order to get things done, like winning two world wars, conquering the Great Depression, building the A-bomb, and sending a man to the Moon. This is a generation that still has an immense amount of faith in institutions, from the church to the government to the military. Patriotism is a given with Traditionalists. Of all the generations, the Traditionalists believed of America that you should always "stand beside her, and guide her." Because Traditionalists were born into a country that lacked the significant social safety nets we rely on today (like Social Security, Medicare, welfare, and the FDIC), the fear of the Great Depression drummed into them the value of a dollar. Their experiences in the military (over 50 percent of Traditionalist men are veterans) taught them that using a top-down approach was the most efficient way to get things done. Today, the management style of many Traditionalists is still modeled on the military chain of command. When the rubber hits the road, Traditionalists understand that leaders need to lead and troops need to follow.

Because Traditionalists are made up of two generations born in the first half of the last century that tend to believe and behave very similarly, the Traditionalist-dominated workplace ran smoothly for a long time without having to deal with a younger, dissenting generation that wanted to shake things up. But based on all the influences and traits of the Traditionalists, you can see where generational collisions began to arise when the Baby Boomers came along. Many Traditionalists probably still long for the 1940s and 1950s, when they were practically the only generation on the job. By the early 1960s, things started to change as the Baby Boomers began busting through corporate America's front doors. From a generational perspective, the business world would never be the same.

The collisions that arise at work when two generations bump headlong into each other are what we call "ClashPoints." The American workplace experienced a major ClashPoint when the "chain of command" military style of management that had worked so well for the Traditionalists crashed headlong into the Baby Boomers' desire to shake things up.

BABY BOOMERS (BORN 1946–1964)

Eighty million strong, the Baby Boomers changed every market they entered, from the supermarket to the job market to the stock market. Influential *people* included Martin Luther King Jr., the Kingston Trio, Richard Milhous Nixon, John Fitzgerald Kennedy, Eldridge Cleaver, Beaver Cleaver, Rosa Parks, Peter Benchley, "Deep Throat," McEnroe and Connors, the Manson family, the Osmond family, Gloria Steinem, Barbra Streisand, John Belushi, Janis Joplin, Captain Kangaroo, Captain Kirk, the Monkees, the Beatles, the Partridge family, and the Stones.

Places varied wildly for this generation as the Boomers careened from tragedy to escapism and then plunged into the real world. Places included the Watergate Hotel, the Hanoi Hilton, Chappaquiddick, and Kent State, on the one hand, and sit-ins, love-ins, *Laugh-In,* and Woodstock on the other. Then came the suburbs, the bedroom, the boardroom, the delivery room, and eventually the divorce courtroom. The Boomers' evolution was marked by a range of *things* that reflected their evolving identity and the exploding availability of consumer products in the marketplace—from bell-bottoms and mood rings to Brooks Brothers suits and Rolex watches, from junk food to junk bonds, and from LSD to the SEC.

Ask any Boomers about the greatest invention of their childhood and their antennae go up. The single most important arrival during the birth years of the Boom was television. In 1952, *four* million television sets could be found in American homes. By 1960, the number was *fifty* million! Gradually the generation gap between Baby Boomers and Traditionalists widened as an entire generation of Boomers could relate to a whole set of reference points (TV shows, characters, plots, advertisers, and products) that were unknown to their parents. As they fine-tuned their sets, the Boomers' generational personality was shaped. Events that were revealed to the public through this highly visual new medium included deep, divisive issues like the war in Vietnam, Watergate, the women's and human rights movements, the OPEC oil embargo, stagflation, and recession. Experiencing these landmark events, whether live or through the miracle of television, permanently changed the Boomers.

We said the key word to remember about Traditionalists is *loyal;* the key word for Boomers is *optimistic.* The booming postwar economy gave the United States of the late 1940s, the 1950s, and the 1960s a sense that anything was possible. The availability of jobs and GI loans to Traditionalist parents, the boom in production of consumer goods, and the promise of a good education for all allowed

Boomers to grow up in a relatively affluent, opportunity-rich world. Traditionalist parents did everything they could to create a world in which their children would have opportunities they had only dreamed of and to encourage their offspring to pursue those dreams. Energy that had been turned outward by Traditionalists toward a world in turmoil was now turned inward by idealistic Boomers intent on fixing what was wrong with America. Educated and able young idealists questioned the ideals of their parents' generation and protested the status quo, pushing for change in the areas of civil rights, women's rights, reproductive rights, and even the rights of Mother Earth, giving birth to the ecology movement.

Another trait that marks the Baby Boomers is *competitiveness.* You can't be born and raised with eighty million peers competing with you for everything from a place on the football team in an overcrowded high school to a place in the college of your choice to placement with your dream company and *not* be competitive. Boomers, while graced with many blessings and privileges, have had to fight for much of what they've achieved in corporate America against the sheer number of their peers competing for the same jobs and promotions. Boomers have again and again been labeled the "Me Generation," in part because they were privileged to be able to focus on themselves and where they were going instead of needing to sublimate the needs of individuals as the Traditionalists had done. But we see a second meaning in this "me generation" label, and that is the deep identification Boomers feel with who they are and what they achieve at work.

Remember that our first ClashPoint began with Traditionalists' belief in "chain of command"? Well, for Boomers focused on what it was going to take to get ahead, it was more like "change of command." They saw the flaws in the way the world was being managed and believed they had the idealism, education, and sheer numbers on their side to change it. Because Boomers were raised in the era of interpersonal communication, information provided by Traditionalists on a "need to know basis" rankled. Clashes arose between the

Traditionalists in control and the Boomers, who seemed compelled to challenge their authority.

> Frank, a Traditionalist supervisor, was sitting at his desk early one December morning when an energetic young Baby Boomer, Jim, knocked at his door.
>
> "What can I do for you, Jim?" Frank asked formally.
>
> "Well, I was hoping to take a look at some of the projects the company has on the calendar for next year, sir."
>
> "And why would you need to see that?" Frank answered sternly.
>
> "Well," stumbled Jim, "I just wanted to, uh, get the big picture, you know, see where I might fit in."
>
> Frank scowled. "I'm not sure you understand, that information is confidential. I will be the one to tell you about the projects that concern you when it is appropriate."
>
> Boomer Jim walked away demoralized by his Traditionalist boss's unwillingness to share information and his controlling style. Jim was concerned about being assigned to more high-profile projects because some of his peers were already being promoted. *This is a free country,* he thought to himself. *I don't know why he can't share a little information!*
>
> Traditionalist Frank felt Jim was trying to break rank and get above himself—a bad sign for anyone who hoped eventually to earn a promotion by "fitting in" to the prevailing culture.

Kaboom. Though probably neither one of them saw the incident as a generational collision, it was a ClashPoint at work.

As Boomers have evolved, they've moved up, out, and into the upper echelons of management, taking their optimism and idealism with them. Along the way, they've learned a tremendous amount from their Traditionalist role models, and together they are manning the helms of most of America's greatest corporations. As they have continued to negotiate ways of sharing power, Boomers and Traditionalists have struggled to unravel the mysteries of the generational collisions that so often stopped them in their tracks. Often, they've formed powerful partnerships that served to fuel the economic boom of the past several decades.

Until recently they didn't realize that a powerful complicating factor was about to appear on the horizon, causing even greater clashes: Generation X.

GENERATION XERS (BORN 1965–1980)

Possibly the most misunderstood generation in the workforce today, this small (forty-six million) but influential population has worked to carve out its own identity separate from that of the Boomers and Traditionalists. For years now Xers have been able to say "Show me the money" and mean it in the business world, ticking off remarkable accomplishments as managers, inventors, and entrepreneurs.

A highlight reel of the leading *people* during the Xers' formative years would include headliners as disparate as the Brat Pack, Bill Clinton, Bill Gates, Monica Lewinsky, the Ayatollah Khomeini, Ted Bundy, Al Bundy, Beavis and Butt-head, the Menendez brothers, Quentin Tarantino, Clarence Thomas, Newt Gingrich, O. J. Simpson, Dilbert, Dennis Rodman, supermodels, Madonna, and Michael Jordan. It's no wonder so many millions of Xers wanted to "be like Mike"—they didn't have too many other heroes to emulate. With the explosion of twenty-four-hour media and tabloid journalism, Xers saw almost every role model of their time indicted or exposed as someone far too human to be a hero. Where was John Wayne, Roy Rogers and Dale Evans, or Walter Cronkite for this generation?

The media expanded the *places* Xers could travel to, taking them from the former Soviet Union to Somalia, from Cannes to Chernobyl, from Lockerbie, Scotland, to Starbucks, and from the International Space Station to the Internet. And as the media exposed it all, and movies about the making of movies were made, much of the American mystique was gradually stripped away.

While Traditionalists were characterized as being extremely *loyal* and Boomers *optimistic,* Xers have been marked by *skepticism.* They grew up seeing every major American institution called into question. From the presidency to the military to organized religion to corporate America, you name the institution and Xers can name the crime. Combine that with a U.S. divorce rate that *tripled* during the birth years of Generation X and you have a generation that distrusts the permanence of institutional and personal relationships. As a result, Xers tend to put more faith in themselves as individuals and less faith in the institutions that seem to have failed them time and again.

While Boomers' childhoods were revolutionized by the invention of a single medium, the television, Xers don't have enough fingers and toes to number the *media* that have sprung up during their lifetimes. Cable TV, digital TV, satellite TV, VCRs, video games, fax machines, microwaves, pagers, cell phones, PalmPilots, and, of course, the most life-changing item of all: the personal computer.

But while these inventions were intended to simplify the American way of life, just ask Xers about their childhood, and they'll tell you it was pretty complex. Violence appeared not just in the news, but close to home in the form of AIDS, crack cocaine, child molesters, and drunk drivers. So much for the carefree silliness of *MAD* magazine. Now your mother was a card-carrying member of MADD. Children mysteriously disappeared from neighborhoods and showed up frighteningly at the breakfast table on milk cartons. The message served up was that the world isn't as safe as it used to be. The number of single-parent households skyrocketed, and Mom no longer waited after school with milk and cookies. Instead, it was off to a latchkey program or home to an empty house to play video games until supper, as the nuclear family went the way of the nuclear power plant.

As a result, Generation Xers are an extremely resourceful and independent generation who count on their peers and themselves to get things done and don't hold out too many false hopes that any person or institution is going to swoop down and save them from reality. While it's great to be a self-starter, throw the skeptical, independent Xers into the mix with the loyal Traditionalists and optimistic Boomers and . . . *kaboom!*

As if the collision between the Traditionalists' "chain of command" mentality and the Boomers' "change of command" mind-set weren't tough enough! Suddenly, the Generation Xers, who learned at an early age to rely only on themselves, are adding a third element to the ClashPoint—"self-command."

A Baby Boomer boss, Mary Jo, is leading a meeting of her department made up mostly of Xers. "How many times do I have to ask you people to turn in your daily activity reports?" she asks impatiently. "They may not mean anything to you, but information is power, and if we're going to pull together and build a strong department, then I need to know what everyone is doing."

Seven blank faces glare up at her in exasperation. Finally, one Xer who is completely fed up with Mary Jo's controlling management style blurts out: "At what point are you just going to let us do our jobs? I mean, we spend more time filling out forms than we do getting the work done! Do we really have to be micromanaged all the time just so you can turn in a bunch of reports to Corporate?"

Mary Jo is furious. She's got four Boomer peers at her grade level all vying for the single vice president job, and she needs to stand out. Plus, her Xer employees don't seem to want to play ball so she can get the information she needs to make her department look good. How did she end up with a so-called team of lone rangers who don't understand her political position or the greater goals of the company?

While Mary Jo debated how to turn the situation around, a couple of Xers did it for her. Instead of handing in their reports, they turned in their resignations.

It's become painfully obvious to everyone at work that as the number of generations on the job has grown, so too has the number of collisions. And with three generational personalities finding themselves butting heads, it is practically impossible to imagine what will happen when yet another generation arrives on the scene with its own set of attitudes and agendas.

THE MILLENNIAL GENERATION (BORN 1981–1999)

The next Baby Boom (seventy-six million in number) has been variously known as the Echo Boom, Generation Y, the Baby Busters, or Generation Next. Whatever you call them, they've been watched closely by everyone from principals of bulging public schools to toy and blue jean manufacturers to college admissions officers. However, prospective employers who must figure out how to attract this smart, practical, techno-savvy generation into the workforce are only now starting to notice the Millennial generation. While it's hard to know what a generation is going to be like in the boardroom when the bulk of them are still wrapped up in Boy Scouts and

Brownies, the leading-edge Millennials are emerging onto the employment scene, and we've been watching them. We've included the Millennials in our generational comparisons wherever we could, based on our research and conversations with companies that are already employing them. In places, we've speculated about what we think the Millennials are going to be like, based on everything we've seen so far. We hope to give you as complete a picture as we can of this fascinating generation so you have a leg up on getting to know them long before they show up for orientation where you work.

A snapshot of some of the people, places, and things that have influenced the Millennials during their short lifetimes reminds many of us of how much the world has changed since we were their ages.

With technology and the media blurring the lines between fantasy and reality, the *people* influencing Millennials often seemed larger than life. They've included Prince William, Chelsea Clinton, Tinky Winky, Ricky Martin, Claire Danes and Leonardo DiCaprio, Kurt Cobain and Courtney Love, Barney, Britney, the Backstreet Boys, Felicity, Buffy, Cartman, Marilyn Manson, Mark McGwire and Sammy Sosa, and Venus and Serena Williams.

Places have been both virtual and tangible, ranging from chat rooms to *Dawson's Creek,* from *90210* to Oklahoma City, and from cyberspace to outer space.

Technology moved even closer to people; in fact, it moved right into their pockets. This is a generation that has had access to cell phones, personal pagers, and computers since they were in diapers. While the Xers were the first to jump on board the personal computer, Millennials can brag about being able to take it for a joyride on the information superhighway. Through the Internet, they have visited virtually every corner of the globe and have been able to choose between hanging out at the local mall *or* the virtual mall.

With information beaming into Millennials' bedrooms on a minute-by-minute basis, Millennials are realistic about the challenges of modern life for a modern kid. Never mind a missing child on a milk carton, how about the fear of a missing classmate from the next desk as the result of a gunshot wound? Millennials have been directly affected by personal threats stemming from violent outbreaks such as Columbine, readily available illegal drugs, and the proliferation of gangs. In a recent poll, Millennials named "personal safety" as their number one workplace issue.

© 2001 Mike Luckovich. By permission of Mike Luckovich and Creators Syndicate, Inc.

The benefit of the optimistic, idealistic Boomer parenting style for many Millennials, however, is that they feel empowered to take positive action when things go wrong. Millennials also have the benefit of the wisdom of each generation that has gone before, prompting Strauss and Howe to predict that they will truly be the next "Greatest Generation." It's as if the Traditionalists have given the Millennials a dose of their *loyalty* and faith in institutions, Boomers have given them the confidence to be *optimistic* about their ability to make things happen, and Xers have given them just enough *skepticism* to be cautious. As a result, the pragmatic Millennials have combined these traits into their own identity. If you want to remember just one key word to describe Millennials, it's *realistic*.

One Boomer client related that her Millennial son was intent on watching every minute of a miniseries called *The '60s*. It seems he was fascinated to see what it was like to experience the civil rights marches, the placards, and the sit-ins. When it was all over, she eagerly asked him, "So, what did you think of the protest movements of the sixties?"

"Well," the Millennial answered confidently, "I thought it was a very inefficient way to make the point."

Try explaining your benefits program to *that* Millennial. If he thought the 1960s were inefficient, what is he going to think about your health care plan?

Combine their confident, pragmatic nature with a workplace that hasn't yet made way for Millennials, and you're going to have a combustible atmosphere that could blow at any time.

Millennials' defining traits include an appreciation of diversity—after all, they've been exposed to many different kinds of people through travel, day care, technology, and the media. We call this "diversification expectation." It means that Millennials expect the workplace to resemble the diverse world they've grown up in.

A Millennial was interviewing for a summer job building Web sites and was turned off by a Traditionalist manager who went to great pains to explain that this company had a "diverse" work environment.

"I finally figured out what he meant by a diverse environment," she explained. "He had, like, two people of color working there. As if that's supposed to impress me. We have more diversity in our high school office than they have in the whole company. I thought, *If you think that is such a big accomplishment, I don't want to work for you.*"

And we expect even these *two* generations at work together? What about when there are *four*?!

Think back to our ClashPoint. We said the Traditionalists came of age in the workforce in a "chain of command" environment, the Boomers were focused on "change of command," and the Xers have fought for "self-command." So what about the Millennials? They would probably say, "Don't command—collaborate!" *KaBOOM!*

We once met a Gen X meeting planner who had to work with a team of Millennials to put on a large trade show for his company. He e-mailed out instructions to the group and asked them to check back in via e-mail at the end of each week to let him know how they were doing at carrying out their individual parts in the plan he had designed. Instead of updates on his plan, however, he received a steady stream of ideas for how he could improve the plan. His e-mail inbox was overloaded with replies from collaborative Millennials suggesting everything from new poster possibilities, to colorful kiosks, to an ecofriendly recycling area, to menu ideas for a vegan snack bar. He closed his eyes. With deadlines pressing, the team had just enough time to work independently and get their individual assignments done. With no time or energy for so much input and group interdependence, he could feel his trade show turning into a freak show!

Raised by highly communicative, participation-oriented parents, the Millennials have been included in major family decisions since they were old enough to point. From deciding where to go on family vacations to which computer to buy, Millennials have always been part of the day-to-day negotiation of their home lives. They'll bring this quality with them in spades when they show up to work. That means they'll be tough to bully because they're used to sticking up for themselves, but it also means they'll be able to contribute and collaborate right from the get-go.

By now, we hope it is obvious that we can't look just at age to define a generation. Instead, we need to look at how each generation shares a common history and how, having lived through certain events and conditions, each generation has adopted its own personality. As the example of our first ClashPoint demonstrated, when these personalities meet around the boardroom table, each one has valid reasons for believing his or her generational perspective is right. In reality, no one is right or wrong . . . just different. By taking time to learn about these differences, companies can gain a competitive advantage in recruiting, managing, retaining, and motivating the generations.

If you read the descriptions of the generations above and felt you were neither one nor the other, never fear. You might be what we call a "Cusper," someone born on the cusp between two generations. Some Cuspers find they identify strongly with one generation or another. Others find they have characteristics of both. Any way you slice it, Cuspers are extremely important in today's business world. If fact, they are so influential that we've given them their own chapter. See chapter 3 for more information about yourself or the Cuspers in your life.

Likewise, your age might place you in one generation when every fiber of your being is telling you that you belong to another. That's okay, too. A generational identity is a state of mind shaped by many events and influences. Only you can define what generation you fit into.

WARNING: THIS BOOK CONTAINS CONTENT THAT MAY OFFEND SOME READERS

We all know the warnings that appear at the beginning of the movies to warn viewers about the use of graphic language, nudity, or violence. (Okay, don't get excited that an X-rated book accidentally ended up on the workplace shelf . . . that's *not* our warning.) In every seminar we lead or speech we give, someone smart, usually a wire-rimmed-glasses analytical type, will ask, "Hey, aren't you two just perpetuating stereotypes when you try to tell us that a member of a generation is going to think or act a certain way? Can you really generalize?" To him or her, we offer two answers.

First, you *can* make generalizations about people. If one generation experienced a divorce rate of *15 percent* during their formative years and a later generation experienced a divorce rate of *50 percent,* you can bet the two generations have been affected by divorce differently. Likewise, if one generation grew up during the Great Depression and another during a long economic boom, we can make some assumptions about how they are likely to believe and behave in the marketplace. The generations can't help but be influenced by the events and conditions that have shaped who they are and how they see the world.

But the second answer is this: We expect that anyone who is interested enough in the generations to read this book has a genuine desire to gain some new tools for dealing with the generations in thoughtful ways. We assume that our readers have the moral sense to try earnestly not to use this information to stereotype people, but rather to become better listeners, better observers of the human condition, better bosses, and better friends. Our goal is not to put people in a box, but to open up the box so that we can all get a better glimpse of who and what is inside.

OUR RESEARCH

We've gotten to know the generations in a number of ways over the past several years. First, of course, we are a Boomer and an Xer who own a company together and know about what it's like to collide. But rather than depend just on our own experiences, we have enlisted a lot of help. We've read numerous books and articles by sociologists and demographers who are some of the more brilliant people we ever hope to meet. We have fielded dozens of surveys both via our Web site and through our work with large and small companies in all sorts of industries. Specifically for this book, we conducted the BridgeWorks Generations Survey, which involved asking a multigenerational sample of several hundred people from all regions of the country and a variety of ethnic backgrounds about their workplace attitudes. The result of the survey has been to help us quantify a topic that can seem very anecdotal and personal.

But for taking the pulse of the generations, nothing beats talking to people. We have consulted with all sorts of companies, from huge Fortune 500 manufacturers to small service organizations. We've worked with for-profits as well as not-for-profits, and through our conversations with top executives, midlevel managers, and frontline employees, we've learned a lot about how people think and feel on the topic of the generations at work.

Often the best snapshots of what the generations think and feel are taken when they come up to talk with us right after a speech. Sure, they might have the odd question or two, but more often than not, what they want to do is tell us a story. Sometimes it's a heartfelt complaint like "Why can't we get these people to work harder?" Or, as a French Canadian Boomer manager in an American plant said to David, "How can we get zees leetle sheets to wise up?!" More often than not, though, it's a story about people who like each other and love working together. They tell us things they've tried that work in their companies. They generously share ways to solve problems, or they make us laugh with examples of what went wrong before they got it right. All of these readings, surveys, interviews, consulting experiences, and most of all stories are what have helped us figure out what to do when generations collide at work.

CAN BRIDGES BE BUILT?

Finding common ground with members of our *own* generation at work is relatively easy. Having lived through the same formative times and shared the same points of reference, we tend to share a feeling of connectedness.

But with members of another generation, connecting can be much more difficult. The same factors that bind one generation can drive apart members of different generations.

While generational collisions may seem utterly impossible to understand in the heat of battle, they can be talked about, understood, and resolved, and they most certainly don't have to end badly. We have organized this book around the key functions in the life of an organization where understanding generational differences can make a direct impact on the bottom line. They are putting the generations to work, recruiting, retaining, and managing the generations. In each section, we provide examples of how the generations see the work world differently, why they see it that way, and the problems that are caused by generational differences. Along the way, we share numerous stories of generational collisions as well as survey findings that show these are not just entertaining anecdotes, but bottom-line management issues. Best of all, we are able to share case studies from our clients and concrete solutions for how these collisions can be resolved and how you can effectively bridge the generations gaps in your workplace.

Eight months after David received his "reprimand," our company received a written memo (with names alphabetized, of course) complimenting David on his attention to detail and letting us know how much fun the client had on the project. Lynne, meanwhile, was gloating with "Video Dude" over the award they had just won at the Houston International Film Festival for the video they created together. And as for David and the Millennial baby-sitter . . . well, after feeling anything but "phat," he and his wife decided from then on they would only hire baby-sitters who drive. Some things do take a little time.

3

THE TIE-DYED PREPPY

We recently received an e-mail that read "I'm 35 years old, am I a Boomer or an Xer?"

Our immediate response was that this person clearly needs a hobby. But as we dug more deeply, we realized this is a very important question, and behind it is a real generational issue as well as an opportunity.

People who e-mail us questions like this are what we call "Cuspers." No, they are not a religious cult or an urban gang. They are individuals who carry an extra strand of generational DNA because they are positioned right between two generations.

CUSPER, THE FRIENDLY GHOST

It comes as a surprise to many who have never noticed them, but we have three different groups of Cuspers in the workplace. The

ON THE CUSP BETWEEN TWO GENERATIONS

dates shown here are approximate. It's up to you to decide where you fit.

Traditionalist/Baby Boomer (born 1940–1945). These are Cuspers who are old enough to relate to the values and work ethic of the Traditionalists, yet young enough to have gotten excited about challenging the status quo along with the Boomers. These Cuspers were too young to fight in the Traditionalist wars, World War II and Korea, yet many were on the leading edge of America's internal struggles, spearheading numerous protest and human rights movements. Many women on the cusp entered a male-dominated work world before the women's movement even existed and blazed a trail for the generations of women who followed.

Older Cuspers may remember gathering around the radio to listen to *The Shadow* but also have fond memories of swinging their hips with Elvis as the jailhouse rocked. About the time their Boomer cohorts aspired to the pastel fashion statements of *Miami Vice,* they were already ensconced in the Traditionalist's dark suit and narrow tie made fashionable by *Dragnet.* And sadly (or luckily, depending on your perspective), "Saturday night fever" probably meant staying up half the night with a sick infant for these Cuspers, rather than an invitation to "do the hustle."

Baby Boomer/Generation Xer. Another group of Cuspers (born 1960–1965) are the men and women who were too young for the protest movements of the 1960s and the disillusionment of the 1970s, but old enough to have seen *Bewitched* when it wasn't a repeat. They may remember the defining Boomer events like Watergate, but as something they saw on the news, not something that changed their lives. Many were still in school during the 1980s and managed to get through school without ever using a computer. And while they were deeply impressed by Gordon Gekko's immortal line from the movie *Wall Street,* "Greed is good," by the time they graduated from college, recession had hit and the greed was gone. They were the ones who had to truly scratch for opportunities in a down economy and the shadow of the millions of Boomers who got there before them.

Many in this group recall their closets filled with John Molloy's "dress for success" clothes, which came in an exciting and colorful array of browns, navies, and grays. At the same time, they remember donning their pink and green polo shirts for leisure wear (collars up, of course) as dictated by *The Preppy Handbook*. These Cuspers can reminisce with the Boomers about nights spent playing Twister, Monopoly, or Risk, but they also pioneered the video game revolution as they led the Xers in mastering Space Invaders and Donkey Kong.

Generation Xer/Millennial. The next group of Cuspers (born approximately 1975–1980) are definitely prime candidates for a bipolar generational personality. On the one hand, they absorbed some of the cautiousness of the skeptical Xers who entered the workforce when jobs were almost impossible to get and were always told they would be the first to do worse than their parents. The younger Cuspers may never have attended a rave, dyed their hair purple, or gotten even a single tattoo, and they resent having been stereotyped with all the negative images heaped upon Generation X. At the same time, they have been imbued with the optimism of the Millennial generation, whose career confidence has been fueled by an unprecedented economic and technological boom.

It's no wonder so many Cuspers we meet have a generational identity crisis. At a presentation to about five hundred sales, office, and photography employees at Lifetouch National School Studios, we asked the Cuspers in the audience to raise their hands. Only about eight people did, and astoundingly they were all sitting together at the same couple of tables. It was not intentional, they told us, but clearly they had something in common that had made them pick one another out of this huge crowd and flock together. Being caught in the middle of two generations can be confusing and even make people feel as if they don't belong at work.

However, while Cuspers may struggle personally, our experience shows that they fill incredibly important roles and may be one of the most precious assets corporate America has access to today.

For example, many don't realize that it was the Boomer/Xer Cuspers who were the first to adapt—and fast—as computers became standard operating procedure in the workplace. Their technological comfort level from the Xer gene made it easier for them to merge onto the information superhighway. At the same time, also being blessed with the Boomer gene allowed them to be the perfect candidates to understand any concerns and help the more computer-illiterate Boomers and Traditionalists get on-line and up to speed! Yet given the perspective and flexibility of the Cuspers, it's surprising how often they are overlooked and undervalued in the workplace.

BRIDGING TROUBLED WATERS

Because Cuspers stand in the gap between the two sides, they become naturals at mediating, translating, and mentoring.

"We have a very fast-paced, demanding group of Xers in our IT department," explained one Boomer/Xer Cusper, "and our senior managers are all Boomers who have an ambitious vision but don't really get the technology. I sincerely believe if I left, there'd be no one to hold everybody together."

We also believe that Cuspers can make the best managers. After all, if you can innately relate to more than one generation, you have the ability to look at the world of work through more than one set of lenses. It can make all the difference when employees feel they are being listened to and truly heard. Whether conducting a performance review, designing a career path, or giving day-to-day feedback, this innate understanding of more than one generation can make Cusper managers both efficient and effective.

One Generation Xer commented on his Cusper supervisor, "My boss is a real mentor. She understands my constant need to talk about my future with the company, but at the same time, she really does a good job of teaching me how to be patient."

Cuspers can provide a voice for those who aren't being heard. They share a common history with the younger generation but possess enough distance to be able to give them perspective. They have the advantage that the older generation will accept a Cusper as "one of them," making them more willing to listen to a Cusper's perspective on touchy subjects like dress codes, diversity, or technology.

While Cuspers should enjoy this, workplaces need to embrace it. Cuspers are invaluable when it comes to designing strategies for recruiting and retaining the younger generation. Without even realizing it, Cuspers may be able to spot workplace or marketplace trends that are going to explode with the next generation simply because they not only get their gestalt, but they get there first.

AND NOW A MESSAGE FOR OUR CUSPERS

So you didn't participate in the March on Washington and were home eating Jiffy Pop and watching *Starsky and Hutch,* or you may have missed out on sex, drugs, and rock and roll because you were in grade school and instead the Carpenters seemed cool to you. But that doesn't mean you didn't have life experiences! The events and conditions that shaped who you are may not be those that everyone in your company can relate to, but there is a unique perspective that only you can provide. What others have to work hard to understand comes naturally to you. One Cusper explained, "Although I'm not really a Traditionalist or a Boomer, I inherited my parents' sense of loyalty. That means I have been willing to stay at this company through thick and thin. At the same time, through the bad times I learned the Boomer quality of adaptability. I appreciate it when I see them challenge the status quo. As a result, I've been able to be both a supporter of policy and a change agent when needed."

At the same time, it is very important that as Cuspers you recognize your stressors, because you may indeed experience tensions that don't affect others around you. For example, you may be a Traditionalist/Boomer Cusper who can't afford to retire because you're juggling kids in college, elderly parents, and your own health concerns while watching child-free, dual-income Boomers younger than you grab their pensions and run. Or you might be an Xer/Millennial Cusper who gets passed over for a job in favor of a seventeen-year-old who's even more techno-savvy than you are. These things happen. Give yourself a break. Your life experiences and perspective made you who you are. That identity may be challenging, but as we see it, it's like having a special degree—it's an extra bullet on your résumé no one ever talks about but that can be worth a fortune.

If nothing else, appreciate that you're the only ones who can use the language and wear the clothes of more than one generation and not look dumb!

4

RACE, RELIGION, GENDER . . . WHAT NEXT?

David always kicks off our workshops on generation gaps at work with the same question: "When I say 'Generation X,' what comes to your mind?" It's amazing how willing people are to immediately call out things like "slacker," "lazy," "grungy," "unmotivated." They do this not only with gusto, but right to David's face!

Now we ask you—what would happen if David were to kick off the seminar by asking, "Hey, everybody, when I say 'Lutherans,' what comes to your mind?" Of course, it would never happen; asking about race or religion is taboo. But when it comes to *generational* stereotyping, anything goes. The good news is that at last there's a form of diversity we can all talk openly about and not worry that the political correctness police will slap us with a violation.

Just as other diversity movements have provided new ways of looking at how to get work done and get along, generational diversity can bring a plethora of new perspectives into the workplace. On

GENERATIONAL DIFFERENCES:
THE NEWEST FORM OF DIVERSITY

the personal front, when employees talk openly about their own generation, it can lead to gaps being bridged and, ultimately, to a more united workforce.

On the professional front, companies that understand generational differences and adjust their recruitment and retention strategies accordingly are reaping bottom-line rewards in terms of an increased success rate with job candidates and higher overall job satisfaction.

Whether it be something as complex as developing a new rewards program or something as simple as changing a few job titles, understanding the generations can be a strategic tool that is relatively easy to work with and can actually be fun.

The bad news is that even with a form of diversity that does not involve tiptoeing or tongue-tying, generational gaffes still occur.

"You're the youngest speakers ever to address our executive committee!" exclaimed the liaison for a Fortune 500 insurance company. The topic they asked us to speak on? How to build long-term client relationships with Generation Xers and Millennials! Go figure.

Other times, David has been asked to visit with a board of directors as a guest expert on generational issues in marketing, sales, or hiring. "Wow!" they always exclaim afterwards. "Why don't we have anyone from your generation on our board?" Seems it never dawned on them that while grappling with how to attract the younger generation of customers or employees, they could actually reach out and recruit one themselves!

The hidden messages are clear to us. It's still uncommon for younger generations to be seen as credible. Yet so often they are exactly the people executives and marketers are failing to listen to in their own workforce or among their own customer base.

On the flip side, too many members of the younger generations assume that youth equates with being the most up-to-date, cutting edge, and in touch. They forget that experience is what gets you up the hill and that not all members of the older generations are over-the-hill.

Often we're far too hesitant or lazy or polite to ask a Traditionalist about her career experiences. Or to ask a Boomer how he got started in his own business. Or to ask an Xer what she aspires to achieve in her lifetime. Or to ask a Millennial what kind of music he likes and why. Are we afraid of the answers? Are we afraid someone is going to bore us with long stories about a bygone war or offend us with talk of the latest hip-hop lyrics? Maybe we need to take a chance; it can definitely be worth it.

Ask Michael Fiterman, CEO of Liberty Diversified, a family-owned group of companies in manufacturing and marketing with over 1,500 employees nationwide. At one of his management retreats, Mike looked around the room, noticed the proliferation of silver hair, and realized that over the next ten years, many of his best people would be retiring. Many of them had been with the organization their entire careers. He saw that the next ten years would require an all-out recruitment war to be fought on several fronts. He would need to find ways to keep his best players in place to keep the company running smoothly. He would need to build bench strength among those qualified to replace his top tier. And he would need to hire a whole new generation of younger managers to begin teaching them the ins and outs of the business *now* if he ever hoped to create a workable succession plan.

This was a challenge. Mike knew that in order to achieve the same high level of tenure with the next generation of managers, he would need to reevaluate the company's benefits package and retention strategies. He needed to make sure the new strategy would appeal to the younger generations, while at the same time, he would never want to do anything that would alienate any of the older generation, who had been so loyal.

Surprisingly, rather than spend hours behind closed doors with the top rungs of the ladder, he decided to stay out of it and let the generations involved tackle the challenge.

"I didn't want to guess what they wanted; I wanted them to tell me," Mike explained. Exactly who did he mean by "them"? For one year, thirty employees made up of a mix of Traditionalists, Baby Boomers, and Generation Xers, ranging from one year with the company to over thirty, formed a team and put their generational perspectives on the table as to what the new benefits strategy should be.

Sound risky? Perhaps. But by taking the risk, Mike Fiterman knew that the benefits plan would take the needs of all the generations into account. What he didn't know was the result would be more than a change in strategy on paper. A change would also occur in the hearts and minds of his multigenerational workforce.

"We weren't too excited about each other at first," commented one veteran of the year-long project. "At the kickoff meeting I looked around the table at all these different ages of people and just didn't know how we were going to relate. But by the end of the project, I'd made lifetime friends in people I never would have considered getting to know before."

At Liberty, some of the strongest bonds were formed between the old and the young. Many Xers have shared what it has meant to them to have an older friend or mentor they could look up to. And many Boomers and Traditionalists have mentioned what a breath of fresh air it was to work with someone younger. Programs are cropping up that help these relationships along for Millennials who may not have access to mentors and those who want to mentor. The San Francisco Bay Area nonprofit Women Across Generations is one such organization.

"Our ultimate goal is to empower teen women," says board member Marie-Jeanne Juilland. "Cross-generational mentoring is key. Research shows that around age twelve young teen girls can start losing their confidence and develop issues with self-esteem. When we as adult women offer our ears, life experiences, skills, and hearts to these young women, they get a glimpse of other possibilities."

The value of generational diversity seems to have gone unnoticed for so many years because when we think of sitting down with someone from a different generation, we imagine the conversation kicking off with, "In my day we trudged ten miles up hill to get to work even during a blizzard!" Sure, the topic lends itself to nostalgia, but why would sharing stories about how we got to work in a blizzard stop once we got there?

The reason the phrase *in my day* is so recognized is that each of us feels we have our own day and our own way of doing things. Every generation of employees walks through the door or punches that time clock with a different perspective, from the way people map out their careers to how they want to give and receive information. This is diversity at its finest! Just because there may not have been a sit-in or a protest around the topic doesn't mean generational diversity doesn't carry weight in the workplace. Sometimes it is the invisible poison that is the most deadly. By no means are we suggesting that other forms of diversity are not extremely important and challenging to deal with. There is still an incredible amount to be done on all the diversity fronts. What we are saying is that generational diversity is not just a trend that will come and go with shifts in the economy, nor is it the type of diversity that affects only a small portion of the workforce. Generational diversity impacts everyone and is here to stay.

Okay, now that we made it sound like a new deadly virus, we need to say that far from being something to be frightened about, generational diversity is something to get excited about. A year and a half after Mike Fiterman set up his task forces, his corporate controller, Irene Rygh, was faced with the challenge of creating more continuity for payroll procedures across all of Liberty's divisions.

What did she do? She put together her own multigenerational task force of employees with varying degrees of experience. As she put it, "We have employees in such different life stages dealing with such different things that unless I listen to all of the generations, I won't know if I am being fair to everyone."

It seems Fiterman gave his employees more than a new benefits package when he put those first task forces together. He gave them a lesson that has improved not only his business, but the day-to-day lives of employees as well.

PUTTING THE GENERATIONS TO WORK

5

WHAT DO YOU WANT TO BE WHEN YOU GROW UP?

It's 1981, and Traditionalist Tom has just been promoted to marketing manager. He pulls out the corporate org chart to review his destined path. Tom feels confident that in less than five years he can become a marketing supervisor and ultimately achieve his goal of marketing vice president before he retires twenty years from now. His career path is set!

If only it were that easy today. No longer can an org chart come close to describing all the possible directions a career might take. With competitive pressures, tight labor markets, and economic upheavals, companies are becoming much more creative in how they plan and manage employees' career paths. Employees who understand where they are going and who can see that their direction is in line with the direction of the organization are much more likely to sign on and stay. Unfortunately, almost 60 percent of respondents in our survey said they did not have "a clearly defined career path where I work." With career pathing such a critical tool for motivating and retaining employees, it's dismaying to us that such a huge proportion of employees are lacking a specific plan.

However, as much as the pressure is on for companies to pull out the career compass for employees, they shouldn't have to do *all* the planning. It's time for employees of every generation to emulate what Gen Xers have been doing for close to a decade—that is, take an aggressive role in creating their own career paths.

When talking through this section, we had one of our typical generational clashes. As a Boomer, Lynne's point of view was that organizations and employees should share equally in the responsibility for developing career paths that are both secure and meaningful. As an Xer, David vehemently disagreed: "I would go so far as to say that employees have 100 percent of the responsibility for their careers and that if the company pitches in, it's only a bonus. The goal is to find champions at work who believe in your path and who will help you make it happen, but ultimately the responsibility is the employee's alone."

Where many Traditionalists were part of paternalistic organizations that took care of employees, Boomers experienced a degree of competition that forced them to be less trusting and more proactive about their careers. Xers, raised in an environment in which the employer-employee contract was written in invisible ink, have taken career independence to a whole new level and seem the least dependent on the company to provide them with a career path. For example, when we asked Xers in our survey, "What activities convince you that your company really cares about your career development?" 36 percent said they get "nothing from the company, I self-manage." This presents a real problem if you believe, as we do, that working actively with Generation Xers to develop their career paths is one of the best ways to retain them. At the same time, mergers, layoffs, and economic downturns have created a workplace environment where every generation is having to take more responsibility for their careers. Employees like Tom can no longer assume that organizations will look after them long-term or provide a career path that's right for them. The payoff is more control over your own life, better ability to respond in stressful times, and a more satisfying career. At the same time, we believe companies can engender a lot more loyalty in employees by making sure they know where they are going.

As both employers *and* employees become the architects of career paths, the really successful players are incorporating generational differences into their blueprints. While all the generations share the drive to get ahead, there are clear differences in the approaches each will take.

Where do you start?

UNDERSTAND THE DIFFERENCE BETWEEN "JOB SECURITY" AND "CAREER SECURITY"

Before we put pen to paper and design career paths for the generations, it is critical to understand the difference between *job security* and *career security*. "Job security" is the model followed by most Boomers and Traditionalists. It says the goal is to find a company where you can stay for a long time, work your way up, become vested, and make yourself increasingly secure by virtue of your accomplishments and your tenure there. This model worked fine when companies were more paternalistic and "lifetime employment" was virtually guaranteed as long as you didn't screw up.

In our presentations, we like to show a video clip from the television show *ER* in which the Traditionalist chief of surgery, Dr. Anspaugh, is trying to retain a Boomer doctor, Dr. Greene, who is threatening to leave the hospital. The arguments Dr. Anspaugh uses to lure Dr. Green are perfectly aimed at a dutiful Boomer focused on job security: "You kept me awake last night." "I do not want to run the emergency department without you." "I could push up your eligibility [for tenure] and consider you in 2002." Guilt, duty, loyalty, and security are all played out in a minute-long scene.

On the flip side, "career security" is what we call the model embraced by Generation Xers. Skeptical Xers have seen too many American institutions crumble to believe any of them will be around for the duration, let alone that they'll reward loyalty with lifetime careers. Thus Xers lack faith that job security exists anymore. The career security model says you should build a portfolio of skills and experiences that guarantees that no matter what cataclysmic event occurs, you'll be able to land on your feet. For Xers, this can make job changing seem like a necessity. Many have told us they needed to move around until they felt they had enough bullets on their résumés to feel employable in case the worst should happen.

To demonstrate career security, we show another clip from *ER*. In this clip, Traditionalist Dr. Anspaugh is again called upon to keep a doctor from quitting. This time it's the quintessential Xer Dr. Carter. And this time Anspaugh switches tactics. No more blather about indispensability and long lead times for tenure. This time Anspaugh focuses on trying to understand where Carter wants to end up long-term. He uncovers that Carter doesn't want to leave the hospital; he just wants to leave surgery. Normally, a Traditionalist like Anspaugh would be tempted to say, "Forget it. You made a commitment, you're halfway through the program, quit screwing around and finish what you started!" But he knows Carter well enough to know that won't work. If Carter can't achieve his goals at this hospital, he'll find another where he can. Dr. Anspaugh wants to keep Carter on the team, even if that means he jumps from surgery to another specialty. The message applies even in real life. Companies that understand the difference between job security and career security are able to be more creative in designing career paths that make each of the generations want to stay.

With the key differentiator between *job* security and *career* security on the map, you are now ready to help the generations navigate their career paths.

"ARE WE THERE YET?" UNDERSTANDING THE GENERATIONS' DESTINATIONS

It's always nice when plotting a course to have an idea as to where the destination lies. Understanding the different generations' goals makes career paths all the easier to navigate.

 CLASHPOINT AROUND CAREER GOALS

Traditionalists . . .	*"Build a legacy."*
Baby Boomers . . .	*"Build a stellar career."*
Generation Xers . . .	*"Build a portable career."*
Millennials . . .	*"Build parallel careers."*

Traditionalists

"Build a legacy." Many in this generation expected to build a lifetime career with one employer, or at least in a single field. That loyalty, combined with the desire to leave a lasting legacy, has guided Traditionalists in planning their next career steps. Organizations make a huge mistake when they fail to recognize the deep sense of personal responsibility felt by many Traditionalists toward the places they work. Rather than view Traditionalists as over-the-hill, we need to see them as still moving along a path that involves service, loyalty, and the desire to give back.

Smart companies are tapping Traditionalists *today* to recareer into roles as leaders, recruiters, and trainers—all vehicles that allow them to retool a lifetime of experience *and* ultimately leave something behind. One of the biggest mistakes we see companies make when implementing career-planning programs is forgetting to include the Traditionalists. When we asked Traditionalists, "What activities convince you that your company really cares about your career development?" 31 percent responded, "They don't seem to care." We think that's an appallingly high number for a generation that's been around and loyal for such a long time. Just because they are close to retirement age doesn't mean they want to retire. And just because they have been traveling down the career path the longest doesn't mean they have reached their final destination. Companies that don't check up on career paths for older employees are just encouraging them to check out.

While telling a Generation Xer to take a proactive role in career planning is like preaching to the choir, Traditionalists tend to be anything but "evangelists." They need to embrace what we call the "fast-forward phenomenon." Traditionalists need to buck their natural tendency to trust the system and agitate for companies to help them create a compelling career direction. When we asked Traditionalists if they "would feel comfortable talking with [their] manager about a different career track within [their] company," 33.5 percent say they would *not* feel comfortable. We think this could mean one of two things. Either the managers aren't making Traditionalists feel they are welcome to talk about such moves, or old taboos about appearing to be disloyal prevent Traditionalists from approaching their bosses. Too many still wait passively for companies to dictate the path to take or hope the best next step will emerge. Traditionalists should never assume it's too late to embark upon a stimulating career path and should push their companies hard for information about where their careers might take them next.

Baby Boomers

"Build a stellar career." Boomers have always wanted to excel in their careers, and many are reaching a critical life stage in which the ticking of the biological clock is being replaced by the ticking of the career clock. Boomers are realizing they have a limited amount of time left to excel and to earn at peak capacity and they are going to want to make the most of these remaining career years. While Boomers are less likely to job-hop than Xers, employers can no longer assume that Boomers will wait forever for top positions to open up. As millions of Boomers move toward retirement age, now is the time for organizations to consider how they will seize Boomers' loyalty. Developing challenging career paths may be the best solution. One thing is for sure: This generation loves to be challenged. The answer, however, isn't to pile on more work and even more direct reports to manage—many Baby Boomers are already feeling burned out. The strategy is to design a path that includes opportunities that will vault them to the next level in terms of opportunity, visibility, or challenge.

At the same time, as many Boomers are preparing for the final assault on their careers' summit, they are increasingly moving into a more contemplative life stage. Baby Boomers are questioning whether or not they made the right career choices and whether their careers have meaning. In our survey, when we asked Boomers who knew that they could make more money elsewhere if they left their current jobs why they stayed, less than 10 percent said they stayed "because I love my work!" We're surprised and intrigued that the number would be so low, and we suspect that over the next ten years Boomers will become less focused on earning and moving up and more focused on finding work that provides satisfaction and fulfillment. Companies that can tap into those desires are likely to have the greatest advantage in retaining top Baby Boomers.

If you're a Boomer listening closely to the career clock tick, and you still want that "stellar career," the solution hasn't changed since you joined the workforce. Just as you did years back when eighty million others applied for your job, you need to stand out from the crowd. Request projects that will put you in the limelight and showcase your unseen talents. Talk to your Traditionalist mentors about new places you might fit, and be willing to hear any career advice or feedback they give you. If you stopped seeking out mentors somewhere along the way, now might be the time to get a new one. Having seen more than one economic ebb and flow, you have the advantage over younger generations to foresee or predict company reactions. If your hunch is that the company is going to be affected by any downturns, think ahead about what you can do now to shore up your value. Ask yourself what you can do to make your contribution indispensable. Do some informational interviewing within your company and outside of it. Look around at jobs you might want to take on next. Although Xers almost appear to walk around their place of employment wearing a sandwich sign reading, "HEY, EVERYBODY . . . I'M LOOKING FOR A JOB!" we see some merit in operating with the normal Boomer secrecy so that you don't send the wrong message about your loyalty. At the same time, don't be too afraid to talk to your bosses about your direction and put them to work on your career path, too.

Generation Xers

"Build a portable career." In the movie *Annie Hall,* Woody Allen compared relationships to sharks: they have to keep moving forward or they die. Generation Xers have tended to feel the same way about their careers. Their switch from looking for job security to career security has made it critical for them to keep building a repertoire of skills and experiences they can take with them if they need to. In interviews, Xers tell us they can't stand the thought of reaching a dead end. Their greatest fear is that they might become stagnant. The rate of change they've seen during their lifetimes and the cynical sense that everything is temporary play into their distrust of

career permanence. In addition, any generation raised with the knowledge that computers become obsolete in a matter of months can't help but feel that way about their own shelf life at work.

The desire to build a résumé that contains a variety of experiences that make them more widely hirable is one reason Xers have made a conscious effort to change jobs (long before a Boomer or a Traditionalist would have). It is not unusual for an Xer to tell us in an interview, "I felt I had to move, I just didn't have enough on my résumé yet to really feel secure." For the older generations, who had a longer job time horizon in mind, and greater loyalty to institutions, this attitude is both foreign and objectionable. It's easy to see why Boomers and Traditionalists often describe Xers as "flaky," "unreliable," or "disloyal." One twenty-three-year-old we interviewed recently left Arthur Andersen after a successful eighteen-month stint because she couldn't see where she was going to be a year later. Whether that was due to her own impatience or her boss's inability to show her a career path she could love, or a combination, the fact remains that she moved on.

But while Xers are focused on career security, that doesn't mean they can't find it within a single organization, if that organization is keeping a running dialogue with Xers about where they're going and what it's going to take to get them there. If Xers feel they are being coached and trained, and that they are building a career portfolio, then they're much more likely to stay. We really do believe this is a generation searching for a place to call home. Mark Bailey, director of staffing and recruiting for General Mills, has seen this shift. "Xers really don't *want* to move . . . they want stability," he explained. "The goal is to show them a place that is willing to invest in them as a person. In return, they give you their all."

The challenge in designing Xers' career paths is to accept that they are looking at the world of work through skeptical lenses. As we said, this might mean job-hopping a bit at first to build some experience on the résumé. Or it might mean bugging the boss every few months about that next career move. But rather than see this as dissatisfied or disloyal, see it for what it is—a survival strategy. When developing career paths, point out to Xers that the career skills they are developing at each step are skills that will serve them in future jobs, even if not with your company. Expose them to assignments that are "résumé builders." Xers may be in your building, but you need to treat them as if they have one foot perpetually out the door when it comes to career paths. Soothing their career jitters by talking about how you're helping them build a portable career is the single best way to make sure they never leave.

If you're an Xer employee, it's one thing to be ambitious and eager; it's another to annoy your superiors to the point where they can't stand to see you coming down the hall. "My biggest complaint about Xers," explained one Traditionalist manager of a consulting group, "is that they assume they are ready to do anything I can do. But I've spent sixteen years gaining experience about our clients, our services, and how to handle difficult negotiations. There's no way they are going to be good at this in a year or two, and it offends me that they are not willing to take the time to learn to do it right." Xers need to embrace the "slow motion notion" by being a little more patient and taking the time to become truly competent in what they do. It may seem as if you are moving in slow motion for a time, but being willing to move in synch with others' timing shows respect for the process and will smooth the way with those who can help you the most.

If you are with a good company and you believe your bosses recognize your talents and see a future for you there, let the process work on your behalf. Companies have their own time frames, and believe it or not, there's often a good reason for them.

MOVE OVER CHUTES AND LADDERS; THE NEW GAME IS *RUBIK'S CUBICLE*

We'll talk about the Millennials and their "parallel careers" shortly, but first we wanted to remind you that once you have the different generations' destinations in mind, it is critical that you remain open to different routes to get there. It used to be that careers had only three directions they could go in—up, down, or sideways. Winners went up, losers went down, and dead-enders made lateral moves. That's old thinking. The two-dimensional career path is out, the multiple dimensions of what we call "Rubik's cubicle" is in.

What is it? It's a model that says career directions are as numerous as the moves in Rubik's cube. And they aren't all upward. Moves can go up, down, or sideways, depending on strategy and fit.

Companies need to acknowledge and support the idea that successful career paths don't always have to go up. But too many managers have it ingrained in their psyches that upward mobility is the only way to motivate or challenge employees. Whether it's accelerated learning, control of project selection, more schedule flexibility, or a lateral move, there are many forms of enrichment that can challenge and excite employees.

Not everyone wants to move up to management. Hair-cutting franchise managers with a national low-cost hairstyling chain posed this question to us in a workshop: What do you do when some stylists aspire to move up (to become supervisors, managers, trainers, franchisees, and so on) and others just want to be stylists? This was an important question because both career paths are highly valuable to the organization. The answer, of course, is to create compelling paths in a number of directions and put resources toward helping employees on each path be the best they can be, whether they are moving up, down, or sideways. And along each of those paths, offer feedback, training, and support. A gifted stylist might want to abbreviate her schedule to have more personal time. She might want to bump up the creative side of her job by going to more classes or giving classes herself. She might want to enlist as a management trainee. She might even want to be tapped for a job at corporate. Thinking outside the box about career paths means imagining all the permutations of Rubik's cubicle and applying those to your employees in the ways that best fit them.

The question is, how willing are you to truly accept that there just may be more than one way to get where you want to go?

TALK ABOUT CAREER PATHS, INCESSANTLY

Once you have the different generations' destinations in mind, and even a variety of routes to get there, it is critical that you keep on driving and driving and driving. In other words, talk about career paths incessantly.

Because just when you think you have a career path set in stone and can put that map back in the glove compartment, guess what? It's time to look at it again. The career path time horizon is growing shorter by the minute, and managers aren't prepared to respond. Whether it's because the older generations are more able to see their next steps or they're just more patient, many Traditionalists and Boomers don't have their own career paths laid out in nearly the amount of detail they are expected to produce for others. Generation Xers are constantly pulling out their career maps to double-check that they are headed in the right direction or, more often than not, to make a detour and change routes. Unless managers are always looking over these maps *with* their Generation X employees, they can be blindsided and find that someone who *is* paying attention has come along and picked the Xer up for the ride instead.

Not only do we have to talk more often about career paths, we have to start talking about them sooner. Beth Leonard, partner and head of college recruiting for the accounting firm of Lurie, Besikof, Lapidus, reported that as a Boomer she's been astonished by Xers' and Millennials' willingness to ask for specifics about their career paths *in the initial job interview!* Beth isn't alone. In our BridgeWorks Survey, we found that one complaint Generation Xers had about orientation at their companies was that career paths weren't discussed. Probably the Boomer or Traditionalist who designed the orientation programs didn't realize Xers would be demanding answers their first day on the job.

Rather than get mad at Traditionalists and Boomers, Xers need to understand that the older generations never had the luxury of demanding such details. They were expected to pay their dues and prove themselves for "an appropriate amount of time" before talking about advancement or risk seeming pushy. Generation Xers are demanding that organizations speed up the duration of career paths. While Boomers generally assumed they'd spend one to five years in a position before being promoted, Xers want to know where they're going to be next month.

Baby Boomer Greg Jensen, a manager at Lockheed, explained the clash this way: "I have a twenty-nine-year-old direct report who is outstanding. I've gone to incredible lengths to keep her—pushing for promotions, trying to get her more money, involving her in challenging projects—and it's really rewarding. But it's also exhausting. The pace of her expectations for her job is completely foreign to me, and the rate of change she expects within the company is just unrealistic."

One disgruntled Xer e-mailed us that he really loved his job but wasn't sure he would be there a long time. As much as he enjoyed what he was doing, it wasn't clear enough to him where it would take him or what his growth potential was. This was making him just too nervous to stick around. Sounds fair, until we tell you that he had been in that job for six weeks!

When we asked in our BridgeWorks Generations Survey, "When it comes to a career path, I believe a person should . . . ," the generations showed distinct differences. Twenty-nine percent of Traditionalists chose "build a lifetime career with one company," compared to 14 percent of Boomers and just 11 percent of Gen Xers. Clearly, the belief that a lifetime career with a single company is desirable, or even possible, is lessening with each generation. But that doesn't mean career paths are hitting dead ends. It just means companies will have to create more compelling journeys for their best employees if they hope to convince them to stay.

Talking incessantly about career paths does not apply just to Xers. With that career clock ticking louder and louder, Boomers are picking up on this career-path impatience. Jan Haeg, a midlevel manager with Lifetouch who had reached a career plateau recently, challenged her company to revamp her career path to help her get reenergized. The company responded by encouraging her to develop a new position she thought would suit her and benefit the company. She is now recommitted to her career path and reinspired to work with her company.

Understanding Boomers' individual needs will be critical to designing their career paths. Some are moving into the most crazed and time-crunched phase of life, which means they may need to slow the pace of work for a while. (Small wonder a recent Del Webb poll showed that the most significant landmark event Boomers look forward to over the next few years is an empty nest!) Others are moving into a peak period of career productivity. Boomers are reaching an age at which their technical knowledge of their job will combine with their vast experience working with people and their ability to visualize where organizations need to go. This buildup of wisdom and passion, and the desire to do it *now* before the opportunity is lost, puts Boomers and organizations under pressure to work seriously on their career paths and build next steps as fast as Boomers can climb. Companies that can capitalize on this career intensity will be tapping into one of their greatest assets.

As we've said earlier, talking about career paths incessantly with Traditionalists means remembering that they can reinvent their careers at any age. Managers should not assume that Traditionalists will be satisfied to stay plateaued. The best idea is to keep a running dialogue with Traditionalists so they know where they stand and so you know what their career aspirations are. They might surprise you. One sixty-five-year-old Traditionalist told us that when she met with her boss for her annual review, she expected to be asked when she planned on retiring. Instead, the boss asked if she'd be interested in a promotion. "I had been feeling unmotivated up until that point, and thinking maybe retirement was the best choice. Taking that promotion was the best thing that ever happened to me!" We'd bet it was good for the company, too.

Traditionalists, Baby Boomers, and Xers have very different destinations, routes, and speeds to consider when mapping career paths. And companies dealing with these differences can definitely relate to the immortal phrase of the Grateful Dead—"What a long, strange trip it's been." But just when we all thought navigating career journeys couldn't get any more complicated, along comes a whole new generation of passengers.

MILLENNIALS "BUILD PARALLEL CAREERS"

If employers are finding Xers to be overly résumé focused, they are likely to be even more shocked by Millennials. This generation is already being coached by their parents to build extensive portfolios for college admission. They already understand the importance of balancing hobbies, sports, and volunteer activities with a variety of work experiences. (There is a reason we are seeing so many concerned child psychologists make pleas to parents to *stop* overprogramming their children.)

Where Traditionalists seek to build *lifetime* careers, Boomers to build *stellar* careers, and Xers to build *portable* careers, the career path ClashPoint for Millennials will be around *parallel* careers. Millennials' programmed lives have made them true multitaskers. Millennials are already quite capable of learning several jobs simultaneously and performing them admirably. Millennials are throwing out the old model that you're either a waitress, a hostess, or running the register. Why can't you be all three? Sound like a crazy way to manage? In a tight labor market, making sure scarce Millennials can cover more than one position is a smart strategy. In a contracting economy, it's cost-effective to put Millennials' multitasking abilities to use rather than hire more employees. Plus, cross-training is a great retention strategy, which reduces the expense of turnover.

Baby Boomer Daniel Mohorc is president and CEO of a Dallas-based travel incentive and marketing company called Galactic Marketing. He was smart enough early on to recognize that his Millennial recruits plan on having more than one career in their lifetimes and that he'd like those careers to be with him. So he created a program called Walk a Mile in My Shoes that is a real win-win. Each quarter, employees choose someone from a different department with whom they swap jobs for at least four hours. The goal is to get a feel for what it's like to work in a different department using a different set of skills. Once the swap is completed, each participant receives a hundred-dollar certificate. Not only does it encourage employees to step out and explore all their career opportunities within the company, but it allows Galactic to build bench strength by cross-training employees. Plus, everyone develops a greater appreciation for what the other people in the company are doing—a giant step for morale!

If managers think the idea of plugging multitasking Millennials into more than one box on the org chart is going to make career pathing a challenge, buckle up! It's only the beginning.

Futurists predict that Millennials will experience as many as ten career changes in their lifetimes. That's *career* changes, not *job* changes—meaning they will recycle their skills and talents and personal preferences into new applications again and again and again. Throughout their careers, this generation will be ready, willing, and able to adapt to an organization's evolving structure.

You're probably thinking, *Great! Just when I was beginning to accept that keeping an Xer for a year was good enough, I have to get ready to see the Millennials come and go in a few months!* Not to worry. In fact, we actually have good news. We believe that Millennials will reject the Generation Xers' distrust of organization and instead judge organizations on their own merit. That will make it possible for them to imagine having a *lifetime* career with one company if they can hook up with an organization that offers the right combination of challenge, opportunity, and even security. And, if managers and employees are willing and able to devise career plans like never before.

CHEW ON THIS . . .

A Millennial graduating from college in 2002 might enlist in the Peace Corps and spend a couple of years abroad, then return to join corporate America to work in human resources, using the people skills developed working abroad. After learning how to recruit and retain employees internally, our Millennial might choose to apply those skills to the customer service unit, where she will be trained to now interact with customers instead of employees. Again, the Millennial is using all the skills already obtained to move in a new direction but will also be acquiring new knowledge as she learns all about the company's offerings. It won't be long before this self-motivated Millennial with people skills and a good understanding of the company's products and services might notice patterns in the types of things customers are complaining about. That would be enough to propel her in yet another career direction—research.

Exhausted? Well, guess what? Our Millennial is now only thirty-two!

If we'd just described this career path for a Traditionalist, that final promotion to research might have taken place when he was in his mid-fifties, or it might never have happened at all, since recruiting, customer service, and research are seldom lined up on the same track. When we talk to Traditionalist CEOs about what Millennial career paths will be like, they immediately turn white . . . or should we say green, as they can't help but think of the dollars involved? Who can blame them for considering that the cost of filling each position will be higher than if that Millennial had stayed in it longer?

Not to mention the cost of providing the training and coaching needed for each skill transfer along the way. But we have no choice. We cannot look at Millennials' career paths as a liability, we have to switch our thinking and look at it as an asset. Yes, recycling Millennials will cost more, but think of the value created. They will not only be a generation that knows the system and how it fits together, they will care. With so many career paths within a company, they will be uniquely suited to becoming missionaries to drive change through the organization and down to the customer.

Under the Traditionalist model, our Millennial might have remained in HR her entire life. Or she might have had the guts to make one career change move into customer service, then found herself moving up through the ranks of customer service manager, customer service supervisor, director of customer service, assistant VP of customer service, and on and on. The problem with this career path for Millennials will be that learning slows to a crawl, and they will very likely become bored. It's hard to imagine so many careers in a lifetime for just one person. Even more important, it sounds stressful, especially for managers who are already struggling hard to map career paths for three generations already in the workforce. But in the eyes of the Millennials, the opportunity to pursue parallel careers might be the trend that most attracts them and wins their long-term loyalty.

A FINAL WORD . . .

Before we close on Millennial career paths, we have a plea. We hate to be like those Oscar recipients who thank the producers, directors, actors, and family members but then also use their platform to tell millions of viewers to stop using aerosol sprays—but we do feel this is relevant. The challenge in writing anything about the Millennials' career paths is to identify which Millennials you're writing about. It's an unspeakable loss to think about all those children who will never participate fully in our workforce because they lack opportunities now. At the time of this writing, the *San Francisco Chronicle* published statistics showing the number of U.S. children living below the poverty level. California, which boasts the sixth largest economy in the *world*, was found to have 25 percent of its children living in poverty. That put California just below *Russia* when it comes to taking care of its children.

Organizations and individuals must do more to reach down and pull these children into the mainstream. We can do a great deal toward helping them by partnering with schools to provide training, mentoring, and internship programs. We can develop internal policies that encourage the hiring and teaching of those who might make outstanding employees if given the chance. We can push policy makers, not just on education, but on helping to educate young people in a way that will enable them to support themselves later on. And we can push ourselves to be more compassionate and creative in reaching out. We can be mentors, Big Brothers and Sisters, friends, coaches, teachers, or employers—whatever it takes. We can all remember that not every Millennial will have the opportunity to use a computer or go to college. In fact, the sheer numbers of Millennials (seventy-six million) will make it even harder on their generation to get the resources they need. Already studies are emerging to show that financial aid will be in too much demand as the Millennial boom hits campuses.

As we think about the career paths for the Millennial generation, we owe it to our future to remember the poor children who are being excluded from the best our system has to offer in terms of food, shelter, medical care, parenting, education, and technology and who will *not* travel down the same paths because they have not been groomed for them, unless we find ways to help.

6

FROM A GOLD CLOCK TO FOUNDERS' STOCK

Judith Cohen, a hard-charging Boomer and president of San Francisco–based CoMotion Corporation, wanted to reward one of her Xer employees for his outstanding performance on a client's marketing communications project. What did she do? She invited the Xer to accompany her on a Friday trip to Los Angeles for the big client meeting. What did the Xer do? Turned her down flat. As he explained, "You know, I have been working such crazy hours lately that I was really looking forward to having a long weekend. Since I'm not really needed there, I think I will pass."

She did mind. "I was rewarding him with the ultimate vote of confidence by including him in a meeting with the president and key executives of one of our biggest clients. To him the reward was being home so he could hang out and start

REWARDING THE GENERATIONS

the weekend early?! I just couldn't get over it. I mean, how could he not appreciate an opportunity like that to get exposure in front of such influential people?"

Ask the Boomer, and the reward was going on an important business trip. Ask the Xer, and it was not having to go at all. Generational differences are making it harder for employers to figure out the best ways to reward employees. Take a reward as common and as simple as time off. . . .

Steve, a twenty-nine-year-old Generation Xer in a food and beverage company, has been logging sixty-hour workweeks. His stress level is high, and he's spent little time at home lately. One day Steve stops in the office of his Traditionalist supervisor to say, "Hey, John, I won't be here on Friday, I need a mental health day."

John's immediate response: "Is that going to be a vacation day or a sick day?"

Steve pauses. "I don't know . . . whatever . . . I just need a break."

"Well, I'll check with Human Resources and get back to you."

Steve rolls his eyes. He doesn't care how the time is logged; he just needs a day off. His boss, on the other hand, can't understand why Steve seems to disregard policies and procedures. John, a Traditionalist with sixteen years of service, is almost never sick and has accrued eleven months of paid leave he can cash in when he retires.

What sounds like just a personality clash is really a much deeper generational collision being felt in companies large and small. Clearly there's a conflict at work here (no pun intended) between the paternalistic model that monitored employees' time off and the PTO, or "paid time off," model, which combines sick and vacation time into one pool of personal days employees can use at their own discretion.

Increasingly, for many companies the solution to the collision is to move to PTO. These plans don't cost any more to implement, can actually save money over time in administrative costs, and can work for companies of any size in any industry. So what's the holdup? Generational collisions.

The older generations have been accustomed to following strict guidelines as to what constitutes vacation time or sick leave. In exchange, they benefit from being able to accrue unused days over many years, with the idea that they'll stockpile them "for a rainy day." If that rainy day never comes, they can usually cash in accrued time on the back end of their careers, having used the value of all those days as a sort of investment plan.

The younger generations believe in using their days, not stock-piling them, and don't want to have to explain to anyone whether they were actually sick or were taking time off to sit around and watch *Oprah*.

The pressure on companies to address these differences has been mounting. According to the Commerce Clearing House (CCH), unscheduled employee absenteeism increased by 25 percent in the late 1990s, costing employers an average of $757 per employee. Yet the CCH found that although there was a rise in unscheduled absences, most employees were not sick, but were taking care of family-related issues. Employees are adopting the "hooky" approach and calling in sick at the last minute to take care of personal matters they knew about well in advance. An unscheduled absence disrupts the work pipeline, creates stress for employees who must carry the load, and affects the bottom line in terms of lost profitability.

If generational differences are getting in the way of rewards as commonplace as time off, how are employers expected to address everything else from on-site day care to school reimbursement?

While we know from our survey that 40 percent of respondents said that in the last eighteen months their companies have had to "offer new kinds of rewards" in order to attract employees, we're not sure they understand how the generations view these rewards. Companies need to assess how the generations differ and adjust recruitment, management, and retention strategies accordingly. This doesn't mean we're telling companies they need to offer completely different rewards packages to each generation. It doesn't even mean that companies need to change what they are doing now. What we're saying is that companies need to be more creative in the ways they are willing to compensate the different generations of employees, and then managers need to be more comfortable applying those rewards in ways that actually will motivate the generations.

THE RETURN ON INVESTMENT

The first step in rewarding the generations is to stop thinking of them as a one-way transaction. Too often, companies see rewards as merely an expense item and not as an investment that actually benefits them as well. A classic example is technology, one of the hottest perks on the rewards scene. It used to be that a company car was the be-all and end-all. Now it's the company laptop with DVD, CD-ROM, and more gigabytes than the FBI's mainframe. Somehow employees who receive technology as a reward continue to get pumped up by it. Perhaps carrying the latest and greatest gadgets just makes people feel cool, no matter who they are. And giving employees connectivity tools makes them feel that they are indispensable. The shocker is that there are still companies that consider portable PCs and company-funded home computers too much of an expense. Yet what could make more sense than giving employees a perk that enables them to put in more hours, work from home, and better balance their personal lives to boot? Like Pavlov's people, the more tools we have for working remotely, the more we seem to log in. In the *American Lawyer*'s first "Who's Wired, Who's Tired" survey of law firms in 1998, Alston & Bird LLP tied for first as the most "wired" law firm because they use technology so well. The firm provides, at no cost to associates, wireless devices for picking up e-mail and cash allowances toward the purchase of laptops—all ways of helping associates stay in touch while away from the office.

This naturally builds a lot of flexibility into the job. As midlevel Generation X associate Jim Casey explains, he can drop his kids off at school in the morning and come in a little later but still be available via his wireless device and cell phone for clients who need to reach him right away. While some might be put off by being continually wired into the office via such tools, Jim and others like him embrace such new technology because it allows them to perform their jobs while maintaining a greater degree of lifestyle flexibility.

Xer Kris Evans Bien, a former marketing manager at Microsoft, says one of her biggest losses when she left the company was the separation from her high-tech toys. "Having the latest technology made me work harder, yes. I could work anywhere, anytime—even at home or while traveling. It enabled me to be very productive. But it also made work more fun, because there's a lot of status attached to having the latest high-tech gadgets. It provided an image of being cool and on the cutting edge."

So rewards should not be looked at as a one-way donation. Whether high-tech, low-tech, or no-tech, companies stand to garner significant returns by understanding how to apply rewards in the right way. And no, we don't mean a nice thank-you card with sunflowers or sunrises. We're talking about a direct impact on the bottom line. General Mills, for example, offers free on-site flu shots, which can be provided at a very low cost to the organization. For workers, this can literally be a lifesaver. But it's also a lifesaver to the company when you think about the domino effect of reducing sick days. Not only do healthy employees come to work instead of staying home sick, but they also don't spread the flu to their families or other workers. Flu shots alone must save General Mills tens of thousands of person hours per year, as well as the medical expenses for those who have to be seen by a doctor under General Mills's medical plan.

Take this a little further and rewards can even make existing programs more cost-effective. One of our clients, for example, has an award-winning employee cafeteria that has begun to offer what the food and beverage industry refers to as "home meal replacement." This means that employees can stop by the cafeteria after work and order a complete family dinner packed to take home. This is a huge reward in terms of time and cost savings for the employee, but it also expands the usefulness of the cafeteria, which formerly opened only for breakfast and lunch. And without having to worry about what to put on the table, employees are actually more available to stay at work later.

THE CAT'S OUT OF THE BAG

Once you can drop the mind frame that rewards are *just* for employees, you can more clearly see them as a true win-win. However, that still doesn't make it easy. How can organizations effectively reward up to four generations of employees when each generation has different expectations for what the rewards should be? If a certain reward is a turn-off for one generation and a turn-on for another, what's an employer to do?

A Generation X Web site animator we know flew to the East Coast from California to spend a day interviewing with one of the hottest firms in the industry. After interviewing with the Boomer art director, he spent some informal time with the Xer designers he'd be working with, comparing notes and getting acquainted. That evening he flew home to California, and by midnight he was back at his computer, e-mailing the Gen Xers he had met that day and asking for more information. By the next morning he'd received responses from all his newfound buddies supplying just the information he needed—their starting salaries, perks, and bonuses all laid out in detail to help him negotiate his own package! In twenty-four hours he'd met his peers, gained their trust, and enlisted them in helping him get the best deal possible. Is it any wonder that Boomers and Traditionalists who might have gone their whole lives never telling anyone what they earned are taken aback by the Generation Xers?

This wasn't always such a problem. The last thing Traditionalists wanted to talk about was how much money they made or any extra perks or rewards they were receiving. These were taboo topics for many. If one received a raise, it wasn't broadcast around the company as if he or she had just won the lottery.

Not so with Generation X. Having operated in the shadow of the Boomers for so long, they've become a little like those hand-picked intelligence units that pass information about the enemy back and forth with extreme efficiency. Xers tend to see tier peers as allies in a silent battle to get out from under the shadow of the Boom. On the other hand, Boomers at the same age often saw their peers at work as the competition for scarce raises and promotions. As a result, Xers in your workplace are likely to know exactly what all their peers are making because they feel knowledge is power. The more they know about what's in the pot, the better their chance of getting it.

One reason for this ease with espionage is what Bruce Tulgan, author of *Managing Generation X,* calls their comfort with the "transactional nature of work." Unlike Traditionalists, who equate work with duty, and Boomers, who see it as a form of self-fulfillment, Xers see it as a way to get compensated. They may love their jobs and be committed to doing them well, but they see no reason to beat around the bush about the financial arrangements and rewards.

As a result of the booming economy, Xers have turned their natural talents at understanding the economics of their own and their peers' professions into a black market of inside information. There's even a Web site called www.greedyassociates.com that encourages Xer associates in large law firms to log on and share the particulars of their compensation packages, then compare what they're getting to what everyone else is getting. In this way, they've managed to gain leverage in an area where senior partners have always held control. There's no way for them to keep it a secret if they offer one incoming associate more bucks or perks than the next. Thus, Xers have empowered themselves financially in ways the other generations never dreamed of.

Rather than get freaked out about what you can and cannot give an employee, it may be best to stop and find out what they even want in the first place. It may be as simple as an extra day off or an office with a window. Companies have to be willing to talk about rewards from a perspective of what motivates *the generations,* not simply from a perspective of what you have traditionally offered.

So what exactly does motivate the generations?

MILES, MUGS, MONEY, AND MORE: REWARDING THE GENERATIONS

 CLASHPOINT AROUND REWARDS

Traditionalists . . .	*"The satisfaction of a job well done."*
Baby Boomers . . .	*"Money, title, recognition, the corner office."*
Generation Xers . . .	*"Freedom is the ultimate reward."*
Millennials . . .	*"Work that has meaning for me."*

Traditionalists

How many times have we heard Traditionalist parents and grandparents exhort us to recognize that hard work is its own reward; that we should work for the satisfaction of a job well done? Most of the time, it was when we were angling to get paid for some onerous household chore.

The younger generations are amazed at the way Traditionalists view their work as the actual award. In fact, it is so foreign to other generations that companies need to wake up to the fact that they are in danger of losing the easiest rewards program ever.

Traditionalists have spent decades amassing great wisdom and are *still* ready, willing, and able to give their 100 percent. Yet more often than not, we see companies let this wealth of knowledge and dedication end up by some poolside in Phoenix. Instead of spending time designing that cherrywood retirement plaque, companies should get creative and find ways to harness Traditionalists' vast capabilities and create a win–win scenario that would keep the best older workers on the job. Traditionalists working toward the "reward" of retirement, for example, might be willing to return to work in a different capacity if the schedule allowed them time for travel or grandparenting. Companies should reward returning Traditionalists with challenges, money, and/or flexibility, whichever appeals most to the individual employee.

The Bonne Bell Company provides transportation to and from the plant for its crew of formerly retired Traditionalists, which removes the stress of maintaining a vehicle, parking, and driving, particularly in bad weather. They also provide music on the plant floor they know their Traditionalist workforce will appreciate. In place of Eminem, Elton, or even Elvis, Frank Sinatra serenades workers over the sound system.

For some, a reward might mean blowing off the commute altogether. Daniel Pink, author of *Free Agent Nation,* makes the point that many Traditionalist workers are opting for what he calls "e-tirement," in which they can continue working from home via the computer and never come into the office.

Joan Halperin of Petaluma, California, is a prime example. At age sixty-three she relocated from Chicago to Northern California to live closer to her daughter and friends and escape the winters. When she threatened to retire from her business, where she oversaw all the orders and bookkeeping for a thriving Chicago-based pay phone company, the rest of the staff balked. Now Joan works from her home office in California and coordinates with the team in Chicago via fax, phone, and modem on a reduced schedule. She feels she got a reward, yet she is still handling most of her former functions from two thousand miles away. "I wanted to stay busy and keep earning," explained Joan. "But I needed more flexibility and freedom. This gives me the best of both."

Alternative scheduling is a great reward for Traditionalists who want to continue working. Deanna Walsh, our program coordinator at BridgeWorks, signed on with the understanding that hers was a four-day-a-week job. After the long hours and high stress of her last position with a large consulting firm, she was ready for a pared-back schedule that would be easier on her health and her sanity. The Tuesday-through-Friday routine allows her some extra personal time for hobbies and her grandson. Now we have a hardworking, happy employee who loves her three-day weekends, and David has come to love not getting nagged on Mondays!

Traditionalists should be mighty proud of their phenomenal dedication and work ethic. There's a lot all the generations can learn from it. Traditionalists were not raised to take having a job for granted. They've never really expected anything more than receiving a paycheck and the standard benefits package. David's dad recently celebrated his thirty-fifth anniversary as a physician for the same hospital. Over the years he has helped thousands of patients, trained hundreds of residents, and has even won the Teacher of the Year Award from his medical school for the past five consecutive years. So what did he get as a reward? A choice between a vacuum, TV tables, or a transistor radio! David isn't sure what is more confusing, the fact that the hospital sees that as a reward or that his dad wasn't insulted and was, in fact, thankful. (Okay, David was also a little confused as to why his dad chose the vacuum, considering he's never seen him operate one.)

To David's dad and his generation, being given the opportunity to practice his profession for so long was more than enough. These veterans of the military and survivors of the Great Depression tend to take work seriously and are often shocked by what they perceive as the lack of gratitude in the younger generations. They have told us they view Gen Xers and Millennials as being spoiled, expecting too much too early in their careers, and having a lack of appreciation for how lucky they are to have a job.

Because Traditionalists have invested years in climbing the rewards ladder (even if at the top there was only a Hoover waiting), they resent seeing younger people come in and demand rewards without seeming to have earned them. Paying dues is just part of the natural order of things. As in a military model, you move up through the ranks and are rewarded when you have put in your time.

When it comes to rewards, Traditionalists tend to value job security above all else. They are focused on making a contribution and are willing to be team players as long as they feel the outcome of teamwork will bring them closer to the goal of security. General Mills recognizes the importance of security as a reward. Mark Bailey, director of staffing and recruiting, said recently that even in the case of Traditionalists, who are near the end of their careers, they find a way to capitalize on their talents. "You may have a Traditionalist who has lost his spark. You can't lose sight of how much they have given to the company for so many years and the skills they have acquired." This person may not be eligible to retire for a few years, but rather than let that person flounder in what time he has left, General Mills instituted a "Bridge Program." The program places these Traditionalists in positions working for a nonprofit while still on the payroll at GMI. This revitalizes the employees by recognizing they can still contribute and reward them for their many years of productive, loyal service. This is a kind of unseen reward that makes companies like General Mills more humane and highlights how thoughtful an organization can be about deploying human capital in humane ways that are both motivating and good for business.

When it comes to saving for the future, Traditionalists hold the winning hand. They continue to save at the highest rate of any generation. Partly because Traditionalists are nearing retirement age, and partly because they have always focused on putting aside a nest egg for the future, companies can do well with rewarding Traditionalists by helping them fund a comfortable retirement and providing benefits that will make them feel safe and well cared for. In our survey, when we asked Traditionalist respondents which benefits would be most valuable to them, their number one choice was "retirement plan." Interestingly, number two was "more pay tied to performance." While organizations might shy away from putting pay at risk for a generation nearing retirement, Traditionalists seem to want the opportunity to prove what they can do and be paid accordingly.

Companies should meet periodically with Traditionalist employees to talk about which benefits motivate them the most and to reinforce the value of the benefits they currently have that promote future health and security, like life insurance, health care, dental, disability, 401(k) plans, matching grants, and so on. Because Traditionalists respect institutions, they feel justified in their long-term loyalty and are proud of being associated with a company that has provided for them in these ways.

If nothing else, reward Traditionalists with recognition. Let's face it: it won't be the Xers who proudly hang a plaque on their walls. Recognition is an underutilized tool for rewarding Traditionalists, particularly those who have been in one place for a long time. Being of value to the organization means a lot to Traditionalists, and even the simplest perks like being written up in the company newsletter, being given a verbal or written commendation, or being awarded something lasting can make a huge difference. And why not take the time and put a little into the recognition? Sure, you can always splurge on a few extra lines of engraving on the plaque, but with so many corporate awards companies out there, you owe it to the Traditionalists to look into rewarding this generation with some new recognition schemes.

Baby Boomers

For a Boomer competing with eighty million others, the satisfaction of a job well done just wasn't enough. Unless, of course, you were willing to announce in a national media campaign that the Boomer had done a good job. For this generation of strivers, rewards came to be about money, title, a better shift, seniority, the corner office, the up-front parking spot, and any other marker that let you and especially others know how you were doing.

> Not long ago, Lynne found herself picking up lunch at an Arby's drive-up window. The teenage boy who leaned out to take her money was wearing a name tag bearing the title "Temporary Assistant Relief Associate Manager." All she could think was, *Wow, clearly some Baby Boomer made up that title as a lame attempt to reward this sixteen-year-old and make him think he was really moving up the ladder.*

As much as we may laugh, it makes sense that Boomers needed these rewards as a way of distinguishing themselves from the pack.

When a large health care organization moved into new quarters in Florida, the greatest hue and cry came from Boomers concerned over who would garner what location in the new space. The human resources manager in charge of the move explained, "I had to deal with a steady stream of mostly Boomers who were completely freaked out at the thought they might lose that prime office location they had achieved over the years. The younger generations didn't seem to care."

Boomers have been groomed from childhood to do better than their parents did. Part of the American dream for Traditionalists was to provide more for their offspring than they themselves had growing up. As a result, Boomers have been well equipped to succeed. About 30 percent of Baby Boomers have earned a bachelor's degree or higher, compared to less than 20 percent of Traditionalists. During the formative years of the Boom, women began to be a factor in the American workplace. The rise in the number of dual-income families allowed Boomers to have even more disposable income. And Boomers have enjoyed spending it. They have spent more and saved less than their parents at every stage of their lives. Visible rewards like company cars, travel, and expense accounts have been popular with Boomers, along with promotions from one salary grade to the next.

Idealistic Boomers have also been motivated by what they can accomplish at work. They wanted to rise far and fast, but they also wanted to do great things. The opportunity to work on exciting projects that might change society or alter the future of the company is a very important reward to Boomers. Boomers take a lot of pride in what they've accomplished in terms of changing the way our society functions. They have fought for equal opportunities for women and minorities, and for environmentally sound business practices. Increasingly, opportunities to tap into the idealism of the 1960s will be an important rewards strategy for Boomers as they become comfortable with what they've achieved and begin to search more deeply for more meaning in their work and avocational lives.

Perks for today's Boomers are shifting gradually from the value of money and things to the value of time. While Boomers tend to believe that they will remain youthful into the foreseeable future and that they will live forever, they are increasingly seeing their time is fleeting. Too many Boomers are suffering from what we call the "sandwich effect"—the pressure being put on them by aging parents and growing children at the very time they may be reaching the apex of their career achievements and earning power. Increasingly, time may become more valuable to Boomers than even money. Companies hoping to retain and challenge Boomers are looking to time as a valuable component of the rewards equation. This doesn't always have to be a difficult reward to implement. For example, employees at Ernst & Young and SC Johnson Wax are rewarded with access to an errand-running service that enables them to have someone pick up a parcel or drop off a legal document. Think of the hours saved when sandwiched employees aren't driving around, usually in after-work, rush-hour traffic, doing these things themselves.

But the rewards landscape is expanding even further for the Boomers. Don't get us wrong—they will always enjoy that nice BMW or Rolex—but as this generation moves into its fifties, the reward will be not having to reduce their standard of living when they retire. More and more companies are providing retirement and financial counseling as a reward for Boomers who are waking up to the reality that they need to plan *now* if they are ever going to have enough to fund their lifestyles for the next thirty to fifty years.

Generation Xers

Forget hard work as the reward, or even fancy titles or corner offices. For this generation, who saw their parents trapped in the web of corporate America, *freedom* is the ultimate reward. Generation Xers' need for freedom has been confusing for many Boomers and Traditionalists. The challenge is that during the birth years of Generation X, the U.S. divorce rate tripled. At the same time, many women entered the workforce, so many more families had two working parents, which meant that Generation Xers came home to an empty house. We then hit the 1980s and suddenly these same latchkey kids who saw their parents spend more time at work than at home saw their parents tossed out on the street by their company

because the economy went sour. Consequently, we have a generation that is simply not willing to pay the same price for success that
they saw their parents pay.

This doesn't mean Xers aren't ambitious or willing to work
hard. They are both. But Gen X is a generation that's already
focused on balance and freedom at an age when the Boomers
wouldn't have given it a thought. In fact, many Boomers linked
"sacrificing" with "success." Want us to come in on weekends for a
special project involving a couple of vice presidents? No problem.
How early do you want us there? The idea that freedom and balance
are bigger rewards than chalking up brownie points with the boss is
a huge frustration to Traditionalists and Boomers who have spent
years paying their dues and proving their value.

Because Xers see the work world as one that is filled with
uncertainty, they are interested in rewards that make them feel safe
now, as compared with Traditionalists, who wanted to ensure they
would be safe *later*. That is why so many companies are rewarding
Xers by helping fund higher education. One Xer we interviewed
currently works as a recruiter in Northern California. At age
twenty-nine, he was making over $150,000 a year. Yet we found him
applying to MBA programs. Why? "I don't really know how long
this high-tech boom is going to last," he explained. "So I'm saving
as much as I can, and I'm going back to school to make sure I'm
employable when the market changes."

And although Xers are interested in rewards that make them
feel safe *now*, they are not ignorant about rewards geared toward
saving for the future. However, when working with retirement
rewards, you must have the attitude "You *can* take it with you!"
Unlike their elders, skeptical Xers have shied away from the idea
that they are likely to remain with one employer throughout their
careers. As a result, rewards geared toward permanence such as
tenure and vesting tend to have less value for Xers. Generation
Xers have a hard time getting excited about a retirement plan that
kicks in at age sixty-five when they aren't sure they'll be around

next month. More and more frequently, Generation Xers are looking for retirement plans and benefits that are transferable or convertible if they leave the company. Portable retirement/pension plans mean that an employee can build toward the future without having to make a future with one organization. This can be a big attraction when it comes to recruiting the young and the restless. We give companies a lot of credit for going as far as communicating that they understand why an employee would value portability when we know it goes against the grain for many employers. This takes a lot of courage and confidence. Because by offering this type of portable retirement reward, they are really saying, "Hey, if you decide to stay with us long-term, it's not going to be because you're locked in to your pension plan. It's going to be because we've offered you something that makes you want to be here. If you have to leave, we want you to have a plan you can put to use. The onus is on us to make sure you want to stay."

Rewarding a generation with freedom can be quite the challenge, considering that "freedom" is not an easy word to define. But perhaps the best way to approach it is to think along the lines of not feeling trapped and feeling more turned on. This may sound like a contradiction, but companies are finding "freedom" to be a way of actually strengthening their level of commitment. Portable savings, investment and retirement plans, continuous training, flexible leave policies, paid time off, accelerated career pathing, even things like relaxed dress codes and open office designs have helped foster a more "free" and flexible sense of the corporate environment, thus making Xers all the more committed.

Millennials

This generation is motivated by rewards that are both tangible and intangible. Taking their youthfulness into account, it's no surprise that they get turned on by tangible rewards that help them foot the bill for their busy lives. The good news is that these are *very* easy for companies to hand out. Many companies that employ teens are using gift certificates, discounts at retail stores, free meals, or tickets to events as rewards Millennials can cash in now and enjoy boasting about to their peers (hint . . . hint . . . go figure that tickets to an amusement park can actually be a good recruitment tool).

Rewarding Millennials requires a lot more work when it comes to intangibles. These include a fun environment, the ability to work in teams with peers, having bosses they can relate to, and being allowed to participate in work decisions.

Millennials also value "résumé-building," since they've been coached since preschool by their "having been there and had to do that" Boomer parents to create a portfolio that will outshine their seventy-six million cohorts to get into the best schools or land the best jobs. If you can make a case to Millennials that the job you offer can add a skill or experience to a crowded résumé, it will be seen as an excellent reward.

Finally, when it comes to Millennials, there is one crucial reward that no industry or place of employment will be able to ignore: making Millennials feel as though they are engaged in work that has meaning. This generation has always been in demand as workers. They want to know their work is making a difference. Since many Millennials don't have to work to contribute to their households, they have had the luxury of looking for work that has meaning. Where before the purpose was to "serve" the client, this generation will want to know what the work actually *does* for the client or what the client will be doing with it. This will not be easy. Managers accustomed to dialogues around working toward that company car will have to consider other aspects of the reward mix, like making the world a better place.

Suddenly the Millennials' job won't be just to get Hamburger Helper into the marketplace; instead it will be to help busy families make a quick meal and get to enjoy sitting down together as a family. Sound tricky? It is. But isn't this reward worth the cost? Wait a minute . . . could this be true? There is no cost! All this will take is for those to be willing to take the time to ask themselves how indeed they are making a difference in the world and then go out of their way to prove it to the Millennials.

REWARDS À LA CARTE DOESN'T HAVE TO MEAN CARTE BLANCHE

As you can see, a one-size-fits-all-generations approach to rewards just won't work. At the same time, we don't recommend giving the generations carte blanche when it comes to rewards, either. We're just saying that rewards should be tailored to the generations. The cafeteria plan, where employees can pick the traditional benefits that suit them best, has worked great for companies. Why shouldn't we use the same approach when it comes to rewards? We call it "Rewards à la Carte." The idea is, simply, tailoring rewards to the generations and life stage of employees in ways that have meaning for them.

We have our own version of Rewards à la Carte at Bridge-Works. For David, a huge reward has been coming in late in order to drive his daughter Ellie to nursery school three days a week. Does this disrupt BridgeWorks in some way? Not really. We cover his calls, and he rearranges his workload. It's just that he gets to operate on Ellie's schedule instead of ours. Cost to BridgeWorks? Nothing. Getting to stop for doughnuts and have some one-on-one time with Ellie? Priceless.

What about Lynne, our Boomer? We noticed that she was going nuts trying to get writing done at the head office, where phones, faxes, e-mail, dogs, visitors, and deliveries keep us in a constant state of chaos. BridgeWorks sprang for a new home office computer setup. Now Lynne can write in the peacefulness of a home sanctuary in the mornings and drive into the office when she's ready to face the material world. Cost to BridgeWorks? Your head if you interrupt her during writing time!

For our Traditionalist, Deanna, we recently juggled the weekly schedule around so she could take a quilting class that falls on Tuesdays. Cost to BridgeWorks? Minimal. Cost to Deanna? Well, David says she owes him a quilt!

Granted, we're a small company, so the Rewards à la Carte program is a bit easier. But big companies are falling in line. Here is a first-class example. Watson Wyatt Worldwide recently rolled out a new program for their various generations of employees and retirees called "At Your Service," which provides "help managing your work and life"—a reward every generation can appreciate. The challenge, however, is that each generation is obviously managing very different life stages.

What struck us when we read through the options was that there was something for every generation. Are you a Millennial buying your first new car? Fine, we'll help you look into financing. An Xer buying your first home or paying off student loans? They've got home improvement resources, moving services, and debt reduction help. Are you a Boomer parent going through a major life change like a divorce? They have life change counseling resources available, and they can even help you choose a summer camp for kids. How about a Traditionalist planning for the future? They offer financial counseling, information on volunteerism, and legal help.

Of course, not everyone can afford to offer these kinds of rewards. Human resources consulting firms can afford the crème de la crème because their profit margins are higher than, say, a grocery chain or a manufacturing plant. Also, when it comes to benefits, they have to walk the walk since they're in the business of talking the talk. Which doesn't take away from the fact that it's a great program. It's just not a program that's going to be realistic for everyone.

But not all Rewards à la Carte programs have to be expensive. In her "Work and Family" column in *The Wall Street Journal,* Sue Shellenbarger recently wrote a compelling essay about a program taking place in the New York offices of the Securities Industry

Automation Corporation. It's a support group for employees caring for sick and dying parents or elders. The group, mostly Boomers and Traditionalists, has been meeting monthly for over four years and is coordinated by the Partnership for Elder Care, a collaboration of the New York City Department for the Aging.

Shellenbarger wrote, "Over the life of the group, Edna Elcock has lost her father, and Edie Costanxo her mother. Louis Maresca has battled exhaustion caring for his eighty-seven-year-old mother, a victim of Alzheimer's disease. Before and after work every day, Paul Graziano stops by the home of his ninety-six-year-old aunt to oversee two in-home aides and to manage her finances, home maintenance, and shopping. Without the group, Mr. Graziano says, 'I don't think I could deal with some of the tensions.' "

The program obviously isn't aimed at everyone but has helped many face unspeakable exhaustion, hard decisions, and, eventually, loss. This is a type of program that costs little to maintain but is an immensely valuable reward to Traditionalist and Boomer employees who would otherwise be suffering, and juggling, in silence.

Another example of Rewards à la Carte is a program offered by Ceridian Corporation called "Due Dates." Aimed mainly at Xers, it helps expectant mothers manage pregnancy, maternity leave, and the transition back to work. They also offer a brochure that answers questions about everything from taking care of the new baby to buying equipment to childproofing the home. Okay, obviously there aren't too many Traditionalists yanking out their reading glasses for this brochure, but what a wonderful and, yes, inexpensive reward for young, first-time Xer parents who are probably sitting at their desk worrying about these very things. And by thinking about the transition back to work, rather than just the medical expense involved in the birth, Ceridian may get some of its best employees back after childbirth rather than losing them altogether.

Each of these companies embraced Rewards à la Carte—providing a range of options tailored to the individual needs of the generations. Some are expensive to implement, others cost nothing more than time. But all of the companies stopped trying to reward everyone at the same time in the same fashion. Is this the job of today's organizations? Yes, for any organization with multiple generations of employees, we think it is.

IN THE FIGHT OVER FAIRNESS, MAKE PRODUCTIVITY THE POINT

The immediate push back we get when we talk about Rewards à la Carte is around fairness. What happens when one employee gets this and another employee gets that and then they both find out the truth? At a recent gathering of Employers' Association Inc., the CEO of a large paint company came up to chat with us after we spoke. "I think I'm great at offering creative rewards," he said. "But my employees don't seem to appreciate it. I have two salespeople, and I knew one wanted to work from home, so we bought her a souped-up laptop. The other one's in her car all the time, so we leased her a souped-up car. Now I have to hear, 'I want a laptop! I want a car, too!' It's making me crazy."

Our survey backs this up. When we asked participants to respond to the statement "When it comes to compensation and benefits where I work, we have issues about fairness," *more than half* of each generation agreed, with Xers and Traditionalists feeling even more strongly about it than the Boomers!

So how do you handle fairness issues? The answer is to tie everything as closely as possible to performance. Then fairness isn't the issue anymore; performance is. Don't focus on who or what . . . focus on why someone is earning a reward.

Management consultant Bruce Tulgan, author of *Managing Generation X,* says: "Start with the work that needs to get done, and treat everything as a business issue. If you look at everything through that lens, it's easier to explain rewards to people. For example, "Mary doesn't have to work Thursday because her sales are much better than yours. You want more flexibility? Here's exactly what you need to do. . . ." It's a very aggressive approach to rewarding, but it's a lot easier if it's all about work.

"Transparency becomes a big issue then because you have to share a lot more information. But why not go all the way? Why not put up a poster: 'Mary gets Thursdays off! Come to my office to find out why!' "

Rewards are tied to what you produce for the company. And increasingly, everyone can be a winner. Grading on a curve might work in grade school, but it doesn't cut it in the workplace. Mary Kay Ash used this beautifully to motivate female entrepreneurs to achieve through selling Mary Kay products. Anyone and everyone can earn the pink Cadillac if they sell enough. There isn't just one company car or best parking space or "Salesperson of the Year" award. Rewards are limitless. If everyone achieves at a peak level, they all win. This is highly motivating to Generation Xers because they don't have to "pay their dues" before they can win. It's also a great equalizer, since anyone of any generation can succeed.

Think about the profit potential. Let's say you typically offer a lease on a Porsche for one year to that year's top salesperson. Are they going to compete hard to get that car? Sure, the top ones will. But those farther down the commission ladder will probably give up on their Porsche potential early in the game. And what if Number One pulls so far out ahead that no one can catch him? Then the game's over and the Porsche's value is wasted on all but the one who won. Let's say the winner had $8 million in sales. What if, instead, you offered *unlimited* Porsches, but to win one you had to do $10 million in sales? Hypothetically, everyone can win. So five or ten or sixteen people make it? Big deal. How much better off are you for having changed the equation?

The best news is that ultimately, fairness isn't the issue, performance is. And this is a real motivator because it levels the generational playing field.

THE TOMB OF THE UNKNOWN REWARD

It blows us away how many times we will meet with a company that has the most incredible rewards and yet so few employees know about them. Even more significant, how few employees actually understand how the rewards program works.

It just doesn't make sense. Why spend all this money on these rewards but not tell anyone? Go the extra mile to make sure all the generations of employees know what rewards are available to them and what it takes to earn them. Older employees might have been around so long that the reward or benefit system has changed, but they were never brought up-to-date on it. Younger employees might never have fully understood the value of what is available. Even worse, recruiters aren't always clear on which perks will mean the most to the generations they are recruiting.

Let's take this a step further. Sometimes it's not even the employees who are in the dark, it's the employers themselves. Companies spend too much time figuring out how to reward the generations when the solution is often right under their nose. The problem is that they are looking at the world of rewards only through their own generation's glasses.

One accounting firm called us in to help them figure out how to attract more Xers. The team we met with happened to be all Boomers. "We just don't have anything to offer this generation," they complained, and they were ready and willing to shell out a lot of money to rectify the problem. However, as we asked them what they do for employees, we slowly uncovered things like free dry-cleaning, or how they provide meals and transportation for families to come in during tax season when you can't get home in time for dinner. "We've been doing these things for years," the Boomers explained. Yet it was never mentioned in interviews or printed in one employee brochure. They didn't need to spend money developing rewards, as much as they needed to spend time talking about rewards they already had.

Talking about rewards is more than just handing them over. Clearly, employees aren't being made to feel good about them, which means companies aren't getting the bang for the buck they intended. In our survey, when we asked the generations about the last time they "received a bonus, raise, perk, or recognition at work," it was great to hear that over 20 percent said it "felt like I had won an Oscar." But 55 percent of respondents said their last recognition at work felt like "nothing special." That leaves a whole lot of room for improvement when it comes to really making sure employees feel good about what they've accomplished.

Low-budget dot.coms have garnered plenty of free publicity by announcing the implementation of wacky perks and radical rewards such as one Scandinavian-owned firm in Silicon Valley putting in an employee sauna! There's nothing wrong with this means of making news. In fact, traditional companies should take better advantage of it. Why wait around until your company softball team wins the league championship, only to have your fifteen minutes of fame buried on page ten of the company newsletter? Many alternative rewards programs that companies support are newsworthy, and companies should take advantage of the opportunity to get some free press. And these programs can help build a more hip image if you're looking to connect with the younger generations. Besides, why let the dot.coms get all the praise for the way they reward when you're undoubtedly spending a fortune on some of the very same things?

WHAT'S IT WORTH, AND IS IT WORTH IT?

When we read that one Silicon Valley company had instituted "Bring Your Parrot to Work Day," we knew the envelope had been pushed over the edge. But we have to applaud companies that have been willing to put just about any reward on the table to see what works in the battle to gain employee commitment. The recent economic boom encouraged companies to invent a host of new ways to reward employees in return for their work product. Sure, many of these perks will fall by the wayside as the economy corrects. Others will fall by the wayside as companies decide they don't work. In fact, in the year 2000, some 25 percent of companies that had adopted casual day returned to formal business attire. Whether the benefits go or stay, the willingness of organizations to explore new, more creative ways to reward employees has been excellent in many ways. If it's caused managers to do a better job of differentiating among the needs of different generations of employees and tailoring benefits to the individuals they hope to attract and retain, it's been worth the experiment. In fact, in the BridgeWorks Survey, 67 percent of respondents said their companies had changed their benefit plans in some way in the last few years to better accommodate the needs of their own generation.

Most important, don't make this about money. That is an excuse. Even if funds are tight, that doesn't mean you don't have rewards to offer.

While laws on overtime payments vary from state to state, Lucia Jones, director of the nonprofit Northeastern Illinois Area Agency on Ageing, told us that when employees work more than the core eight-hour day, they can bank the hours for time off. As she said, "We may not pay for that time, but our employees have such busy lives with so many demands that they tell us that time off is a reward worth more than money."

And sometimes just taking a little time not for you but for a co-worker can be the best reward of all. At the International Speakers Bureau in Dallas, Texas, all the employees got a sheet of paper on which they were to write something nice about each person in the office. Every employee then received all the nice things people said about them inside a bottle—they call it "the medicine bottle."

When employees feel down, they can pull a piece of paper out of the medicine bottle and read something positive that a co-worker said about them.

As Harvey Mackay says: "Little things don't mean a lot, they mean everything."

7

SCORING A PERFECT "10" ON THE BALANCE BEAM

A couple of years ago, we had the opportunity to be interviewed by a senior editor at *Fast Company* magazine. It was a great opportunity for us, but it kicked off a huge generational collision:

Lynne: My conversation with the editor went great, and at the end of it she said, "Hey, Lynne, I'm under a really tight deadline, but I love this topic. Is there any way I could interview your Generation X business partner?"

"Absolutely! We'll make it happen," I responded, and I proceeded to set up an interview for her with David that Friday at five. Fine, so I thought. But when Friday evening rolled around and I hadn't heard a word from David, I was really worried. Dying of curiosity, I finally gave him a call (by now he was at home).

WHAT "BALANCE" MEANS TO THE GENERATIONS

"Hey, David, what's up, how did it go with the editor?"

"Oh, uh, yeah," came his response. "Well, I had to blow her off."

Here we were with a once-in-a-lifetime media opportunity and he was *blowing her off?!* You can imagine how my blood pressure started to rise and how I responded.

David: Whatever, Lynne. I didn't blow her off. Here's what *really* happened:

Friday afternoon rolled around and I was waiting at my desk, but there was no phone call. Five-thirty, no call. Six o'clock, still no call. Finally around six-thirty the phone rang, and when I picked it up, the editor just dove into the interview. A little annoyed that I didn't even get a "Sorry I'm late," I asked her when her story was due. She said it wasn't until the end of the following week. So I said, "Do you mind if we do this first thing Monday morning? I am happy to clear off my schedule for you. But you see, if we do this interview now, I won't get home until after eight o'clock. I've been out of town two nights already this week, and this will make it the third night I don't get to put my kids to bed, and honestly I'm just not willing to do that."

She said it was fine, we rescheduled, and I flew out the door to make it home. Well, later that night I was lying on the couch (Lynne was obviously still at her desk . . . separate issue) and my phone rang, only for me to receive a tongue-lashing from Lynne that was worse than the time I let off a stink bomb in the school cafeteria in seventh grade!

Lynne: Do you want to know the *really* annoying part of all this? About two weeks later I called the editor to see if she had everything she needed, and the first words out of her mouth were, "Oh, Lynne, I just love your Generation X partner, he has the best values!"

Excuse me? As a Boomer, I was taught that you call your

> husband, delay dinner, cancel plans, stay at your desk, and get
> the job done, no matter what the cost.
>
> Now we're not going to take a vote or anything, but I ask
> you—who has the best values?
>
> **David:** I say we take a vote!

While we still make fun of each other about that one situation,
we both will agree that it taught us that neither one of us has better
values, they're just different. And by talking about these differences,
we really learned about where each of our generations is coming
from on the topic of balance.

It was a real eye-opener for David to realize that when Lynne
was his age, she never would have had the luxury of "blowing off"
the editor. If she didn't do it, there would have been eighty million
others right in line behind her. As a result, for a lot of Boomers
trying to stand out from the crowd and competing for the same
jobs, workaholism became a badge of honor. Putting in those extra
hours was a way of showing we were making it. And Boomers
all know those little digs and jabs we used to show everyone else
just how hard we were working. Like the classic "Say, did you
know the air-conditioning in our building goes off at six A.M. on
Sunday?"

At the same time, Lynne stopped being mad at David when he
made it clear as day that his generation does not *live to work*, but
instead *works to live* . . . and a balanced life at that. Why? As a direct
antidote to the unquestioning dedication of the Traditionalist workforce or the dog-eat-dog ambition of the Boomers, they have refused
to sign a corporate contract that says you have to give up a balanced
life to have a decent job. They simply don't want to pay the same
price for success that they saw the previous generations pay. It has
nothing to do with being willing to work hard, but to an Xer it's just

not worth putting your children in day care or, worse, ending up divorced. In fact, in a recent Harris poll commissioned by the Radcliffe Public Policy Center, more than 80 percent of men ages twenty to thirty-nine (Generation Xers) interviewed said that "having a work schedule that allows me to spend time with my family is more important than doing challenging work or earning a high salary."

RAISING THE BALANCE BAR

Years ago, balance was never an issue. As long as men worked to support their families and women stayed out of the workforce and handled things on the home front, families achieved a form of balance. Traditionalists were never a generation to gripe about having a job. They were grateful to be employed and felt they owed their employer a good day's work. With fewer women in the workforce and a lower divorce rate, the Traditionalist family had several advantages. Men could focus more exclusively on their jobs, and women had the time to keep the household running. The households weren't taxed with child care costs because the mothers usually provided the child care (and were seldom paid for it). It's no wonder they all loved Lucy.

And think about the other ways in which balance was easier to achieve:

Families lived closer together, so a relative was often available to be home with kids during the day. And when Traditionalists were young, it was more affordable for a family to manage food, clothing, and housing on only one income. Traditionalists had lower interest rates, and many were able to take advantage of the GI Bill for help in completing an education or buying that first home.

In addition, while they've always been hardworking, many Traditionalists worked an easier workday. In fact, numerous studies have shown that the American workday has continued to get longer throughout the second half of the twenty-first century. So Boomer and Xer families have been faced not only with higher housing costs, higher interest rates, and longer work hours, they've also had to juggle the nation's 50 percent divorce rate, meaning most parents now have to work, leaving many more kids in day care. The result? More stress, more costs, less personal and family time, and more worry. This isn't to say that Traditionalists had it easy or that the old way was even remotely fair to women. Neither is true. It is simply to say that the old model was more favorable to "balance."

Then, too, for Traditionalists and their parents, expectations were lower. The middle class of forty years ago might have been quite content to stay home on a Saturday and clean out the garage. A big Saturday night might have involved getting a baby-sitter so the parents could attend a cocktail party at the neighbors'. There they could toss back a gin martini, down some rumaki (bacon strips wrapped around a piece of liver and run through with a festive toothpick, for those who don't remember it!), and dance the night away to Frank Sinatra, Dean Martin, and the mellow sounds of Herb Alpert and the Tijuana Brass. Today, choices abound. Besides keeping up a house and yard, parents are chauffeuring vanloads of children to soccer, baseball, and dance class, dashing by the senior care facility to visit Grandma or Grandpa, running stepkids to and from the homes of birth parents, and racing home to download the latest backlog of e-mails from work. And if the PalmPilot shows a gap in the schedule, leisure choices abound. Rather than spending Sunday with a trip to church followed by Sunday dinner with the relatives, today's families have time and cash-consuming options like skiing, a trip to the cottage, or a spin on the boat. Aunts, uncles, and cousins who used to live down the block are now two thousand miles away. Attempts to bring whole families together involve more planning than and cost almost as much as Desert Storm.

And the complexity of the relationships!! Read or listen to any advice expert, from Dear Abby to Dr. Laura, and the most common laundry list of problems stems from today's ever-changing and always challenging extended family. Do I invite my ex-husband's second and third wives to our child's confirmation? Do I pay for the grandparents to attend the family reunion when they live in Nome, Alaska, and our kids have never met them? We laugh, but the changing face of American families has put more stress than ever on our free time and our free will.

Balance today implies everyone is supposed to do everything and be good at everything. Men are supposed to be physically buff *and* know how to cook. Women are supposed to be able to trade a few stocks on-line while looking like a Victoria's Secret underwear model. Kids are supposed to be smart, well-adjusted, great in school, and in line for imminent Ivy League admission. And grandparents should be agile, in shape, smiling, fun, attentive, and, of course, rich!

It's stunning to imagine that we're supposed to do all this while still holding down a job!

BEYOND THE BATTLE FOR BALANCE

Marketers have been quick to tap into the struggle for balance as a great theme for selling products. Think about the AT&T television commercials of the 1980s. You'd have the successful guy in the back of the limousine with two telephones, a pager, and a fax machine. And the message was all about being able to get work done better and faster before you even got to the office.

Now AT&T's done a complete change in strategy. They're still demonstrating how their products help people achieve success, but now they show it can be done while having balance in your life. Think about BridgeWorks's favorite AT&T commercial. It's the mom racing around the kitchen getting ready to go to work while explaining to her little girls that she can't take them to the beach because she has a meeting with a very important client. Then comes the clincher—innocent blue eyes look up at Mommy and a sad little voice asks, "When do I get to be a client?" Ouch! The mother's torn and guilty expression says it all. She hesitates a second and then looks down at her AT&T cell phone before responding: "You have

five minutes to get ready for the beach or I'm going without you!"
The ad then cuts to the girls playing in the sand while Mom is
reclining in a lawn chair. Her cell phone rings and she answers just
as the littlest girl calls out, "Hey, everyone, it's time for the meeting!"
It's embarrassing, it's cute and funny, and it's a set of emotions we
can all relate to. What if a cell phone really could allow us to spend
more time with our kids *and* get our work done?

While tapping into this yearning for balance as a way to sell
products has scored a touchdown in the marketplace, helping the
generations achieve balance has been more like a fumble for many
employers in the workplace. There are many reasons:

Some companies simply don't have the culture that supports
balance initiatives easily. In unionized settings, for example, each
new initiative must be negotiated and agreed upon by all sides
before it can be offered. This can make it difficult to experiment
with options and tough to drop programs that fail. Other types of
workplaces can't be as flexible because of the nature of the work.
Teachers, for example, can't exactly decide to work nights instead or
work from home if the baby-sitter doesn't show up. But just because
the job doesn't lend itself to being able to work more flexible hours
doesn't eliminate the company's need to fight for balance. Organizations may have their hands tied, but sometimes all it takes is throwing the challenge into the lap of the employee. Many in those
situations know exactly what it will take to get more balance in their
lives and are willing to do the legwork to make it happen. It might
be as simple as spreading out the workload. The point is that it's not
just about balancing one's *time;* it's about balancing one's *mind.*

Many organizations do have flexible work policies in place, but
employees don't make use of them. In many cases, we've seen it come
down to one simple fact: employees just didn't know about them.
David recently delivered a keynote address to a group of hospitals and
complimented them for having an 80 percent work option where
employees could work four out of seven days a week. Suddenly there
was a stir in the audience. No, there weren't any problems with the

program; it was that the majority of the employees hadn't even known the program existed until David told them. If a keynote speaker is more in the loop than employees, there is definitely a problem. Failure to communicate flexible policies is the kiss of death.

But there is a deeper reason why some flexible work policies do not get utilized. Many times it is not a case of not knowing about it, it is more about being afraid to take advantage of it. The Families in Work Institute studied 188 companies and found that while most offered part-time shifts, less than 5 percent of employees made use of them. Often this is because men fear being seen as wimps, and women fear being put on the proverbial "Mommy track."

So it's one thing to *offer* the benefit of balance, and it's another to encourage and support it. The challenge of embracing a new way of working goes much further than simply writing and communicating a new policy. If managers don't embrace new policies and figure out how to work with them, they aren't likely to fly.

YOU CAN'T CHECK YOUR LIFE AT THE DOOR

The employees we interview as we visit all types of organizations are dedicated, caring, and ambitious. But they are also concerned with how to keep their lives running to the best of their ability so that they are *able* to work at peak effectiveness. It used to be that workers were told they needed to leave their life at the door and they could return to it when the workday was over. But let's get realistic. How do you do that when your child is sick, or your elderly parent needs care, or your spouse travels on business while you need to cover the home front, or you're struggling with chronic pain, or you're juggling day care, or someone you love has just died? An employee may be battling alcoholism, a death in the family, a runaway child, or money woes . . . you name it. The great unspoken truth of the go-go American workforce is that at any given moment a huge percentage of the people in any workplace are struggling with personal difficulties that take their minds off the job. Yet the workplace is often the last place where these things are acknowledged.

And what about those who aren't dealing with a tragedy or a lot of outside commitments? Their need for balance must be addressed as well. The single Gen Xers who deliberately keep their lives simple so they can focus 100 percent on work, the child-free Boomer couples who both are dedicated to their careers and don't have to juggle work with family, the empty-nest Traditionalists who are in good health and have never been more energized by their jobs . . . in many situations, these are the people who feel the most snubbed. The "balanced workplace," if there is such a thing, has to make sure that these individuals aren't penalized for showing up and taking on a huge share of the workload.

> "I think it's unfair," reported one Gen X supervisor in a large manufacturing company based in the South. "I resent all these parents who have to leave right at five to pick up kids at day care, or who take dozens of personal calls every day from the baby-sitter. I don't have kids, and I feel like I'm always the one cleaning up the mess."

YOU CAN'T EXACTLY CLOSE THE DOOR, EITHER

The most consistent complaint we hear from company leaders is that the company doesn't run if the work doesn't get done.

One Traditionalist business owner commented: "People want this day or that day off, or they want to work just part-time. But we have demanding clients. It's not our responsibility to tell our employees how to manage their personal lives. It's our responsibility to make sure that we service our clients. We pay people a lot of money to be able to balance their workload with whatever else they have going on."

If companies are running inefficiently, then balance becomes a moot point. So we agree that any approach to balance has to be from the point of view of the bottom line.

Too often employers interpret the quest for balance as a lack of desire or appreciation for the work that needs to get done, when in reality, the search for balance has little to do with whether or not employees want to work hard and everything to do with also wanting to live hard. In fact, there's evidence to show that Americans are working harder than anyone else in the world. According to a 1997 study by the International Labor Organization, fathers were working an average of 50.9 hours, while mothers were working 41.4 hours per week.

We've found that the companies that are the most flexible about helping employees achieve some level of balance seem to have an easier time recruiting, managing, and retaining employees. In addition, we believe that these companies have lower turnover, a less stressed workforce, lower absenteeism, and better morale. We've also found that balance doesn't have to cost a fortune. We've interviewed managers and employees in small government agencies where the workload is large and the pay is not great, and we've found happy, committed people who like their work and have carved out meaningful careers because they've been able to achieve a balance that works for them.

Sometimes all it takes is showing a little support for employees' avocations. For less than $500, our company has funded a kayaking class for David, bought Lynne tickets to the Westminster Kennel Club Dog Show during a stressful trip to New York, and paid for Deanna to join a fitness center—none of which applies to the work we do, but all of which we believe helps the work get done. How? Companies are increasingly recognizing that avocations keep employees sane, mentally stimulated, and, in many cases, fit. It's worth supporting these for employees even if the avocations can't be completed after a traditional workday or on weekends. Employees know they have a job to do and will really appreciate the vote of confidence that you are sure it will get done.

Former Ceridian CEO Larry Perlman was interviewed by the Minnesota Center for Corporate Responsibility in August 1998, and he really nailed it when he said, "What was always the right thing to do has become the smart thing to do." Increasingly, the generations are putting pressure on organizations to "do the right thing" and help them balance their busy lives so that they *can* be more effective at work.

A BICYCLE BUILT FOR FOUR

When people learn to balance and ride a bike, it becomes so easy that they never have to think about it again. But what happens when you have four different people riding that bike? Balancing becomes a lot more difficult.

Probably one of the biggest obstacles in achieving balance in today's workplace is that we have four generations not only wanting balance, but coming at it from different directions and colliding. On the subject of balance, the workplace is rife with resentments.

Time and again, Traditionalist leaders ask us, "If we give in to all these demands for balance, who's going to do the work?" Boomers comment, "I can't believe Xers have the nerve to demand something I would never have dreamed of asking for when I was that age." And Xers say, "If they can't understand I want to have a kick-ass career and a kick-ass life, then I don't want to work here."

The attitude at traditional companies has been that it's mostly the overindulged Generation Xers, particularly the techies, who are demanding those outrageous new work options. For many, the unspoken hope is that Xers will somehow outgrow this antiestablishment stage and fall in line as they mature.

But the Xers' attitude toward balance in the workplace, far from being just annoying, is beginning to be a catalyst. After all, if you let your Xers leave at five to have enough time to go home and be with their families, at some point you're going to want to go home and be with your family as well.

As Nancy Ball, business human resources manager for Weyer-haeuser Company, explained: "It's not just the young ones who want these options anymore. Traditionalists and Baby Boomers are at a stage in their lives where they need more flexibility, and they are beginning to see that alternative work arrangements can be valuable for them, too."

But even though all the generations are beginning to see the upside of balance, the discomfort around such arrangements is often a result of generational differences. These generational differences translate directly into workplace collisions as organizations struggle to implement alternative work arrangements.

A classic example is a study that was completed by Ceridian Corporation in 1999 called "The Boundaryless Workforce."

The study defines boundaryless work as "new work arrangements that include . . . telecommuting, virtual teams, flexible work plans, and the use of temporary professionals."

What the study uncovered is that the success of implementing various balance initiatives is hampered by attitudinal differences expressed by the generations. For example:

Rewards

"The Boundaryless Workforce" found that "respondents age 19–39 [mostly Generation Xers] were more likely than those forty and older to endorse boundaryless work arrangements as a means of rewarding valued employees." If older workers don't view flexible work alternatives as a reward for those they manage, how successful will they be as the stewards of those programs?

Reporting

The study found that managers over the age of forty (Boomers and Traditionalists) were much more likely to foresee reporting problems as a result of boundaryless arrangements than those under forty. If the generations can't figure out how reporting will work when they are not at work, how will managers and employees keep track of work flow and measure performance?

Respect

The Ceridian study found that respondents fifty and over (Traditionalists and older Boomers) were more likely to view boundaryless workers as "less respected than traditional workers." This finding not only highlights the most ingrained generational collision getting in the way, but will take the most effort to overturn. The older generations' model was that those who aren't visible on the plant floor or at their desks are more dispensable. As virtual work options become more commonplace, will older workers be able to truly value a virtual workforce? Even more important, will they be able to value an employee for what really matters?

Generation Xer Dylan is a fifth-year associate in the patent department of a large law firm. He meets all of his deadlines, works until late at night, and stays in close touch with clients. Yet, at his most recent review, Dylan was informed he was no longer on a partnership track. It seems his Traditionalist boss didn't think he was "working" hard enough. You see, Dylan operates out of his home office two days a week.

As each generation begins to see the value in balance, the pressure on organizations to adopt and adapt more flexible work arrangements is increasing. But the work to be done isn't just putting these initiatives down on paper, it is working on our generational biases and truly changing hearts and minds. If these initiatives are going to succeed, we need to find ways to get *all* the generations on board. And those that do a good job of it will have a distinct competitive advantage, both in recruiting and retaining the best employees. The challenge is that the generations view the concept of balance in somewhat different ways.

BALANCING THE GENERATIONS

CLASHPOINT AROUND "BALANCE"

Traditionalists . . .	*"Support me in shifting the balance."*
Baby Boomers . . .	*"Help me balance everyone else and find meaning myself."*
Generation Xers . . .	*"Give me balance now, not when I'm sixty-five!"*
Millennials . . .	*"Work isn't everything; I need flexibility so I can balance all my activities."*

A Traditionalist might say

"There's a reason we keep business hours—that's when we do business!" Traditionalists became accustomed to a military model of the workplace and showed up when they were assigned to work. Anything other than that upset the natural order and reflected a breakdown in discipline. Many Traditionalist workers even received awards or a medal of honor from their employers for perfect attendance. Should we be surprised that it's a challenge for a fifty-five-year-old who's spent a lifetime showing up when the rooster crows to relate to a younger generation that sees no problem in rolling in around ten A.M.?

At the same time, Traditionalists are waking up to the fact that while they've kept their noses to the grindstone, the younger generations have been sniffing out all sorts of ways to ask for and achieve more balanced lives. If handled poorly, this can cause intergenerational resentments to arise. In our survey, twice as many Traditionalists felt that work/life balance was not handled with fairness as did Boomers or Xers. While the emphasis has been on creative hiring and innovative incentives for the younger generations, it's important to remember those who have been around a while.

But as they near retirement, some Traditionalists are feeling increasingly that they've reached a point of financial and career stability where they are able to ask for more balance. In fact, one HR director for a medical supplies company said she has been shocked lately to discover that when you offer an assignment to a Traditionalist, more and more of them are asking, "How much time do you think this will take away from my family?"

What is a labor-strapped company to do when the one generation they have always counted on is becoming more willing to actually use the "snooze" button on their alarm clock?

Support them in shifting the balance. Companies should not panic. Trust that Traditionalists' devotion will always prevail. This generation's loyalty to companies has been so strong that many of them are not ready for free time once they actually have it. Traditionalists worry about their self-worth after retirement because they are so accustomed to feeling "needed" on the job. Therefore, it can actually be dangerous for people to work, work, work their whole lives and then suddenly just stop.

Companies can play an active role in avoiding abrupt life

change. For Traditionalists, balance is going to mean getting some help with the transition into retirement. What a shame to put in so many hours and so much of yourself for so many years, only to end up finding yourself lost.

Many companies are catching on. If nothing else, providing resources for balancing this life transition will go a long way. Ceridian Corporation recently rolled out enhancements to their Work-Life Products aimed at helping employees who are coming close to retirement. Diane Piktialis, director of Work-Life Products, explained, "Dealing with retirement means more than just worrying about the money factor. We have found that one of the biggest issues on retirees' minds is how they will spend twenty to thirty years in a meaningful way. Our product helps them figure that out." The Life Works Service helps with other issues that many upcoming retirees are concerned about but don't know how to address until it hits them dead-on. "For example," Diane explains, "many of them have worked with the same people for so long that they need to think about how they are going to replace the personal relationships and 'community' they've had at work for so many years. Since dual-earner families are the norm and many people are working longer than prior generations, retirees can't count on having all of their neighbors around to replace the community they've had at work. We can help them understand the importance of developing new social connections before they leave the workplace." With resources like this, companies can really show that they not only respect the life change many Traditionalists are about to experience, but can actually help them navigate the transition.

A Baby Boomer might say

"Forget work hours, the best time to leave the office is ten minutes after the boss leaves." For Boomers, "face time" wasn't

optional; it was a standard operating procedure. Competitive, politically savvy Boomers used face-to-face opportunities as effective
ways to boost a career. Leading meetings, making presentations, and
dropping by the boss's office were accepted ways of showcasing
skills. Hard to do when you're working from your living room!
AccounTemps became famous for its commercials in which a
worker stays home sick, only to be replaced by the ubiquitous
"Bob," who thrills the boss with his sterling work ethic and flashy
accounting techniques. The message plays perfectly off the Boomer
fear of the consequences of missing a day.

But as hardworking and ambitious as Boomers have been, they
have entered the twilight zone—not the twilight of their years; the
twilight of their disposable time. For Boomers, there simply isn't
enough to go around. As hard as it has been for Boomers to seek
balance, many are realizing they just don't have a choice.

"Help me balance everyone else and find meaning for myself."

With single-parent households, growing kids, aging parents,
demanding jobs, and retirement looming on the horizon, Boomers
are finally throwing in the towel and admitting they can't do it all
without a little more help on the supply side. They are looking more
and more to their employers to help make "having it all" easier to
manage. But for Boomers, there's another piece to the balance puzzle. Always an idealistic generation, Boomers are reaching a stage of
middle age in which they are beginning to question where they've
been and where they're going. Balance, for these introspective, questioning Boomers, will include the search for meaning.

The 1999 Academy Award–winning film *American Beauty*
touched on this very nerve. Many Boomers could relate to Lester
and Carolyn, the couple played by Kevin Spacey and Annette Ben-
ing, who found themselves questioning everything from their marriage to their careers. Who can forget the moment when Lester gets
fed up with his mind-numbing job selling advertising and actually
goes to the local drive-through and asks for a job. "But sir," objects

the teenage interviewer, "we don't have any positions in management right now."

"Good," replies the exhausted and disillusioned Lester, "I'm looking for the least possible amount of responsibility." Whether or not people liked the movie, they could relate to the search for meaning that his "perfect" life wasn't providing.

Whoa . . . what is a manager supposed to do with Boomer employees who are questioning the purpose of their lives and the value of their work? This isn't exactly on the forms for the annual performance review. In order to help Boomers balance the search for meaning, however, managers may have to venture into that touchy-feely side. Traditionally this has been a no-no for this career-driven generation. Yet in focus groups, introspective Boomers tell us that sometimes all they need is to have a manager or mentor who is willing to talk about the meaning of life and not just the P&L statement. As awkward as it may seem, you may not have a choice. Balancing the search for meaning and the value of their work is only going to get more important as Boomers look toward retirement. You have to ask yourself, wouldn't you rather lend an ear than find yourself conducting an exit interview?

A Generation Xer might say

"Why does it matter when I come and go, as long as I get the work done?" Freedom-loving Xers resent the corporate compulsion to have meetings about meetings about meetings. They hate to be micromanaged, and they struggle to understand why it's so important for someone to see them if they are getting the work done satisfactorily. For Boomers, face time is a strategic tool, but Xers see it as a waste of time or, put more frankly, an attempt to kiss up to the boss for no reason. Rather than pucker up, many are choosing to play their own game of cover-up. One of our favorite examples comes from an international law firm. Generation Xers who leave in time to get home for dinner will actually place their suit coats on the backs of their chairs and keep their computer monitors turned on. That way, if the boss walks by, it looks as though they are still at work but have just stepped away for a moment.

Xers have brought balance to the forefront of today's work-place. In our survey, when asked, "Which generation is the best at finding work/life balance?" all three generations picked the Xers by a landslide. Yet many Xers we've interviewed still complain about bosses who perennially watch the clock and note whether an employee came in a few minutes late or left a few minutes early. "As long as I turn in good work," explained one, "who cares?" This is in part because many Xers (37 percent in our survey) still don't believe they've achieved the level of work/life balance that they are searching for. With so many Xers still searching, we believe they will continue to put pressure on themselves and their employers to find it.

Jean Compton was a software trainer for a midsize tech com-pany in San Diego, California, until she got so fed up with the cor-porate culture there that she quit. "It was a great study in how generational interactions go wrong," she told us. "The three owners were all very classic Baby Boomers who implemented rigid work-place standards and made sure the managers enforced them. There-fore, if I walked in at 8:02, I would have an e-mail waiting for me that said, 'Our workday starts at 8:00 A.M., not 8:02.' Of course, it didn't matter that I would be skipping lunch and working an hour overtime that night. This mentality just felt too rigid."

A few months later, Jean was feeling a lot more balanced. She had moved on to become a technical support representative for Cardiff, a Vista, California, software company that makes forms pro-cessing software for use in all kinds of industries. "It's a very differ-ent environment here at Cardiff. We may come in a few minutes late, but they know how hard we work and that those minutes will be made up, and then some, throughout the week. They focus more on making us feel wanted, and as a result, it's a place I want to stay."

"Give me balance now, not when I'm sixty-five!"

What has been so amazing is how Gen Xers have taken their quest for balance with such short résumés and limited job skills to the street and have had the nerve to demand that they take vacations when they want them, work fewer weekends, and go home on time. Yes, the strong economy has given Xers the power to make these kinds of demands. But to their credit, they were making them even when the economy was in a recession in the early 1990s and jobs for recent Xer graduates were scarce.

Generation Xers are listening to every word companies say when it comes to balance. Often the biggest challenge isn't for managers once Xers are in the door, it's for the recruiters who are trying to get them to knock on the door. As much as they want to know about the job of their dreams, they also want to know right off the bat whether or not workplace policies will give them the lifestyle they crave. And even if recruiters are are well versed in policies, Xers still want to see that the company embraces balance. Sounds crazy, but suddenly recruiters have to talk about time off with as much zest as time on the job.

But in these conversations, watch the amount of stereotyping. Don't assume Xers are running out the door and jumping on their mountain bike or skateboard. Organizations need to understand that Xers aren't just carefree "kids" anymore. They have adult concerns, and they want the time and flexibility to take care of these, perhaps better than they saw their parents do. Xers are starting families, and with that comes the inevitable worry about the best way to juggle work and kids.

And as Xers enter into their management years, it will be interesting to see whether or not their "just say no" mentality will continue to be feasible. Especially when you throw in more kids and bigger mortgages. However, one thing is for sure: For now, they've lit a fire under balance that will only continue to heat up the discussion for years to come.

A Millennial might say

"Work isn't everything; I need flexibility so I can balance all my activities." Guess what? You're never too young to have issues with balance!

Traditionalist and Boomer parents have been engraving the concept of balance into Millennials' heads since birth. This is in part because of the competitive pressure to beat out the other seventy-six million Millennials to get into the best schools—if you hope to get in, you have to show a balance of interests and accomplishments on your college applications. Traditionalist and Baby Boomer parents want their kids to take advantage of as many activities and opportunities that are available to them as possible. It's not uncommon these days for high school students to spend a summer on an archaeological dig in the Andes, while at the same age, their parents would have been happy to get a lifeguard gig at the YMCA! As a result, this has become the most overprogrammed generation ever. From after-school sports to foreign-language immersion to learning instruments to part-time work to volunteering and—oh, yeah—to getting your schoolwork done as well, the choices and pressures are overwhelming.

The challenge will be that Millennials will carry over their activity-laden lives into the workplace, and like homework, the workplace will be just *one* of many important activities rather than top priority. As a result, employers are dealing with everything from "no-shows" to employees who fall asleep on the job.

And as if competing with all these activities isn't enough, suddenly you are also competing with the ones who told them to "get busy" in the first place—their parents!

Divorced and working parents see their Millennials kids far less than they'd like. And they are fighting back. *Newsweek* reported on a group in Wayzata, Minnesota, called Family Life 1st! that "has asked coaches, teachers and leaders of youth groups to cut back on required games and practices—especially during holidays and vacations," so families could have more uninterrupted time together. Okay, that's fine when you are encouraged to miss the odd cheerleading practice, but what happens when that rolls over into the workplace?

At a training conference sponsored by Buffalo Wild Wings restaurants, franchisee owners and managers reported struggling with these very issues with their Millennials. As they explained, *they* are now the ones responsible for working around the employees' Christmas dinners and not the other way around. How many Boomers or Xers can remember carving the turkey after eight P.M. because the mall was open late and you had to work? We hear stories where guilt-ridden Traditionalist and Boomer parents are even offering to supplement their kids' wages themselves if it means they can spend more time at home. What a mixed message!

Obviously, companies are not about to get involved with family dynamics. Nor are managers about to send notes home to the parents pinned on their Millennial employees' clothes. However, they won't be able to avoid competing for Millennials' time as they balance family, activities, and work . . . perhaps even in that order. With the push to keep family at the forefront, the picture is complicated by the fact that it's no longer the traditional family.

Successful employers of Millennials say the best way to help Millennials find balance is flexible scheduling. Yes, it's a headache. But we are already learning from the booming service sector, which relies so heavily on Millennial workers that employers have to flex because they can't do without Millennials. As one supervisor put it, "We have to be willing to get really creative about scheduling, if nothing else, just so they show up and work!"

A MonsterTRAK.com poll asked college students to pick the most important benefit among flexible hours, stock options, more vacation time, ability to telecommute, better health plan, and a large signing bonus. What was number one? Flexible hours. Time is a big issue with overscheduled Millennials. For example, sixteen-year-old Jonathon Holzapfel of Sonoma, California, was happy at the bakery where he worked part-time. But he was also serious about becoming a professional snowboarder. When his repeated requests for specific weekend days off were denied, he quit. Millennials are used to being busy, and they tend to do better with work schedules that allow them to juggle. This mentality does not just affect fast food or retail stores. Whether it's a call center or a manufacturing plant, companies are going to have to get very flexible and creative in terms of scheduling Millennials. No longer will three to four main shifts be enough to choose from. It may even take forty. Consider doing what American Express does and develop a bevy of possible schedules that could fit anyone's schedule, no matter how sandwiched they might be. In fact, American Express call centers now host up to forty different schedules per week in order to field customer calls twenty-four hours a day and keep workers sane.

If you are thinking that this is something to pay attention to down the line as more and more Millennials creep into your workplace, our message is to start now. Never mind flexible schedules for just the leading-edge Millennials entering the workforce; what about the parents of the millions of younger Millennials who are still pressed to attend ballet recitals, school concerts, t-ball games, conferences, and on and on? We heard a story on NPR not long ago in which two parents worked in the same manufacturing plant, but on two different shifts so someone was always available for the Millennial kids' busy schedules. Great plan, except for one thing: There was only fifteen minutes between the time one parent's shift ended and the time the other parent's shift began. That meant that in order to hand off the kids, the parent at home had to get ready for work, get the kids dressed and loaded in the car, drive to the plant parking lot, and wait until the other parent emerged. Then they had about three minutes to do a complete handoff of kids, clothes, homework, the day's news, and so on before parent number one had to be inside starting the next shift. This is just the kind of craziness that can be avoided by adopting more flexible scheduling policies. The benefits of a less stressed, more balanced workforce can be measured in terms of lower absenteeism, fewer work-related accidents, and greater customer satisfaction. But the biggest benefits may be in hiring and retaining hard-to-find workers. If the choice is between two similar shift-work jobs, and one offers a plethora of balanced scheduling choices, which would you choose?

This may sound like a balancing nightmare on the employer side, but for the Millennials, you can be a dream come true. Not a bad way to start off getting to know an entirely new generation of workers.

THE BALANCE PRESSURE COOKER

The search for balance is elusive and frustrating. Part of this stems from our restless American culture—the one that says we should have it all and be all that we can be. In reality, most of us are lucky to be just *some* of what we can be, like maybe have a good performance review and get the dishes done on the same day.

Expectations, driven by the media, are too high and soaring higher. It's no longer enough to be a decent employee, a responsible parent, or a good friend. Now we're supposed to be "balanced."

This struggle is not going away, and companies that are trying to implement balance initiatives will find it an excellent strategy for attracting workers, retaining the workers they have, or enabling workers to be more effective by reducing the amount of stress and distractions in their lives. But the most strategic companies will be those that realize that balance means something different to each of the generations. Part of supporting balance at work is getting your arms around how the generations perceive balance. Otherwise the workplace becomes a pressure cooker that continues to build up steam.

We don't know if you've ever seen what happens when you forget to turn down the heat in a pressure cooker . . . let's just say it's not a pretty scene.

We were in Phoenix, giving speeches over a two-day period. At the end of the long first day, a vice president asked if he could meet with us to discuss ideas he had for a conference to be held ten months later.

Inasmuch as David had come to Phoenix from Minnesota in the dead of winter, he loathed the thought of spending the few remaining minutes of daylight indoors when the sun was shining brightly outside. But in fear of the look he'd get from Lynne if he dared try to postpone the meeting, he sucked it up and trooped down to the lounge, where they were to meet the client.

"Hey, David, great to see you," the vice president boomed enthusiastically. "It seems it's going to be just you and me. Lynne left me a message saying she couldn't make it because she had already scheduled a massage!"

Touché.

8

SITTING ON A PORCH SWING DRINKING METAMUCIL?

Barbara Quigley retired in January 2000 after a stellar twenty-one-year career at Carlson Companies, parent company for Radisson, TGI Fridays, Country Hospitality, and Carlson Wagonlit Travel. Most recently she had worked as the right hand to Curtis Nelson, president and CEO of Carlson Hospitality Worldwide. We interviewed her when she retired, and she told us the following:

I was turning 62 in the year 2000 and figured that was a good time to call it quits and do some things I've always wanted to do. The retirement itself went smoothly, except for the inevitable tears and good-byes leading up to my last day. But I did find myself surprised by one thing: the reactions of the different generations to my decision to retire.

HOW THE GENERATIONS ARE REDEFINING RETIREMENT

"The people my age, the Traditionalists, understood it. They treated me like I'd earned it. They were happy for me and proud of my accomplishment. They were excited I could enjoy the fruits of my labors and do some of the things I'd been putting on hold. The Traditionalists didn't ask too many questions about my future, rather they spent the time reflecting with me on my twenty-one-year career at the company.

"The Baby Boomers, on the other hand, couldn't stop asking questions. They were so focused on what my goals were and what I was going to do with myself. It didn't seem to be enough for them when I said I just wanted to enjoy my life. No matter what answer I gave, from grandparenting to traveling, they seemed disappointed. I almost think they were worried about me. They didn't seem to know who I was going to be.

"I was surprised to find that it was the Generation Xers who were really the most excited for me. They were sad I was leaving, but really thrilled for the freedom I was going to have. As I think about their reaction, I believe that a lot of them don't plan on working forever, and they were really supportive of my decision to move on—to not work any longer than I really had to. They weren't remotely afraid or intimidated by the lack of structure, and weren't at all concerned about my identity as a retired person.

"Wow! I never thought that three generations could have such divergent attitudes toward retirement. I hope my observations can in some way help you enlighten today's workplace as it tries hard to prepare each of the generations for this life stage."

TIME TO RETIRE "RETIREMENT"?

Never before has there been a more inadequate word in the English language than "retirement." *The American Heritage Dictionary* defines retirement as "withdrawal from business or public life." *Roget's The-saurus* lists such synonyms for "retire" as retreat, recede, quit, resign, and seclude oneself. Whoa . . . did we say "retirement" or someone sitting in his living room in the dark, waiting to take his next dose of Prozac? It seems that the English language hasn't kept up with the new ways we define retirement or what happens when we move on after our primary, lifetime career comes to an end.

If a picture is worth a thousand words, it's worth at least that many stereotypes. Hear someone is retiring and you immediately conjure up images of a person grabbing that cardboard box, plunking it on the desk, and then slowly filling it with pictures of family members, fancy pen holders, and crystal paperweights engraved with dated motivational sayings like "Success is not a destination, it's a journey!" Then there's the slow final walk down the corridor, nodding solemnly to co-workers who are all too busy to get off the phone to say good-bye. The elevator opens . . . the retiree gets in . . . and the door closes. Maybe the retiree is worthy enough for that big farewell dinner at Red Lobster, where the gang pigs out on surf'n turf while roasting the guest of honor, telling dumb stories, and presenting gifts like a lifetime subscription to *Bass Fishing.* The evening ends with the granddaddy presentation of the cherrywood plaque, which will most likely end up in the box next to the paperweight.

The media hasn't done much to provide us with a better image. We have scanned marketing campaigns, looking for how retired people are portrayed, and we definitely uncovered a theme: retirees were all sitting on the porch swing doing absolutely nothing! Or technically they weren't doing nothing, they were usually sipping a nice glass of iced tea or Metamucil.

Why is it that when we think of retiring, we generally picture a mindlessly contented duffer dealing out dispassionate hands of bridge or churning out colorful, crocheted potholders? Even Martha Stewart is trying to cash in on this stereotype. In a recent episode of *Martha Stewart Living,* she demonstrated how to turn old woolen business suits into, ostensibly, brown, scratchy, hot, and uncomfortable quilts to adorn the living room sofa! However, if you stop and think about the people you know who are experiencing this life stage, these images couldn't be further from the truth.

Clearly we need some new ways of visualizing and talking about retirement. Without an adequate definition, how can we expect organizations to talk to employees about retiring and, even more important, help them plan for it? But in looking for the updated definition, one thing is for sure: We need to give up looking for just one. As the generations are making plans for what to do when employment ends, each is writing a new definition as to what it truly means to "retire."

CLASHPOINT AROUND RETIREMENT

Traditionalists . . .   *Reward.*

Baby Boomers . . .   *Retool.*

Generation Xers . . .   *Renew.*

Millennials . . .   *Recycle.*

Traditionalists: Retirement as "Reward"

Traditionalists have worked hard, planned and saved, and deferred gratification to a later time when their kids are launched and their debts are paid. Justifiably, they see retirement as a well-earned reward after a lifetime of service to company, country, and family. In a recent BridgeWorks Generations Survey, one Traditionalist defined retirement as a time when you can "do, enjoy, and appreciate all the things in life you didn't have time for while working."

And that they do! Close to 30 percent of Traditionalists are enrolled in school. If they are not in class, they are on the road, making up 80 percent of luxury travel. But not the stereotypical senior tour that includes shuffleboard tournaments or bingo. From cross-country RV journeys to European walking tours to volunteer stints in underdeveloped parts of the world . . . this is the healthiest, wealthiest, best-educated generation ever to retire.

While Traditionalists will always be a fiscally conservative generation, they are ready to treat themselves to experiences they postponed during their working and child-rearing years. Unlike the Baby Boomers, they started their families early and will not find themselves supporting a lot of dependents in their golden years. However, because Traditionalists are likely to live longer than their parents, they are concerned about outliving their savings. This factor, coupled with the fact that many find themselves in excellent health, isn't exactly leading them to slam corporate America's doors on the way out. We were surprised that in our survey, 72 percent of Traditionalists said they planned to continue working in some capacity after formal retirement. It makes sense, since a healthy sixty-five-year-old might live another thirty years, and it seems increasingly silly to assume that one-third of a person's life will be lived without work. This is basic math, yet so many organizations are failing the test.

The numbers are there to support the need to recareer Traditionalists. Watson Wyatt's 1999 survey on phased retirement found that 70 percent of employers "agreed that implementing a phased retirement program, along with other flexible options for workers, such as job-sharing and telecommuting, is a viable strategy for addressing labor shortages." According to the survey, employers' primary reasons for offering phased retirement were to retain skilled workers and give them the ability to retire gradually. In other words, they can slow the brain drain internally while helping employees with the transition.

The state of California has developed a program in which retired state employees can return part-time to serve as mentors and make sure their expertise is passed on. More than just an opportunity for the Traditionalists, it's a very strategic move for the state. As the Traditionalist/Boomer retirement exodus begins in many organizations, there are simply not enough able-bodied leaders being groomed to take their places. It scares us to see how many companies are still not addressing the question of who's left behind to fill the shoes of today's managers.

"Other-centered" Traditionalists often see the "reward" of retirement as an expanded opportunity to give back and to focus even more energy on community, family, and nonprofit concerns where they can make a contribution. Organizations should consider whether they can retain "retirees" in a paid or unpaid capacity to run important programs like blood drives, the company's United Way campaign, or the annual Habitat for Humanity stint. Volunteers are in short supply in all areas of the nonprofit world. Traditionalists who already know the ins and outs of your program, whether nonprofit or for profit, might just be too valuable to lose. Companies that can identify the "keepers" among the eligible-to-retire Traditionalists would do well to think ahead about what is going to get them to stay.

Baby Boomers: Retirement as "Retooling"

Baby Boomers tend to view retirement not as a well-earned rest, but with ambivalence, even discomfort. The stereotype of Hawaiian-shirt-clad retirees sipping tropical drinks stuffed with little umbrellas is anathema to ambitious Boomers who have always identified themselves by their professional accomplishments.

In fact, the American Association of Retired Persons (AARP) has been stymied by the Boomers, many of whom seem to be too hip to read *Modern Maturity* (AARP's magazine aimed at those

fifty-five-plus). Should they be surprised? This is the same generation who wouldn't be caught dead on the subway reading the large-
font version of *The New York Times,* even though they have to hold
their reading material a mile away from their faces. This is a generation that refuses to believe it's getting older, and any mention of
retirement offends them. So how does the AARP attract Boomers
who are raging against aging to join their association? They've
launched a new magazine called *My Generation* aimed entirely at
Boomers age fifty to fifty-five. "How could we be old if we're still
out there Rollerblading and listening to Radiohead?" editor Betsy
Carter wrote in her column in the premiere issue.

The message? "Hey, we're for active, with-it people like you."
Articles focus on travel, exercise, plastic surgery, great careers, sex,
and famous people who have turned fifty—many of whom, thanks
to travel, exercise, plastic surgery, great careers, and sex, still look as if
they're twenty!

The language in AARP's new print ad campaign shows a
marked deference to the Boomer drive to be active, decisive, and
independent. One ad shows a woman named Rosemary McCallum.
Next to her picture is the title "AARP member, rock climber, hiker,
and gardener." The text goes on to explain that Rosemary "knows
age is just a number, and life is what you make it." It concludes with,
"Today's AARP helps you make the most out of life, with the
choices you want, and the voice you need—to keep being yourself."
Quite a change from congratulating a retiree on that senior discount
at movie theaters! Boomers like Rosemary are parasailing into middle age, and AARP is working to find the right way to keep up.

While we think the American Association of Retired Persons is
off to a good start, who knows, maybe to truly reinvent itself, the
association may eventually have to change its name. Just like Ken-
tucky Fried Chicken renamed itself KFC to get rid of the ubiquitous word *fried,* and Salted Nut Rolls became Pearson's Nut Rolls
for obvious reasons, AARP might just need a hot new name that
drops the "R-word" entirely!

Boomers obviously balk at many of the images of slowing down that go with being retired, because they imply taking a less important role in the hustling, bustling scheme of things. Boomers want to retain their youth, yes, but even more important, they want to retain their influence. Could you imagine Donald Trump or Hillary Clinton ever quitting and disappearing from their professions? Baby Boomers want to be able to earn and achieve at any age and at any life stage. We predict that Baby Boomers, who have identified themselves so closely with who they are at work, will continue after "formal" retirement to accept a series of alternative careers that will continue to provide self-definition. One Boomer woman recently invested hundreds of dollars having a logo designed and stationery printed for her recently retired executive Boomer husband. "He's not entirely sure what's he's going to be doing yet, but he needed business cards he could hand out when he's in social settings—he really needed an identity."

We call this trend toward working well into retirement years "retooling."

In the BridgeWorks Survey, one Boomer described it like this: "Retirement for me may well become a withdrawal from a consistent career and entry into a series of consultation-style jobs until I am comfortable enough to take a sabbatical, followed by another job when the bucks run low. And because of how tight the labor market will be, in thirty years an eighty-year-old might be quite welcome in the job market, unlike today."

Boomers might easily be lured away from their current companies to take on a new challenge or learn a new skill set. The key attraction will be if a new opportunity can allow them to get away from the fifty-hour-a-week grind while capitalizing on their value in the marketplace in new ways. Employers need to pay attention to this threat now, and find ways to provide new challenges and new learning to Boomers who might be bored or burned out.

The threat becomes even greater when attitude surveys show that many Boomers will leave the nine-to-five routine completely and become free agents. This generation's youthfulness, ambition, energy, and good health will be marketable long past traditional retirement age. Their considerable level of education and work experience will make many of them sought-after leaders, consultants, and mentors. Boomers have already begun to learn the skills of free agency that will enable them to keep working after retirement. Since the invention of the laptop computer, they've brought work home, answered e-mails, and juggled school conferences with conference calls, all from the kitchen table. As Boomers move through their forties and fifties, they will test the feasibility of being free agents by taking on small freelance assignments or telecommuting a few hours a week. They might even start a small business on the side, working out of that newly equipped SOHO (small office/home office) they paid for with their last corporate bonus. While *American Demographics* reports that two million home-based businesses are currently being started each year, it's only a matter of time until the retooling Boomers blow that number into cyberspace! In fact, a Del Webb survey found in 1998 that while the median age at which Boomers expect to retire from their primary career is sixty-one, two out of three say they will continue to work afterward. Most said they plan to work part-time, and 36 percent intend to run a home-based business.

Regardless of what Boomers want to do with their careers, a contributing factor in the retirement scenario is obviously money. A key feature in the Boomer retirement equation will be their inheritance. Boomers' inheritance is very important in retirement income calculations. Even inheriting enough money to pay off the mortgage can substantially crack the monthly nut Boomers will need to cover in retirement. The limiting factor, however, is information. Too many Boomers aren't sure where they stand.

Boomers are beginning to assume the mantle as heads of extended families. As their parents become too old or infirm to host family gatherings and make important decisions, Boomer offspring are taking charge. This gradual change in the chain of command will put Boomers increasingly in charge of parents' finances. And we hope this will enable them to learn to what extent their retirement income will be supplemented by inheritance. We know that the wealth of Traditionalists has been estimated at some $10–$12 trillion, so it is likely that Boomers and their offspring *could* find themselves relatively well provided for. However, it seems the only ones *not* reporting in on this transference of wealth are the ones holding on to it. The generation we prefer to call Traditionalists has also been referred to as the "silent" generation, and for good reasons, on the money front. Most Traditionalists would rather talk about erectile dysfunction than their financial situation. Boomers were seldom told what their fathers earned or how much their parents had saved for a rainy day. No big deal if they didn't have this information on the playground, but flash-forward twenty to thirty years and Boomers find themselves in middle age with little idea of whether their parents are going to leave them princes or paupers when they die. This has created some uncomfortable planning dilemmas for Boomers, who want to know the family situation but don't wish to invade parents' tightly guarded privacy. One fifty-five-year-old Ivy League–educated bank president we know finds himself providing aid and support to two ailing parents in their nineties. Of course, he is allowed to change their bedpans, but try to get them to tell him anything about their assets or investments and they would rather be . . . well, you know.

So for many Boomers, the "silent" generation has left them still unsure as to whether or not they will be able to afford to retire on what they've saved. Boomers' real income has fallen, their pension plans will be worth less than those of the Traditionalists, Social Security will provide less, and investment income will hold steady. In addition, many Baby Boomers will be supporting dependents long past the age of fifty. The costs of raising and educating children will eventually disappear for Boomers, but not nearly as quickly as they did for Traditionalists, who had their children at younger ages. Boomers who held off childbearing until their late thirties and early forties will be paying for college until well into their sixties.

So are the Baby Boomers ready? When asked, "Do you know how much money you will need at retirement and how you are going to acquire it?" over 40 percent of our Boomer survey respondents answered, "No." But dig a little deeper and—surprise, surprise!—every Boomer seems to feel it is someone else's problem, not theirs. In a survey by Mathew Greenwald & Associates for the American Council on Life Insurance, 75 percent of Boomer respondents said they believe most people aren't saving enough money to live comfortably in retirement. Yet 64 percent said they themselves were well prepared to support themselves in retirement. Hmm . . . it seems aging isn't the only thing Boomers are denying.

A lot of this equation depends on how much money the Boomers perceive they will *need* in order to retire. Financial consultants we've interviewed said consistently that Boomers tend to grossly underestimate how much money they will need in retirement, often assuming that monthly expenses will drop by as much as half once they are no longer working. In reality, living expenses tend to stay about the same. Retirees still need homes to live in and food on the table. As for how the Boomers' predictions are going, the Del Webb study found that the median income Boomers expected to receive in retirement was a modest $35,700. Let's break that down a little further: Boomers think they will need only $2,975 a month to happily enjoy their retirement years.

We're not Charles Schwab, but this does seem to be quite a stretch for a generation of consumers who have always believed in treating themselves to a variety of luxuries, whether it's a $2 bottle of water, a $4 caffè latte, or a $60,000 car. Retirement years will not exactly be a time when Boomers stop indulging, even if they ease off on the Evian. They will still take vacations, perhaps even more frequently once they have disposable time, and many will want to treat themselves to that vacation home they have always wanted. Older Boomers seeing both parenting and career duties nearing an end are far from downsizing the nest. In fact, another Del Webb study found that about a quarter of new housing starts in 2000 were due to Boomers who were actually buying larger homes, even if most of the bedrooms will go unused much of the time.

But don't assume upsizing is a result of looking for more wall space to hang expensive art collected on a recent jaunt to Europe. This is due to another trend—that of "reuniting." As we said, Boomers are gradually taking on the role formerly held by their parents, that of the matriarchs and patriarchs of the family. Because those families are likely to be spread out geographically, and in many cases consist of "blended" family members (stepkids, stepparents, half-brothers and -sisters, and so on), Boomers are building the "place to come home to." They want to create a place where the family can gather for important occasions and relive the feeling many of them had growing up in intact, two-parent households where the extended family tended to live close by.

So Boomers aren't exactly doing the math when it comes to predicting what they will need in the checking account for their retirement years, but that doesn't mean we are about to see eighty million people jumping out of windows. They may be spenders, but they're not stupid. The media tends to focus on the *leading*-edge Boomers as the trendsetters for what is to come. However, the fattest part of the python was born in 1959, meaning at this writing, the bulk of the Boomers are still in their early forties. That means that the bulk of the Boom has at least a decade or two left in which to prepare financially for retirement. Early in the 1990s it did appear as though the Boomers were not preparing for a safe retirement. But that seems to be changing, and Boomers are now paying more attention to preretirement planning and saving. They are also looking for help from their companies. When asked what their company's role should be in helping them prepare for retirement, almost 70 percent

of Boomers said it should be "financial, plus planning and education," as opposed to merely making financial contributions to a plan
or simply paying employees and letting them do the rest. An opportunity exists for companies to endear themselves to Boomers by
offering them training in how to prepare, both financially and emo-
tionally, for this next big transition. Not only is this the humane way
to manage, but it might open up a dialogue that convinces peak-
performing Boomers to stick around a bit longer.

Generation Xers: Retirement as "Renewing"

Generation Xers are worrying about their 401(k) plans at the
same age Boomers were still doing disco. Research shows that this
generation is saving money at a younger age and faster pace than
the Boomers ever did. Xers know the importance of saving for a
rainy day. In fact, the research group Third Millennium actually
found that skeptical Xers believe they have a greater chance of seeing a UFO in their lifetime than a Social Security check! With
thirty-plus years left on the job and an unprecedented entrepreneurial spirit, it would be surprising if we find Xers needing those
senior discounts once they are eligible. This is a generation that has
had the lesson of compound interest pounded into their heads
since birth.

When we asked Generation Xers about "the company's role in
helping employees prepare for retirement," we expected Xers to be
an independent group who either did not count on their employers
to help them plan and save, or weren't quite ready to think about
retirement yet. Contrary to our predictions, 66 percent of Xers said
their company's role should be a combination of making financial
contributions and helping with planning and education. This gives
some support to the idea that Xers are thinking about retirement at
a younger age than Boomers did and that help with retirement
might grow in importance as a valuable perk to offer Xers while
providing a good entrée for talking with them about their futures.

Gen Xers may be skeptical of institutions, but not so skeptical that they won't appreciate a little help.

The biggest difference in the way the generations perceive retirement is in the retirement concept itself. Rather than viewing retirement as the ultimate *reward,* or as a chance to *retool,* Xers focus on retirement as a chance to *renew.* They aren't planning to wait around to age sixty-five or even forty-five to do the rewarding, retooling, or renewing. They want to enjoy the things that are important to them *throughout* their career, not at the end of it.

Recruiter Teri Bloomquist recently left a recruiting gig with BarterTrust.com with enough money saved to take three to four months off before starting a new position. "I've been working ungodly hours the past eight years, and I've scarcely unpacked the boxes in my new house. It's time to take a break and destress before I jump back in again," she explained. Having seen the Baby Boomers and Traditionalists work so hard and sacrifice so much for their careers, and having observed the devastating corporate layoffs of the 1980s, Xers are not willing to sacrifice themselves on the corporate altar. Xers will take time out during their careers to travel, try a new interest or vocation, or spend time with family.

Therefore, we're seeing a lot of Xers plot their careers around large chunks of time off that enable them to do things they've always wanted to do. That might mean working for two or three years, saving up, then quitting to backpack around Southeast Asia before returning to paid employment. Or it might just mean taking a significant chunk of time off between jobs to regroup. It's not uncommon for Gen Xers to find a new job but delay the start date for one to three months to give them time to downshift before gearing up again.

If you are thinking, *That's fine now, but just wait until they are older and have more responsibility,* we highly recommend that you don't blow off this section and skip to the next chapter. Understanding and even embracing Generation Xers' definition of retirement might be your biggest strategic move in the recruitment and retention game.

Generation Xers' desire and attitude to renew themselves is not going to diminish with age and in fact will only become all the more critical when additional responsibilities load on. Having seen Traditionalists thrown out and Boomers burn out, they would rather walk out than find themselves in the same situation. But how will they be able to get away with it? As annoying as it may be for older generations to accept, the thing to remember is that Xers have the numbers on their side and will always be in demand to fill the void when the Boomers move up and out. Regardless of how the economic pendulum swings, Xers will always find jobs.

The "renewing" concept may sound like an ad for a day spa, but it goes way beyond one's skin tone. Freedom-loving Xers resent the idea of being "trapped" by a job, and they fear the burnout they saw their parents suffer. A program that offers Xers an opportunity for a sabbatical, for example, might just make Generation Xers more loyal and productive than you assumed possible. For example, more companies should explore sabbatical programs as a way to help Xers renew. Too often these programs have been seen as expensive perks offered *only* to senior folks based on tenure. What if any age employee could earn a sabbatical based on his or her performance? The point is that companies need to take a new look at rewarding peak performers with the greatest gift of all—*time.*

A sabbatical doesn't have to mean nine months in the Himalayas at full pay. Sometimes it can be as simple as a brief change of pace or even scenery.

Best Buy Company's information systems department has been smart enough to pick up on this. They offer what they call "educational sabbaticals." Employees with five years of service can take a two-week professional development sabbatical to study a topic in business, leadership, or technology. Darcy Hemping is the program's director. As she explained, "The younger generations of associates at

Best Buy are given the rare opportunity to take advantage of a program historically offered only to older associates who have worked for the same company for ten-plus years. We feel everyone should have the opportunity, and by taking this approach we have watched our sabbatical policy become a key part of our recruiting and retention strategies."

Is it working? Just ask Generation Xer David Frost. After six years in mainframe development, David was beginning to feel less challenged. As he put it, "I had been a mainframe developer my whole career. I felt that opportunities were running out and I didn't want to get stagnant." So David took a sabbatical and learned a whole new software called Visual InterDev. Suddenly David felt as though his career were starting all over. He saw new opportunities and, more than anything, felt challenged again. "It felt so good to prove to myself that I could learn something new. I returned feeling reenergized. On my first day back, I found as many managers as I could to ask them for new challenges." More than anything else, David felt all the more committed and loyal to Best Buy for giving him the opportunity.

Allowing an Xer to take a sabbatical might mean covering for a missing employee for an extended period, but that still has to be better than dealing with an extinct one. One thing is for sure: They will come back to the job all the more committed. And (you may need to lie down for this one) you might even get an Xer to believe she actually owes *you* one.

Let's take the sabbatical concept even further. Taking a break to renew oneself might mean taking a new job to learn a new skill, meet new people, or work on a different project. Therefore, organizations should consider welcoming good employees back even if they quit to work for a competitor.

In *Winning the Talent Wars,* Bruce Tulgan suggests that companies should let employees know unequivocally that they are welcome back no matter where they go off to in between. Tulgan suggests that companies stop thinking of employees who have left as "turncoats" and think of them as "alumni" or even "boomerangers," welcoming them back when they're ready to return. This makes sense to Xers, who often leave companies with no hard feelings, just a desire to get their needs met. And even though the Xer may have never stopped working, he will see the "break" as a type of retirement and chance to renew himself.

If an Xer is a peak performer in an area that a company needs, organizations must consider the *renewal factor* in understanding how to keep that person motivated and turned on. It might be something as simple as allowing a little longer vacation or the use of a corporate apartment in another city. Or it might mean arranging for that Xer to take a few months off to welcome a new child or pursue a passion. Sam Zeszut, a San Francisco–based employee of Charles Schwab, is taking three months off to focus on his first love—composing music. Because his work is critical to his department, his managers at Schwab are prepared to welcome him back into the fold when his three months of "renewal" are up.

The bottom line is that the attitude that the "great reward" happens at the end of a long career will *never* make sense to this generation. It's the job of both managers and employees to learn to talk about this new definition, because understanding how Xers define retirement will be key to keeping them motivated over the long haul.

Millennials: Retiring Retirement

As Generation Xers turn the concept of retirement upside down and inside out, they will still be arguing their definition with preceding generations who have the older version of the dictionary. The older generations may always perceive Xers' need for renewal as annoying, but as Xers grow into leadership roles within companies, this will be a good thing in the eyes of the Millennials.

As Millennials demand to be involved in work that has meaning, and expect to have fun along the way, they may never fully understand why a person would need to reward, retool, or even renew in the first place. As they will see it, those are things you do every day of your lives. And you certainly shouldn't wait around until some magic age to *start*. Of course, it seems strange to even talk about the concept of retirement and the Millennials when many of them are just tackling that first job selling Girl Scout cookies. But it is interesting to note that this might very well be the generation to actually erase the word *retirement* from the English language. Imagine that Millennials may reach the age of sixty or seventy without even using that word. After all, the leading edge of Millennials are college age now; that means they have forty years in which to forget a concept that no one seems to agree upon.

REWARD, RETOOL, RENEW . . . AND EVENTUALLY RETIRE

The better job companies can do of understanding what makes the generations tick when it comes to retirement, the better job they can do of managing and retaining them. We used to think of retirement as the end of the employer/employee contract. Now we're realizing it's an important clause in that contract throughout the relationship. Learning to deal with it will make a huge difference in the way organizations relate to the employees they have and those they hope to attract and keep.

Six months after we interviewed Barbara Quigley, we received a postcard. On it was a beautiful picture of a sunset. The other side was inscribed . . .

Dear Lynne and David,

Loving retirement! Don't you wish you were here?

Miss you, Barbara.

Hmmm . . . we wish we were there, too! We just have to figure out what our definition of "there" is.

9

IS FUN REALLY THE "F-WORD"?

When it came time to write about fun in the workplace, we had a real generational clash. David felt it needed its own chapter, since time and again Xers and Millennials have told us they don't understand why it's not okay to have fun at work.

Lynne, on the flip side of the "fun at work" equation, wanted to skip the topic altogether. She was adamant as she explained:

> I don't really see why we have to make such a big deal about fun in the workplace! I mean, as far as I'm concerned, fun is irritating. First of all, it wastes time. Second, you're usually doing things someone else thinks is fun and you don't, like attending a baseball game en masse, or playing air hockey in a stinky cafeteria, or staying late for cold pizza when you could be having a decent meal at home. Or worse yet, you're forced into a planned "team building" activity that's supposed to be fun, like dangling on a rope over a sixty-foot cliff or running about in the

*woods shooting each other with paint guns. Boy, you can't have
too many of those experiences!*

She took a deep breath and then made the mistake of uttering
a soon-to-be-immortalized phrase that David has never allowed her
to forget: "You know, there's a reason they call it the workplace and
not the funplace!"

While David held a big letter *L* to his forehead, standing for
"loser," Lynne held her ground. And after raising our voices a little
(which actually was kind of fun), even David would admit that Lynne
had a point. The problem with fun in the workplace is twofold. First,
not everyone agrees on what fun is. And second, the generations
don't share the same views on fun at work. Yet for many employees,
"fun" is a vital aspect of a meaningful, productive workplace.

WHY SO DIFFERENT?

An obvious reason for different generational attitudes on having fun
is the nature of life stages. The older generations tend to have more
to go home to. If you own a house and have a family to take care of,
there's a lot more reason to try to get out of the plant or the office
on time rather than staying late for a foosball tournament.

But that's life stage. There are "generational" reasons why people differ on the fun front.

Traditionalists and Baby Boomers had a lot of competition for
their jobs and believed that they were being judged by the serious-
ness with which they did them. They wanted to be seen not as friv-
olous, but as professional and competitive. The workplace that many
Traditionalists entered was a formal environment with specific dress
codes and rules of conduct, both written and unwritten. Men wore
suits, ladies wore stockings, bosses were addressed as "sir" or "ma'am,"
and only certain approved-of items were appropriate for desktops.
Protocol and formal ways of behaving at work created a consistent,

professional environment for fledgling organizations that were trying to grow and expand during the earlier part of the last century.
Much like the military model many businesses were designed to
emulate, setting norms of dress and behavior for all encouraged the
conformity necessary to achieve organizational goals. Companies
were formal in the ways other institutions were formal. For example, women would never have worn slacks to church, just as they
would not have worn them to an office.

Xers and Millennials, on the other hand, seem much more predisposed to include some fun as part of the mix. Members of the
younger generations saw their parents come home night after night
exhausted and stressed from jobs that demanded a lot and gave little
in return. Somehow, seeing Mom and Dad come home crabby, fall
asleep at the dinner table, or end up divorced didn't make work
seem much fun at all. More than one child vowed never to work in
the sweatshop they saw their parents march off to day in and day
out. That's why one of the best things parents can do today for their
children is talk about work with them in ways that help them hear
the positives as well as the downsides so that children can develop
a realistic attitude about the world of work. It helps children
immensely to learn about what their parents love to do and why
they love it. What better way to teach kids to follow their dreams
and find work to do that they are good at and genuinely care about?

At the same time, many Xers who came from fractured families
have told us that they often view their peer group as an extremely
important "replacement family." So in working with their peers
today they would naturally want to include play as part of business as
usual.

There's yet another aspect to why the younger generations
believe we need to loosen our neckties on the job. They have
watched Boomers in particular compete with one another to such a
point that they have grown to believe it is anything *but* a game. As a
result, part of the Xers' vision of remaking the American workplace
has been to create a more casual atmosphere where peers get along

and help each other, where the constant pressure of competition is downplayed, and where fun is a natural part of collaboration. At the same time, technology has lowered the barriers between work and home. R. J. Pittman is a twenty-eight-year-old San Francisco millionaire and entrepreneur. One of his ventures was converting a warehouse into an incubator for high-tech start-ups. In designing the workplace for tenants, he put a game room/break area right in the center. From La-Z-Boys to laser tag, it was a place to hang out, have fun, and just relax. Should we be surprised that when potential tenants looked at the space, that was their favorite part? "If you're going to spend sixteen hours a day at work," explained R. J. Pittman, "you might as well be able to have fun there. People want to be able to work hard and play hard, all in the same environment."

Unfortunately, as many Xers have tried to transform their own workplace into more of a "funplace," they are finding some similarities to their childhood board games Sorry! and, for some, even Trouble. One Generation X employee was shocked when he got reprimanded by his Traditionalist boss after pushing hard to have at least one casual day a week. "Look," the boss snapped, "we already have casual day; it's on Sunday!"

WHY "FUN" IS NOT THE "F-WORD"

Everyone needs to blow off steam from time to time. Whether it's after a long period of running a manufacturing plant around the clock, or after the completion of a huge software installation, or even after making a huge sale, it is important that we stop to recharge the battery. Accomplishing tasks like these can be very stressful. Regardless of what generation you are from, or how many big projects you've put to bed in your career, all the generations need to blow off a little steam.

We need to get to know each other in a different way. As much as Lynne scoffs at those experiential team-building exercises, the truth is they are an amazing way to break through barriers and let people get to know one another. One reason the television show *Survivor* was such an immense hit in the year 2000 and again in 2001 was that viewers were intrigued to see how the challenges would be met by such diverse personalities working together. It was fascinating, and somewhat gratifying, to watch the survivors struggle. We're not saying you need to have a larva-eating contest in the employee lunchroom, but we are suggesting there can be a great benefit from seeing one another in a different light from how we see each other day to day. We all need the opportunity to let our hair down and communicate on a different level, to find out things we might never have known about one another. Fun deepens the learning and deepens the bonds, especially among people of different generations who might normally never encounter each other on that level. We've noticed that in general the generations tend to have a pretty narrow bandwidth of tolerance for one another. We give our peers much more leeway than we give someone from another generation. Fun lets us get to know one another on a deeper level, expanding the bandwidth. This pays off when a crisis erupts and we need to count on each other.

We also need to celebrate together. Just as we work so hard to achieve a common purpose, we need to find ways to celebrate its conclusion. If you work for NASA and you get a space shuttle safely up in the air and then bring it down again, all without a hitch, odds are you are going to party down. But you don't have to be a rocket scientist to have a celebration. When a major or even minor accomplishment takes place, the generations of employees need to celebrate together that job well done. But even more than an opportunity to high-five one another, it can serve as a very critical memory at a later date. The next time you find yourself colliding with a member from a different generation, that brief moment of celebration and fun can remind you that the luminous gap you are experiencing *can* and *has* been bridged in the past.

But finding ways to celebrate together isn't always that easy.

What if you're a group of teachers, each battling it out in your own classroom, divided by walls and problems and left to your own devices to find the answers? Celebrating takes on a different tone then, because you have to find a time and a place, and you have to discover your common ground. Yet generations of teachers, who fight unimaginable battles every day of their teaching lives, need that connection, too. They need a way they can celebrate.

FROM ZERO TO HERO—WITH A LITTLE FUN

Case in point . . .

Generation Xer Karen Whiley was recently promoted to nurse manager at Fairview-University Medical Center. She was excited to be in management and work with a team of skilled nurses and professionals. During her first few weeks on the job, she noticed that a lot of people came to work with their heads down, dragging their feet and dreading the work ahead of them. And at the end of the day, forget having a chance to chat with the night crew. As soon as a shift ended, they were out of there. Karen could see employees were unhappy, and several even shared with her that they were looking for new jobs. Turnover was at 16 percent and on the rise.

"The bottom line," explained Karen, "was that no one was having a good time. This just didn't make sense to me."

So what did she do? Karen formed a fun committee, whose task was just that—to figure out ways to have more fun. Reactions were mixed. "At first the older generations of employees were quite skeptical and even a bit irritated. After all, this was a hospital and nursing is a profession that should be taken seriously." Karen's response? "Says who?" (Does she sound like a typical Xer or what?)

Over the next few months, the committee tried everything from creating screen savers with pictures of employees' family members, to organizing lunches and birthday celebrations, to decorating their sterile-looking unit. Over time, all the generations came on board and began to enjoy themselves. They even held a scavenger hunt for the golden egg during the week of Easter that got to be so much fun, the patients themselves were joining in. "Suddenly a little fun designed to help us through *our* day was reaching people who needed it a lot more," Karen explained proudly.

Ultimately, was this disruptive to the nursing unit? Not at all. If anything, it disrupted other departments as employees sneaked over to join in the fun.

And the committee didn't stop there. It was important to them to extend the fun to activities outside of work as well. They met for happy hours, attended plays, and organized golf tournaments. "We were having a ball, but soon realized that many people from the older generations weren't showing up because they had too many family commitments. So we started holding family festivities that included spouses and kids. Before you knew it, everyone was joining in the fun."

Twelve months later, Karen's turnover had gone from 16 percent to zero and patient satisfaction soared from 62 percent to 83 percent. Score one for the idea of having fun!

From "wear green to work" day to pot luck picnics to starlight bowling, you name it . . . we have seen companies try it all. We truly commend senior executives for letting the hair they have left down over the past decade. Given all the gripes about the work ethic of the younger generations, we expected the Traditionalists who participated in our survey to say that today's employees needed to buckle down and put their noses to the grindstone. But when asked whether they thought people had enough fun at work, 30 percent of the Traditionalists said they thought people where they worked needed to have more fun. Is this because Traditionalists have reached a life stage where they are loosening up, are the Xers rubbing off on them, or have Traditionalists always valued fun at work without the other generations giving them credit for it? We don't know the answer, but it's a great question to ask at your next bowling party.

Of course, there are always those employees who have to complain about something or go out of their way to let it be known they are *still* bored. Unfortunately, rather than make executives feel good about allowing a little fun on the job, this only leads them to wonder if it is truly worth it.

Well . . . it is.

Fun on the job is one of the best ways to make employees feel that it's more than a job. When people have fun together, tensions ease and generation gaps get bridged. If you're trying to build a high-performance team, throw out the lecture on group dynamics and go have some fun instead. You won't regret it.

And by the way, if you are ever in Dubuque, Iowa, on a Friday afternoon, one of our clients, Johnson & Johnson, has a surgical center there that hosts a wild crocheting party!

RECRUITING THE GENERATIONS

10

FINDERS KEEPERS

A couple of years ago, we were asked to help a Fortune 500 manufacturing company do a better job attracting and hiring Generation Xers. Their top management tier was made up entirely of Traditionalists and Boomers who would be retiring over the next ten years. They didn't just need to develop some bench strength, they had to go out and find it.

Knowing that the World Wide Web was most likely the first place Xers would go to learn about the company, we logged on to its Web site to see how the company represented itself. The site talked about the company's long history, its founders, and its legacy. It contained sepia-toned photos of the first employees standing in front of a horse-drawn cart loaded down with raw materials. It provided a historic timeline that marked off decades of service, struggle, and survival. The company proudly touted its size—thousands of employees in hundreds of

HOW THE RULES OF THE RECRUITING GAME HAVE CHANGED

locations in dozens of countries around the world. They
described a plethora of products and services, many of which had
been invented over a century ago and were still going strong!

While Allan, our Traditionalist CFO, was impressed with
the company's history, and Boomer Lynne was intrigued by the
career opportunities that were available, Generation Xer David
would have preferred to do community service rather than
apply for a job there. Focus groups later bore out what David
had felt at first glance. Xers scanning the globe for opportunities were passing this Web site by as a historical artifact, not a
vibrant, challenging place that would compel them to attach
their latest résumé and hit send.

Don't get us wrong. This was a great company. Their products
served most of the known world, and their earnings history was
unmatched. These were tremendous accomplishments that anyone
would be justifiably proud to have achieved. But seen from the perspective of Generation X, the company came off as slow moving,
impersonal, out-of-date, and, to a certain extent, *boring!* It wasn't difficult for us to see why this organization was battling hard, and losing, the war for talent.

What was missing? Targeted messages that would appeal to the
hopes, dreams, values, and expectations of the younger generations
the company was struggling to attract.

Instead of all the emphasis on what happened in 1876, why
weren't they talking about where they'd be in *2026?* Instead of
focusing on the founding family that was six feet under, why weren't
they highlighting the young, dynamic leaders of today whom Gen X
job seekers might admire and emulate? Instead of highlighting size,
where was any mention of the agility, flexibility, and change agentry
that would propel this company into the future? Instead of tradition,
where was any talk of innovation?

We had our work cut out for us. By no means would we ever suggest that this Fortune 500 company dump the values that had made it a world leader. But if the workforce they were trying to attract wasn't appreciating those, then, Houston, we have a problem.

We see this collision between the values of one generation and the expectations of another cropping up in all parts of the recruiting process. From the recruiting materials companies produce, to the way they search for candidates, to the people who conduct the interviews, to the questions they ask, to the way they follow up and get a candidate in the door, the process is rife with opportunities to make the generations either tune in or turn off.

Recruiting has gotten tougher for everyone from McDonald's to McDonnell-Douglas. Companies that boasted in 1990 that they'd never had to struggle to find employees were showing up hat in hand in 2000 at college campuses and recruiting fairs. Over one-fourth of respondents in our BridgeWorks Survey said that in the past eighteen months their companies had actually had to "lower our standards for whom we hire" in order to fill open positions. And while dips in the U.S. economy are bound to bring some relief, the truth is that the recruiting picture has gotten a lot more complicated. Organizations that hope to hit a home run with any generation of workers will have to step up to the plate with a clear understanding of the generational trends that have changed the rules of the recruiting game.

FLATTEN THE SPEED BUMP

Along with the pace of just about everything else, turnaround time in the recruiting wars has kicked into warp speed. Technology and Gen X-pectations have changed the pace of the game. Younger workers in particular are no longer willing to wait week after week to find out whether you're planning to make them an offer. Dawdle too long and they're long gone. While the pace will naturally cool off somewhat as the economy slows, there's no getting around the fact that Xers and Millennials have been raised in a culture of instant results—instant cash from ATMs, microwave meals, drive-through windows, and instantaneous information from TV and the Internet provided twenty-four hours a day. Finding out that the company of their dreams can't answer an e-mail request for information within a couple of days can cool an Xer's employment ardor pretty fast. Increasingly, the other generations have moved into high gear and expect the same accelerated pace from employers.

Getting a handle on pace often means changing processes. If an employer doesn't call top candidates within seventy-two hours, it "probably shouldn't bother," says Barry Deutch, a Los Angeles executive recruiter for CJA-Adler Group Inc. A *Wall Street Journal* article entitled "In the Race to Fill Job Vacancies, Speed Demons Win" reported that moving too slowly is the reason his corporate clients lost the talent race in roughly half of two dozen searches handled during the previous six months. Delays can telegraph the idea that you're not interested in the candidate or that you're a slow-moving bureaucrat. To combat this, employment manager Judy Fox of Allergan Inc. ordered internal recruiters to reach the hottest prospects within forty-eight hours.

These days you have to assess résumés quickly, jump on the best ones aggressively, hustle people in for interviews, rush those background checks, and make offers in double time. To speed up the process, companies should give all approvals for hiring in advance, so when recruiters have the prospect on the line, they can reel him or her in without hitting any snags. As Mark Bailey, director of staffing and recruiting at General Mills, explained, "We've had to become very fast with our offers. During a typical day of interviewing, if the candidate is a keeper, we work frantically to put together a package so by the end of that same day we can make the offer right there on the spot."

As a result, General Mills is taking a radical step to pick up the pace and make an immediate, personal connection with candidates who approach the company via the Web. They are preparing to implement a system where applicants can go to the company's recruiting Web site and answer a set of questions about their background and job goals. As soon as the site captures enough information about their interests, it can route candidates to the appropriate person in-house to start a chat on-line. Before they even leave the Web site, candidates have made a personal connection with an actual person within General Mills—a great way to pick up the pace and put a human face on a high-tech process.

FORGET GRAY HAIR, PRIME JOB CANDIDATES MAY NOT EVEN HAVE CHEST HAIR!

The expansion of technology in every industry is changing the face of whom we hire. There is hardly a business today that isn't incorporating an "e-" into some type of business practice. From serving clients to internal communications, e-business is affecting not only how work gets done, but who does it. In early 2001, even with a tightening job market and layoffs occurring in some high-tech markets, it was estimated that 450,000 tech positions would still go unfilled nationally. And this continuing, urgent need for technology workers isn't happening just at those dot.coms that are so far out in the technosphere that we don't even understand their TV commercials! Even the most traditional industries are incorporating high tech into their manufacturing processes at a rapid pace, meaning they need to fill new types of positions they've never even entertained before with people younger generations never dreamed of hiring. For example, *USA Today* ran a feature on the Willamette Industries Sawmill in Dallas, Oregon, where technology has revolutionized the way wood is processed into lumber. Recently, recruiters were getting ready to interview for a variety of production positions. If you were picturing brawny lumberjacks lining up to showcase their skills by performing a few log rolls, think again. The mill spends several hundred thousand dollars to several million dollars every year to upgrade software or install new high-tech machines. This has put a premium on recruiting a younger, techno-savvy generation of workers who can keep things buzzing.

This new emphasis on technology has forced almost every industry to learn how to recruit the younger generations or how to retrain their older generations of workers to fill emerging positions. The same recruiting messages, processes, and techniques that worked for a generation of Paul Bunyans won't work for the generation that brought us *Inspector Gadget*.

"I'LL SEE YOU THREE MILLENNIALS AND RAISE YOU FIVE XERS AND A TRADITIONALIST"

Just because there are four generations in the workforce doesn't mean there are *more,* when it comes to the availability of workers. Major population fluctuations have altered the availability of workers on certain rungs of the corporate ladder. The demographic bulge that occurred during the prime birth years of the Baby Boom enabled companies to cherry-pick from among millions of highly educated, ambitious workers, often at bargain rates. But as the peak of the Boom eases inexorably toward retirement, companies will be scrambling to replace them from a dramatically smaller cohort of Xers. As a result, organizations will also have to dip into the massive Millennial pool of talent that will unfortunately still be wet behind the ears. And never mind only reaching *down* the ladder. To compensate for lack of experience, companies will also have to find persuasive ways to reach up and re-recruit Boomers and Traditionalists to stick around or dive back into the job market.

The Human Resources and Risk Management Department of the University of California at Davis, for example, recently published a "Model Employer Report" describing what it will take for the university to compete for employees in the future. As they uncovered, "By 2005, employment projections show the number of Baby Boomers retiring will outstrip the number of available replacement workers."

If you haven't identified the generation gaps in your recruiting plan, now's the time. Understanding what attracts *all* of the generations to the workplace, not just one or two of them, will become imperative as demographic shifts intensify the war for talent.

AROUND THE WORLD IN TWO WORDS: "WE'RE HIRING!"

As we enter an era in which as many as seventy different languages may be spoken in a single school district, never mind just tweaking recruiting messages, try translating them. Over the years, each successive generation has experienced more diversity on the job. But the thing to realize about recruiting the workforce of the future is that the younger the generation, the more diverse the population. The invention of the Pill and widespread fear of a population explosion have had an inhibiting effect on the U.S.-born population in the last three decades. The U.S. birthrate is now less than two children per woman, meaning the one true population growth area will be through immigration. Companies are just beginning to realize how much more frequently they will be looking to America's newest arrivals to fill jobs. As a result, companies will not only need to utilize multilingual recruiters and produce recruiting materials in more than one language, they will have to find the appropriate channels for reaching out to the generations who are members of these unique populations. Hispanics, for example, have an array of Spanish-language television and radio stations and newspapers they rely on for information, but how many businesses are tapping into these to find employees? And do they understand which generations are tapped into which media?

Smart organizations are figuring out not only how to recruit the younger generations of diverse workers, but also how to adapt business practices to accommodate them. McDonald's Corporation, for example, desperate to staff its fast-food restaurants, has hired a growing number of Asian American and Hispanic Millennials who possess the people skills and work ethic McDonald's needs. The challenge was how to bridge the often significant language barrier, especially at the drive-through, where employees and customers can't make eye contact and the scratchy microphones make speech in any language unintelligible. Solution? McDonald's has installed digital screens at many drive-through order stations that confirm an order visually. If you can't understand the transaction via the microphone, you can confirm your order right on the screen. This smart solution not only helps the company overcome the language barrier, it prevents mistakes in customer orders and allows employees to serve customers faster. As the diversity flame continues to burn hotter, the smart companies are rethinking recruiting processes to make sure they don't get burned.

"YOU'D RATHER WORK IN A *GARAGE* THAN IN OUR WORLD HEADQUARTERS?!"

Where it used to be that your biggest competition for the top job candidates came from your biggest competitor across town, today's field has exploded with competitors you might never have thought of. This makes understanding generational differences all the more important in trying to gain a recruiting strategic advantage.

Lifetouch National School Studios, the company that takes all those millions of school portraits around the country, for years relied on stay-at-home Boomer moms to staff their part-time photographer positions. The work occurred during school hours, was usually close to home, and involved being with kids—a perfect combo for mothers looking to supplement their family's income without taking much time away from the home front. Except that the surge of women into the workplace, the booming economy, and the aging of Boomer moms has effectively dried up that pool. So Lifetouch has had to expand their definition of the ideal candidate for a part-time photography position. As a result, they've been getting to know Generation Xers who want to be their own bosses, and they've been forming relationships with Traditionalist retirees who want to return to work. Both options have forced a reanalysis of how Lifetouch can connect with the right candidates and what it's going to take to make them a permanent part of the picture.

But the competition goes deeper. For starters, people are able to find out about jobs much more easily than in the past. Where an employee used to have to wait for the Sunday classifieds to tempt them with a change, the advent of the World Wide Web has made temptation a daily, or even hourly, threat. When asked in our Bridge-Works Survey if they scan the Web for job postings, about 30 percent of Traditionalists, 40 percent of Boomers, and 60 percent of Xers said they did. And a whopping 27 percent of those Xers said they search on either a daily or a weekly basis.

With information so much more available than in the past, applicants can learn about jobs from Okefenokee to Okoboji with the push of a button. That means bigger is no longer necessarily better. Many of the Davids can get their recruiting messages heard right alongside the Goliaths of the job market. Choices abound. Traditional companies are now competing against start-ups, smart-ups, and upstarts. Although working out of someone's garage doesn't exactly sound elegant, small businesses can often offer more flexibility and freedom than their much larger cousins. And while many may believe it is just the Xers who have always been willing to job-hop, today even Boomers and Traditionalists are increasingly willing to make a move in order to be more satisfied at work.

Above and beyond being tempted to work for a smaller company, recruiters for businesses of all sizes—big to small—are also competing with the candidate's desire to go start one himself. When we asked respondents in our BridgeWorks Survey whether they "intend to start their own business one day," 42 percent of Boomers and Xers, and a surprising 29 percent of Traditionalists, responded, "Yes." All the generations are realizing that if you want to have ultimate freedom and flexibility, then being your own boss can provide both in spades. The economic boom of the 1990s even allowed many Millennials to wear an entrepreneurial hat before they even put on a cap and gown!

The ability to counteract the lure of all these competitors depends on the ability to understand more deeply than ever before what attracts the generations to your place of business. It's not enough to offer a job and a paycheck. The generations today are considering a plethora of new choices not formerly available. Suddenly work conditions, location, flexible hours, levels of technology, family-friendly policies, and many more options are influencing employees' decisions as to where to work. And every generation responds differently to these options. This means employers have to be much more savvy about pinpointing which generations they really want to hire and understanding how to effectively wave the red flag that will make them charge the front gates.

WE'RE TALKIN' 'BOUT A RECRUITING REVOLUTION

Organizations must be able to respond to changing market conditions and competitive pressures, whether that means school districts staffing up because of a population boom or a manufacturer staffing down because of a competitor that can make the same item more cheaply overseas. Just as employees are becoming more agile at landing on their feet when employment scenarios change, employers are learning to expand and contract the labor force as the economy and business strategies dictate.

All these are reasons why, when it comes to recruiting, it's so important to understand generational differences.

The other reason is wasted resources. When we ask employers what they do when they fail to meet their recruiting quotas, they tell us they typically redouble their efforts. They place more ads; interview more candidates. That's as ridiculous as the old fallacy of the best way to look for your lost keys. When people lose keys, they search frantically in all the usual places—the front door, their pockets, their purse, the top of the dresser. When those options have been exhausted, what do they do? *They go search all those same places again!* Some people actually repeat the exercise three and four times before they give up. It's a colossal waste of effort. The same holds true for recruiting. If looking in all the usual places isn't getting you what you want, then redoubling your efforts is a waste of time and money. Why throw more and more resources at recruiting the same people in the same old ways, if it's not working? What you need to do is stop the perpetual motion and say to yourself, "Looking in all the 'usual' places is getting us nowhere. We need to look in a different way, in different places, or we're never going to find them."

Some companies are stepping up to the plate when it comes to trying new recruiting approaches. Our BridgeWorks Survey found that over 40 percent of respondents said their companies had "tried new recruiting tactics" in the past eighteen months. But in answering a related question, 57 percent of respondents said their companies are "not creative enough" when it comes to recruiting. New tickets may be the tactics, but pushing the ticket is the solution.

Becoming a "recruiting revolutionary" means taking time to analyze whether your recruiting process will actually build a generational bridge or just widen the gap. You don't have a choice. We now have to reach out and touch four generations of knowledgeable employees who view the world of work differently from one another.

What appeals to one recruit won't always fly with someone from another generation. Every company knows that we've entered the age of niches in the marketing world. Just take a gander at the magazine racks, where there's a pitch aimed at everyone from body art enthusiasts to orchid growers. Why would anyone assume that a "one size fits all" approach to recruiting would ever work for all the generations?

Eight months after we'd first been contacted, we all reconvened to check out our Fortune 500 client's new Web site. Allan, our Traditionalist CFO, was engrossed in a section all about the company's financials. He especially loved the ability to have it presented in a variety of charts and graphs. Lynne, our Boomer, was making us nervous by having way too much fun in the "career builder" section, where she could actually map out her own potential career path with the company. David, our Xer, was off in his own world, watching an MPEG video clip that highlighted the latest inventions the company would be introducing to the market over the upcoming year.

As the three of us clicked away in our sections, we couldn't have been more satisfied. Sure, we'd eventually surf around and check out the rest of the Web site, but the company had scored by giving us options to access the information each of us cared most about. Best of all, we were dazzled by the way the company had tailored its recruiting Web site to what would appeal to each of our generations.

11

WHY WOULD ANYONE WANT TO WORK FOR YOU?

Close your eyes (okay, keep one open so you can still read) and think of all the reasons your customers buy your products or services.

Our guess is that these incentives were quite easy to bring to mind. They make up what we call the "customer value proposition," the benefits your product or service can offer that the target customer really values. Every product provides some sort of value to its customers—cheaper price, better quality, faster delivery, more color choices, and so on. Any employee in any company should be able to tell you the value proposition for that company's customers or clients.

Now close your eye again . . . this time, think of all the reasons an employee would want to work at your company.

Our guess is that these didn't spring to mind as easily, and even if they did, you probably weren't considering whether or not these reasons would also appeal to a generation other than your own. We find that to be true of most people and most companies. They have

CREATING EMPLOYEE VALUE PROPOSITIONS FOR THE GENERATIONS

no problem describing what their value is to the customer, but it's a lot harder to describe the company's employee value proposition for employees.

What exactly is an employee value proposition? We define it as "a persuasive statement of what you have to offer aimed at appealing to a particular generation of recruits that is focused on the audience, not on the organization."

Our belief is that a value proposition isn't just for customers and that companies need to spend a lot more time than they do now developing the employee version. After all, without the employees on board, you won't have any products or services to offer in the first place. We talked in the last chapter about targeting recruiting efforts to the generations. Knowing the right employee value proposition to attract potential recruits is not only the key first step, it's the most important one.

Just ask the army. The U.S. Army used to attract Traditionalist recruits by focusing on masculinity, patriotism, and pride in serving our country through slogans like "Uncle Sam wants *you*." These remarkable values saw our country through the hardships of wars and the national sacrifices that had to be made to win them. But attitudes toward military service have changed.

At the end of the Vietnam War, the draft ended and an all-volunteer army was formed. Recruiting was a challenge given the unpopularity of Vietnam, but the slots were filled because of the large Baby Boomer enlistment-age population. In an attempt to communicate a feeling of a new, more permissive, congenial military the Boomers could relate to, the army introduced the slogan "Join the people who've joined the army" in 1973.

When the Xers came along, the army was smart enough to understand that they had to recruit this independent, disillusioned generation differently. Xers who felt adrift and hadn't received much structure from their fractured families were drawn to campaigns that focused on helping them find direction and develop self-discipline. So in 1981, the slogan "Be all that you can be" was born.

It focused on helping individuals make something of themselves and it served the army successfully for twenty years, even being named by *Advertising Age* as the second best slogan of the twentieth century (McDonald's "You deserve a break today" was number one).

As the Millennials arrived on the front lines, the army found itself face-to-face with a whole new generation that had never even known a cold war. With no enemy to fight, patriotism was hardly a lure. And, unlike the Xers, Millennials feel they can "be all they can be" *without* joining the service. After failing to meet recruiting goals three out of five years between 1995 and 2000, it was time for a change. So the army not only had to change the message, but figure out which values would speak to Millennials that would be consistent with the army's values. The latest slogan? "The power of one." Why? Because it is a perfect value proposition for a generation that believes in the power of each individual to make a difference. Traditionalists have scoffed at the new slogan, believing it shifts the focus away from teamwork and loyalty. But that's just the point. The army is trying to go after its target using the right ammunition, and so far it's working. As of this writing, recruiting numbers are up.

But the U.S. Armed Forces didn't stop there. Creating a compelling recruiting value proposition sometimes means taking into consideration that you have more than one generation in your audience. In the case of recruiting Millennials, a successful value proposition must often speak to their parents as well. Boomer parents take an active role in helping their kids decide what they are going to do. Unfortunately for the U.S. Armed Services, because of conflicted feelings about the war in Vietnam, many Boomers grew up with a strong antimilitary sentiment. Convincing Millennials to join up is going to mean convincing their parents that a military career is a respectable choice for their child's future. The U.S. Armed Forces recently launched full-page, full-color ads in major magazines like *People* aimed at selling parents of Millennials on the benefits of having their child in the military. One beautifully designed ad shows a well-dressed African American Boomer couple beaming at their daughter, who proudly wears the Coast Guard uniform. The caption reads: "She's not just my daughter. She's my hero."

We learn from the ad that "Tammy" can benefit from 150 career paths, eight different ways to earn college credits, and "the rare opportunity to make the world a better place." Not to mention the "classic lessons in confidence, courage, self-discipline, and character." The ad effectively speaks to the key Boomer values—careers, education, changing the world, and becoming a better person. What more could a Boomer parent ask for from a value proposition?

Unlike the U.S. Armed Services, too many companies think they are doing a stellar job at creating recruiting materials because they have produced a fancy four-color brochure that lists loads of reasons why someone should come on board. Or maybe they've developed a state-of-the-art Web site that includes a video message from the CEO. The problem is that just because a company has found cool ways to get the message across doesn't mean it's the right message. And in many cases, companies are forgetting to look at these messages from a generational perspective. Too often Traditionalists, Baby Boomers, or Xers write an employee value proposition that speaks to their own generation without taking into account that subsequent generations coming in the door might see that same proposition more like a "Do Not Enter" sign than a welcome mat.

Two Boomer ad agency execs were assigned to spend the day at a local job fair to attract Gen Xers to join their firm. In preparation, they spent hours on designing table tents, posters, and handouts. Before going to the fair, they asked a couple of Xers in the agency to look at what they'd produced. The response? Two thumbs-down.

The Boomers had created classic Boomer messages about the size of the firm, the company's prestige, and the types of accounts it represented. The materials were black and white and heavy on type. The Xers redesigned the materials to focus on the fast-paced learning environment, the mentoring, the chance to make a difference on major client projects, and the innovative ad campaigns they'd designed. "We couldn't believe it," said the Boomer recruiter, shaking her head. "Here we are in the advertising business and we didn't know how to market our own business to Generation X. We were designing everything around what a Boomer would want to see."

To compete for the most desirable employees, organizations have to stop trying to create a one-size-fits-all recruiting message. Instead companies need to first spend time identifying what they have to offer. Then they need to really understand what appeals to the different generations. Finally, they must put the two together to create an enticing value proposition that a potential recruit can't walk away from. The generations' reasons for joining a company vary widely, ranging from an organization's history and tradition to a hip and cool culture, from family values to a liberal sabbatical policy, from the opportunity to innovate to the opportunity for training . . . whatever it may be, if companies have a clear understanding of the target they are going after and what they have in their arsenal, they are much more likely to hit a bull's-eye.

A MULTIGENERATIONAL APPROACH

The immediate reaction we hear when we talk with people about value propositions in recruiting is, "Fine, but what do you do if you are recruiting more than one generation?" That's easy: You have to be willing to highlight more than one value proposition. What might be extremely enticing to one generation might be ho-hum to another.

Usually the next question will be, "But what are we supposed to do if we are creating just one recruiting brochure—you can't expect us to produce four of them!" That, of course, is up to you. We've seen great examples of a single brochure that included something for everyone. And we've also seen examples of companies that used different messages in different print pieces, one packet being used to recruit Millennials coming out of college, another to lure Xers away from the competition, another for Boomer executives considering making a move, and a fourth approach for Traditionalists being lured back into the workforce. There's no right or wrong way to promote your value proposition. What's most important is to be aware of whom you're going after and to make sure you're putting the right messages front and center, whether on paper, on the Web, in advertisements, or in person.

"DON'T SOME VALUE PROPOSITIONS APPEAL TO EVERYONE?"

Absolutely! Certain value propositions have tremendous cross-generational appeal. The trick is knowing how to propose that benefit to each of the generations. Flexible scheduling, for example, might appeal to all four generations but for different reasons.

■   Hank, a Traditionalist, loves the flexible scheduling options at his new company. He'd been hankering to retire for the past few years but wasn't quite ready to go cold turkey. Instead he wanted to find a place where he could phase in his retirement. Now he can have every Friday off to take the courses necessary to pursue certification as a master gardener, a hobby he intends to turn into a business whenever he decides to quit "working" for a living.

■ Boomer Steve has been aching for a little flexibility to take the pressure off other areas of his life. He's entered the stage where his kids are committed to a full slate of activities and need more chauffering, but he's never really felt comfortable leaving work before everyone else does. Steve was overjoyed to find a company whose policies, programs, and managers are in accord on flexible scheduling. Though he still works long hours, he feels it's okay to rearrange his schedule to meet his children's needs without being penalized or winding up stalled on the "Daddy track" at work.

■ Xer Jennifer has always been a self-starter and wants loads of control over her own schedule. She's striving for what the book *Rocking the Ages* refers to as not having just a "killer career," but a "killer life." Jennifer is willing to work hard but wants to decide when, where, and how. Flexible scheduling is one of the most attractive benefits her company was able to offer to engender her loyalty. The recruiter who placed Jennifer understood that finding a company that was willing to let her go would ultimately keep her coming back.

■ Millennial Ashlee is in total agreement with the over three thousand Millennials surveyed by the *San Francisco Chronicle* who ranked flexible work hours, the ability to telecommute, and the option to live in a specific region of the nation as more important than income or signing bonuses. "I was an exchange student in France in both high school and college," she explained, "so I don't want to be tied down to just living in one place forever. The place I ended up working is okay with that, and they even offer transfers to international locations for employees who earn them." Clearly, "flexibility" is taking on a new meaning for this mobile generation.

It's so important to train managers and recruiters not just on the benefits that are available, but on how those benefits might be perceived by each generation. Only then can they be fully armed and ready to persuade the generations to come on board.

So how exactly do you create a compelling recruiting value proposition for the generations?

JUST WATCH TV . . .

We've all watched the multimillion-dollar commercials that air on Super Bowl Sunday. You know the ones:

Fade up from black. An old hound is lying on the front porch of a run-down shack, watching people stroll by. Eventually he heaves himself up, saunters over to his water bowl, and laps up some water. Then he ambles back and flops down. The voice-over says, "Where do you belong?" Ninety percent of the viewers are left sitting on their couches, scratching their heads and wondering, "What was that about, and who in the heck was it aimed at?"

No, you didn't miss it because you're dense, you missed it because you weren't supposed to get it in the first place. Why? The ad wasn't aimed at you. Commercials like these, aimed at offbeat denizens of the Web world, have specific targets in mind and use specific strategies to speak to the consumers they want to attract. As recruiting gets tougher, companies are finding they need to use approaches that are just as targeted as the ones marketers use.

Basically, there are two key steps. First you need to know your audience, and then you need to understand what their values are. Sound easy? It should be. But nine out of ten times when we do this exercise with clients, they go back and look at their current materials and find a big disconnect.

WHO ARE YOU GOING AFTER?

Seems pretty basic, but the first step in developing value propositions is to figure out which generation(s) you need to recruit. So many companies just assume they are going after anyone and everyone. But if a company is willing to take a little time to ask whom they predominantly need, they might see that it is not all four generations, perhaps it's just one or two.

Michelle Lemmons-Poscente is president of the International Speakers Bureau (ISB), based in Dallas, Texas. Nearly all of her sales associates are Generation Xers. As a result, she can tailor her value proposition directly to their needs. As she puts it, "I feel I have it easier than other employers. I can come up with rewards that work for everybody pretty simply because all of my employees are of the same generation. For example, we lease a convertible BMW, and each month we have a hot contest where the winner gets to drive the BMW for one month. They like that, and everyone gets excited about it." From the workplace environment at ISB to the corporate culture, the rewards system, the company parties, the way commissions are structured, even the music they pipe into the offices, Michelle can create a value proposition that is a match for her ideal employee because she knows exactly whom she needs to attract and motivate.

It's not so easy for everyone else. If you do need more than one generation of workers, you have more work cut out for you when it comes to honing value propositions that will appeal to your target audiences. But at least once you get to know those targets, you'll be able to take solid aim rather than shooting blindly, wasting time, money, and ammunition.

What the generations look for in recruiting communications, whether in print materials, on video, on the Web, or in person, is a deliberate, thoughtful focus on *them*. Prospective employees need to know in no uncertain terms that you think they're the bomb. (Regardless of whether they're old enough to think you mean the A-bomb!) UBS PaineWebber recently produced an ad aimed at recruiting customers age fifty-plus. It shows a smiling Xer on the right side, arm in arm with a beaming Traditionalist. It says, "You're psyched about the future. You're full of new ideas. You're looking to start a business. You're the guy on the left." Surprise! They're talking to the older fellow! That could be as great a recruiting ad as it is a marketing campaign.

What are your ads, Web sites, and brochures saying to the generations? Hopefully it's our paraphrasing of the simple recruiting concept immortalized by Sally Field at the Oscars a few years ago: "We like you, we really like you!" But more than that, they need to say, "We recognize and value your generation, and we're speaking to you!" Once you know whom you are going after, you can then dive into step two.

WHAT IS THE RIGHT VALUE PROPOSITION?

Advertisers have only fifteen to sixty seconds to convince a consumer watching a commercial to take action, so you'd better believe a lot of time goes into figuring out what the most important messages are. Like advertisers, companies need to be sure they know which messages will get not only the right recruits' attention, but their application.

A classic example is the Peace Corps. Considering there is a good chance that new recruits will end up sleeping in a hut with mud floors and no running water for a significant portion of their tenure, the value proposition the Peace Corps offers had better be an attractive one. Over time, as their target recruit has changed, their value proposition has, too.

In the sixties and seventies, the Peace Corps attracted millions of Boomers by aiming their value proposition at high-minded, adventurous idealists who wanted to "change the world." And for a generation that believed they could, messages about going off to save the planet had an impact. But by the 1990s, skeptical Xers had seen the failure of everything from the war on drugs to the war on poverty, and were a lot more skeptical about any huge bureaucratic organization being able to save the world. But that doesn't mean Xers don't believe in pitching in. Their approach is to try to make a difference one person at a time. Thus, the Peace Corps's new value proposition offers skeptical Xers the more realistic opportunity to make a difference in the life of an individual and not necessarily an entire country. Here's the wording from one of their newest recruiting ads:

> *Assignment:*
> *You will travel 9,800 miles and exchange your experience for*
> *experiences.*
> *You will work with students.*
> *You will work with small-business owners.*
> *You will help a former factory worker refine and repackage his*
> *skills. And he will begin a new career in the local office of a*
> *multinational company. And though your résumé might never*
> *truly reflect what you've accomplished, the résumé of a former*
> *factory worker will.*
> *How far are you willing to go to make a difference?*

Organizations like the Peace Corps have done a brilliant job over the years of tapping into the values of the generations they are trying to recruit so they can make a proposition that makes sense *to them*. DeDe Dunevant, acting marketing director of the Peace Corps, commented, "We created this ad with a generational concept in mind. As a result, our recruitment offices have told us that applicants have walked in and mentioned that the ad meant something to them and they wanted to hear more about how they could make a difference."

How far are you willing to go to create a value proposition that will make a difference?

For some companies, the answer is *too far.* They forget that the value proposition can't just be attractive, it has to actually be authentic. It's a colossal waste to advertise your organization as fast paced and innovative when the last new idea you implemented was changing your letterhead in 1983!

But imagine yourself as a highly motivated forty-something Boomer in the midst of a career transition, with two kids, a working spouse, a mortgage, and aging parents who need your attention. Then imagine you read the American Express Company's recruiting Web site and you see this message:

> *A Career Called Life: Where is the line between work and life? At American Express, we realize that you have responsibilities outside of work. Often these are your most important deadlines. They speak not only to who you are, but to who you will become. Many of our best people successfully balance their lives at work and beyond the job.*

There's no way we would have heard any American corporation use this language ten years ago. Who was going to tell the Boomers they wouldn't have to bust their behinds to get ahead? Yet if you want to speak to the best of the Boomers, you might have to admit that Boomers are looking to get ahead *and* get a more balanced life. And when American Express uses this value proposition, they aren't just making it up. We've talked with a number of their employees, and the company really does put its values where its mouth is.

In most cases, coming up with a decent value proposition just means looking outside your own generation's values. When a recruiter or an executive takes the time to ask the other generations what keeps them on the job, they are pleasantly surprised by what they find out. Organizations tend to have many attractive value propositions to put on the table; they just don't always realize it.

At a recent seminar for a research company, the Traditionalist CEO asked us how his firm could do a better job attracting Baby Boomers. When we split the workforce into groups by generation, we asked each group to brainstorm and list all the best things about their place of business. The Boomers shared that although they worked hard, they felt they had an extremely desirable work schedule. Because most of the clients they serve are banks, when the bank closes, they get to go home as well. That meant dinners with the family on bankers' hours. Also on their list was the fact that they don't usually take work home with them and rarely work weekends. The interesting part was that when the Traditionalist CEO read his own list of what he thought was best about the firm, it was completely different from the Boomers' list. Items on his list included the stability of the company, not having to worry about job security, the large-scale projects to manage, a strong reputation in the industry . . . all very important, but all very different from the items that were top of mind for the Boomers. So what's the point? This Traditionalist can't expect to recruit a Baby Boomer who is going to be a great fit for his firm if he doesn't know which values might get a Boomer excited about working at his company. He definitely had a great value proposition to offer the Boomers; should we be surprised that when we read over his recruiting materials, we couldn't find it?

As companies take the time to understand the recruiting messages that are likely to appeal to different generations of employees, one of two things happens—either they uncover hidden treasures or they have to go digging to find them.

As in the case of the Traditionalist CEO's research company, sometimes it's a matter not of reinventing the company, but of repackaging what you already have. One of our favorite clients, a midsize manufacturing firm, came to us in a funk. The company was ninety years old and very traditional. Their business was making boxes, hardly the sexy, sizzling value proposition you'd expect to dazzle the younger generations. Yet they wanted to create a Web site that would speak to Generation X and give them a compelling reason to investigate the company further. In brainstorming with this company, we discovered all sorts of buried treasure. The company was heavily committed to recycling and owned a state-of-the-art recycling plant, their designers were equipped with some of the hottest tools around, and they had an A-list clientele that was giving them carte blanche to develop dynamic packaging solutions to sell products in all sorts of new ways. The box company had never realized what an incredible value proposition for Generation Xers was lurking right there under their noses.

However, other companies may discover that it takes more than just repackaging to bring in a new generation of workers with different values. Sometimes strategic changes need to be made. Until recently, for example, NASA was experiencing unacceptably high turnover among talented Generation X and Cusper engineers. It seems they were using NASA as a launching pad, then leaving the agency's orbit to pursue high-flying careers in private industry. NASA understood that these people had joined the space race because they liked to design, invent, and test things that would eventually fly. But because of budget constraints, NASA had been forced to do the designing, then farm out the building and testing of their space age inventions to private aerospace companies. The solution? They brought over an important piece of the huge International Space Station project, the escape module, and kept it in-house for their young engineers to invent, design, test, and fly under their own direction. When we visited the agency and spoke with these engineers about their project, the excitement and commitment were palpable. Listening wisely to the values of those they wanted to attract and then changing the way work gets done allowed NASA to attract and retain the future superstars of that organization.

NOT JUST WHAT, BUT WHY

While we applaud everyone who has taken the time to learn what all the generations value on the job, here's a note of caution. It's not enough to make a laundry list, although that's a good first step. Once you find out what the values are, you need to go the extra step and find out why they are so important to your generations of employees.

Let's take a commercial break. Think about the last commercial you saw for toothpaste. We bet it didn't focus just on fluoride. No, any advertiser with sense would also boast that the fluoride will help fight cavities. In other words, it's not enough to talk just about features; you have to talk about benefits.

How does that work when it comes to recruiting? Imagine telling a Generation Xer about your organization's *features.* "We have one hundred offices in forty countries around the world." You might be indecently proud of that factoid. Maybe you even helped open a few of those offices yourself. But the Xer is thinking, *Man, this is probably the biggest, most bureaucratic place outside the IRS!*

What if, instead, you understood the values that motivated that Gen Xer and you also talked about the *benefits?* "One reason we're so excited about our presence in forty countries is that it enables us to provide our employees with an opportunity to live and work abroad if that's what interests them. And of course, our technology is incredible. All the countries are linked by an amazing intranet, so the networking and learning opportunities are stellar. Plus, it's really expanded the size of projects we can take on. So even while you're in a U.S. office, if you're interested in Latin American business issues, you could be working on one of their projects." Thus, one company has taken a feature and, by understanding how it might affect the target audience, has turned it into a benefit for Generation X.

Never assume that your benefits will speak for themselves. It's up to your recruiters, managers, and employees to speak for them.

TWENTY-FOUR-HOUR-A-DAY PROGRAMMING

Fortis Financial produced a series of print ads to assure their insurance customers that they will be there when disaster strikes. One photo shows a whole bunch of school kids pitching in to push their stalled school bus toward a gas station. The text reads: "A community that isn't afraid to get out and push teaches us something about effort and commitment."

When David saw the ad, he was enchanted. What a compelling recruiting message! It took him a moment to realize that Fortis was advertising its services to potential clients, not its values to potential employees. In his mind, David linked "Fortis" with "teamwork," a message that really drew him in. After we got to know the people at Fortis, we realized they really do thrive on teamwork. The consumer ad with the bus could easily be converted to a recruiting ad.

What companies don't realize is that all the marketing they aim at customers also influences the way people think about them as a workplace. Is there anyone alive who doesn't believe that Apple is a place where you'd be encouraged to "Think Different"? We wonder if Huggies has even thought about using their great slogan in recruiting ads. "We're behind you all the way" sure applies to more than diapers!

Whether or not you like it, you are already communicating your value proposition to generations of potential employees. From word of mouth from current or past employees, to your billboards, to your Web site, to the ads you write, to your company logo, to the publicity you receive—you name it—you are communicating with prospective employees every day.

A Millennial college student responded to an ad she saw in the campus newspaper about summer internships for a health care provider. The industry was smart in trying to expose this generation to the health care industry at an early age, and the ad was perfect: "We need your energy, ideas, and desire to help those in need. Flexible schedules are available. . . . After all, even a little help can go a long way." The value proposition was a perfect match, and the Millennial immediately picked up the phone and dialed the 800 number. After three rings, a recording answered: "Hello and thank you for calling. If you're calling to schedule an appointment, press one. For billing information, press two. For public affairs, press three. For directions to one of our facilities, press four."

Unless they were going to say, "To tell us how annoying our phone system is, press five," she wasn't going to wait any longer. So she immediately punched in "0," praying she could bypass the roll call and get an actual operator. Nope. Instead she got, "I'm sorry, the number you dialed is not an option. . . . Hello and thank you for calling. If you're calling to schedule an appointment, press one. For billing information, press two . . ."

Not only did she hang up, she never applied.

12

READY, AIM, HIRE!

"Thank you so much for coming in," the Xer recruiter commented as he wrapped up the interview with a high-potential Boomer he really wanted to hire, "we'll be in touch soon."

"Uh . . . that would be fine," the Boomer lied.

As they shook hands and she quickly gathered her briefcase, the Xer could tell that unless he coughed up more stock options than their CEO had, there was no way he'd ever be printing business cards with her name on them.

After seeing her to the door, he poked his head into the office of a fellow recruiter who happened to be a Boomer.

"Wow, did I blow that. No matter what I talked about, I couldn't get her past polite. I mean, I told her we'd give her free Internet access, a pager, unlimited cell phone privileges to stay in touch twenty-four/seven . . . I even threw in a laptop so

PUTTING VALUE PROPOSITIONS TO WORK

she could work from home—which you know we don't usually do until the second year. She couldn't have cared less. But she's so perfect for this, we can't lose her. Would you please call her and see what it would take?"

Two weeks later, the Xer noticed his dream Boomer candidate seated in the front row at orientation. With his jaw at his knees, he ran to the Boomer recruiter's office.

"How did you do it? You're amazing!"

"All I did," she replied simply, "was tell her what it's like to work here."

"Gee," replied the Xer, "I thought I did that."

Where did the Xer go wrong? When recruiting attempts fail, the cause is almost always that the employee value proposition was a bad match or that it wasn't communicated successfully to the candidate in question.

The Boomer, a busy working mom with a house full of active offspring, had no interest in hearing from the Xer recruiter that she would have a bag full of gadgets that would add more noise and confusion to her household and enable her to work even harder during what was supposed to be family time. But when the Boomer recruiter shared with her what a family-friendly company it was and how she had seldom missed her kids' games or recitals, her attitude changed.

The Xer either didn't ask or didn't listen to uncover the value proposition that would make sense to the candidate sitting across the desk from him. The moral is, it doesn't matter how much time you spend developing a stellar employee value proposition or how much money you spend financing it. If you don't have the right people and processes in place to communicate that value proposition, you'll never reap the dividends of your investment. Employee value propositions are amazingly powerful weapons, but only in the right hands, applied correctly. In the BridgeWorks Generations Survey, employees who were asked about the effectiveness of their company's recruiting messages saw definite room for improvement. To the question "When I think about the messages my company communicates in recruiting (in brochures, Web site, etc.), I think . . . ," a pitiful 30 percent of total respondents answered, "My generation could get excited about working here."

Surprisingly, when you look at the responses of just the Traditionalists, only 17 percent felt their generation could get excited about the messages. We have often assumed that companies whose messages are being written by Boomers and Traditionalists would favor those generations, but it appears that any generation can be excluded or ignored when it comes to value propositions. Here are a few rules of the road to help you put your value proposition to work with as much success and as few casualties as possible.

I MIGHT WANT TO WORK FOR YOUR COMPANY, BUT I SURE DON'T WANT TO WORK FOR YOU!

Today's recruiting experiences are a far cry from the flattop-sporting, suit-and-narrow-tie-clad lineup outside the college recruiting offices that many Traditionalists experienced in the 1950s. Today it's more varied, more creative, and more tailored to the style of the individual company and the needs of the recruits. However, the hitch isn't whether to serve salsa or sushi at your company's next recruiting open house. It's who's going to serve it. Your company may have written the best interview questions in the world, but if the wrong people are asking them, it won't make a difference. More and more, achieving the right match between recruiter and recruitee is a delicate balance.

Have you analyzed whether you're matching the right recruiters to the generations you hope to attract into your flock? In many cases, matching the generations can be very effective. You have to admit that if a Millennial has concerns about being the youngest employee around, it helps if he gets a glimpse of someone his own age during the interview.

When a Southern California office of Arthur Andersen wanted a great college recruiter, they hired—guess who? A great college recruiter. Millennial Rachel Callaghan had just graduated from USC, where she had been recruiting high school students who were considering different colleges. She joined Andersen's human resources department at the age of nineteen to help them target and win the best college candidates. After all, who would know what persuades a high-potential college graduate better than one of his or her own? And putting her own spin on the recruiting process is exactly what she did. Bye-bye, informal chats in the student union over Hi-C served in Dixie cups. Why not talk about working for Andersen at a bowling party? It was a match made in heaven.

But while Rachel probably could connect with college recruits of her own generation better than some of the Traditionalist partners, that's not true across the board. Companies should be careful of making the "age mistake" by assuming that to recruit younger generations, they should always use younger recruiters. Big Bird might be turning thirty this year, but he'd still make an awesome recruiter for Millennials. After all, who knows them better than he does? Ultimately, it doesn't matter what generation a recruiter comes from. What matters is that organizations choose recruiters who have the ability to establish a rapport with whomever they are trying to recruit, regardless of generation. It comes back to knowing each generation and understanding the value propositions that are likely to turn them on. Some people have the knack for reaching across the generational divide and making an immediate connection. The trick is to make sure those are the people doing your recruiting, not someone stuck in a generational time warp.

A Traditionalist human resources manager for one of the largest counties in California found himself walking back to the parking lot after work next to a young woman he had noticed earlier in the day. She was twentyish and sported several body piercings, but she seemed smart and self-confident. Besides, the manager had known enough Millennials to understand that an external fashion statement did not determine the internal qualities of the person. The two struck up a conversation, and he learned she was working as a temp just across the street at the State of California. He said, "If you ever want a long-term assignment, think about coming and seeing us at the County. We use temps all the time, and we could keep you as busy as you want to be."

She responded, "I would never work for the City or the County on a long-term basis. To do the simplest thing in my job I have to go from A to B to C to D and then back to A again to get permission. I can't stand that."

The Traditionalist couldn't disagree with what she said. It was only after she walked away and he had stewed about it all afternoon that it hit him: *Hey, wait a minute. We might be slow-moving and bureaucratic, but what about our management trainee program and our awesome new technology, not to mention the amazing benefits we offer, besides casual dress and a nine-to-five workday!*

He'd never inventoried what they had to offer an ambitious Millennial who was looking to make a difference. Next time, he vowed, he wouldn't make the same mistake. Nor would anyone else in his department.

"I THOUGHT *I* WAS SUPPOSED TO BE INTERVIEWING *YOU!*"

For Traditionalists and Baby Boomers, it used to be that the interview was all about being buttoned down and buttoned up. These generations wouldn't have dreamed of wearing anything more casual than a dress suit for an interview, and they wouldn't have been caught dead asking about money or vacation leave in the first interview. Those questions might have implied that your values weren't in the right place or you weren't prepared to work hard.

Well, times have changed, and now it's not uncommon for recruiters to find themselves in the hot seat, with candidates firing off questions as fast as the recruiter can answer. Interviewers report being stunned by having the tables turned on them, especially by skeptical Xers and self-confident Millennials who aren't shy about demanding to know who, what, when, where, how, and why before they've even proven they're qualified. "Suddenly *I'm* the one being cross-examined," exclaimed Beth Leonard, a Baby Boomer and head of college recruiting for the accounting firm of Lurie, Besikof, Lapidus, "and that takes some getting used to!"

But because the last decade has created a sellers' job market, it's no longer just Xers and Millennials who are willing to turn the tables during an interview. All the generations of job candidates have become more willing to ask the tough questions. While an economic slowdown might mean the generations will have to be less choosy, they are becoming more and more assertive about learning everything they can before making a decision. Queries like "What would my title be?" are being replaced by "Give me three good reasons I should join your sales team and not that of your biggest competitor!" Job applicants are increasingly basing their decisions on whether they *hear* the right answers, not on whether they *give* them.

ARM YOUR RECRUITERS

Interviewers who are prepared to *be* interviewed are faring better than those who are prepared just to ask the questions. The problem is that few companies are making sure their managers and recruiters are prepared. It amazes us that companies will train an entire sales force for weeks on how to sell their $29.99 product but have no problem sending an untrained manager out there to put a $50,000 offer on the table.

No good soldier should march into the war for talent unarmed, but too often hiring is conducted by people with obsolete weapons, rusty skills, and outdated battle plans. The reality is that most businesses don't rely on professional recruiters who are boning up on hiring and compensation strategies on a daily basis. In fact, when asked what measures their companies had taken over the past eighteen months to recruit new employees, very few of our BridgeWorks Survey respondents indicated they had hired new recruiters. Instead, most companies rely on managers, team leaders, and supervisors to do the interviewing, and many of them haven't studied the employee benefits manual since the days when you could still smoke at your desk.

Ask the average employee to outline his or her own basic benefits package and you'd think you'd asked them to explain the electoral college. If employees can't explain their *own* benefits, how can we expect them to zero in on the ideal items to highlight to craft the best value proposition for someone from another generation?

From the 401(k) to whether or not wearing jeans is okay, recruiters need to be coached on *all* you have to offer potential candidates. In addition, as companies figure out the value propositions of the generations, recruiters need to be in the loop on who might be motivated by what. A Generation Xer recruiter might never have heard of bereavement leave or give an R.I.P., but a Traditionalist candidate might be deeply impressed by such a benefit, and be grateful to know about it. Most Boomers and Traditionalists may be past the on-site child care phase of life, but such a benefit might mean a lot to an Xer whose parents consigned him or her to a day care facility miles away from where they worked. The recruiters obviously won't know what's most important until they initiate a dialogue with the candidate, but they can't have that dialogue in the first place unless they know what they are talking about and are prepared to do a lot of *answering* along with the *asking*.

IS ANYBODY LISTENING?

A Baby Boomer supervisor recently complained that he lost a stellar Traditionalist candidate who signed on with a company located nearer his home. Apparently he was tired of having a long commute. The supervisor's comment to us was, "Heck, I could have put him in a different location. I just didn't know that was so important."

What went wrong? It seems the Boomer did most of the talking and the Traditionalist did the walking.

When we ask job seekers about the things that derail job interviews, the most common complaint we hear is that the recruiter or manager did all the talking. This is particularly common when the interviewer is older and the recruit is younger. Bosses tend to see the interview as the perfect opportunity to reminisce about how they joined the company in 1902, when there were just three employees and they calculated their monthly earnings with an abacus! But people of any generation can be poor listeners. One Boomer told us he never went back to a company for a second interview because he didn't feel the Generation X supervisor he met with could relate to what he had to say.

The best recruiters are long on listening and short on lecturing. They understand value propositions, and they do their best to put the most relevant messages out there so the recruit can visualize the organization as a perfect fit. Their motto is like the *USA Today* slogan: "Not the most words, just the right words."

But the other part of working with value propositions is inviting candidates to reveal what's most important to them. After all, there's probably a good reason we have two ears and only one mouth.

A Boomer IT manager was sitting in an interview with a Generation Xer. She saw on the Xer's résumé that he had taken time out from college to help set up remote offices around the country for a nonprofit agency. When she asked him to talk about the experience, he seemed excited, focused, and confident. "You know," she said, "we have a department that sets up computer networks in offices all over our system. It involves a lot of problem solving. You might want to look into it."

Even though the Xer had been convinced he wanted to work for a smaller organization, he suddenly found himself getting excited about the potential for entrepreneurship with a larger company. A few weeks later he was hired.

FOCUS ON THE FUTURE

Asking the right questions doesn't just help the recruiter, it makes the process much more enticing for the interviewee. Good interviewers tune in to how to frame questions for each generation of job candidates to get them turned on. For example, an entrepreneurial Generation Xer who doesn't believe in dues paying and who expects to hit the ground running would be thrilled to be asked, "What kind of projects and clients would you be most excited to work on, and why?" The same Xer might be less enthralled to be asked a question better suited to a loyal Traditionalist, like "What kind of a contribution could you make to building this organization for the future?"

One of the best-kept secrets in putting value propositions to work in interviews is to stop spotlighting the applicants' past and focus on their future. Sure, it's important to know where they've worked before, why they left, and why they've shown up at your door. But that's what's important to *you*. Getting applicants to look to the future is a great way to focus on *them* and get them to start envisioning a future together.

Ask applicants where they want to go, why they're interested in your company, what their hopes and dreams might be, what they think they could do for you, and what's their idea of a perfect job. What motivates them? How do they work best? What sorts of projects do they love the most? What types of clients/co-workers/bosses are the best matches for them? This type of questioning makes the job seem more tangible and uncovers what makes a candidate tick. With four generations bringing different experiences and expectations to the interview, smart companies are rewriting their interview questions to pull out the different values that are important to each generation.

For Traditionalists . . . questions about the future will carry extra weight because Traditionalists often feel they are seen as out-of-date and dispensable. Discussing the future communicates that you expect them to be around for a while and you have faith in their ability to be productive *at any age.* The biggest challenge might be making sure they feel comfortable talking. Traditionalists tend to be very patient with an interviewing style where the recruiter carries most of the conversation. They respect authority and expect the person in charge to lead the conversation. They are unlikely to jump in without being encouraged until they feel truly at ease. Traditionalists also value history, and they expect to take the time to get to know about a company's past before learning about its future. Traditionalists might hold back more in a first interview than the other generations because they tend to view job transitions as a long process that builds over time. Recruiters who want to draw out Traditionalists should make sure their questions are open-ended and not dead-ended and allow enough time to build a solid comfort level that helps a Traditionalist feel respected.

Baby Boomers . . . it's important to recognize that they currently have the most personal, professional, and financial responsibilities weighing on them that they will ever have. At the same time, they've retained their competitiveness and they need to feel they'll continue to move up. These reasons make future-focused discussions appealing and appeasing to the Baby Boomer. The Boomer objective in interviews has always been to appear polished and professional and impress the interviewer with a sincere desire to get the job. Because Boomers were often up against dozens or even hundreds of other able applicants, looking for the *perfect* opportunity wasn't usually in the cards. Boomers tried to keep the discussion on a fairly general level while they scoped out what the job actually entailed, before they committed to describing their credentials. This enabled them to shape their job experiences to whatever the employer was looking for. Once in the door, Boomers could always learn the necessary skills or try to reshape the position into something more to their liking. The goal was to get hired first and worry about particulars later. Rocking the boat wasn't the best way to stay afloat in the interview process, so Boomers worked to avoid the really tough questions until they'd tested the waters. Even today, Boomers tend to hold off and scope out the political territory before they reveal too much about themselves. Where Xers are perfectly willing to be honest about crooked career paths, Boomers agonize over how to explain even slight gaps in their résumés. If a Traditionalist asked, "Where exactly *were* you employed during the Summer of Love?" it was pretty tough to explain that you'd dropped out to work for minimum wage in a bong shop. Recruiters need to ease into the interview process and encourage Boomers to drop the habitually cautious facade so you can really get to know their present-day goals and values.

Generation Xers . . . are going to want to talk about the future, because they are always worrying about it. It's not unusual for Xers to tell us they're concerned about where they're going in a company when they've been there only a few weeks! Beth Leonard, of the accounting firm Lurie, Besikof, Lapidus, found that Generation X recruits wanted to know about exactly what they'd be doing if they came to work at her firm, rather than accepting the fact that in large accounting firms the senior partners typically decide on assignments. In particular, they were consumed with knowing if they'd be on the right career path right away. Instead of asking them exclusively about their education and experience, Beth started asking more questions about what they wanted to work on, what types of clients excited them, and how they wanted to see their careers develop over time. The whole dialogue changed. When focused on the future, Xers became engaged and began connecting with the firm in a much more tangible way than if they'd talked in generalities about why they majored in accounting.

Generation Xers always have built careers with an eye on establishing enough experiences to make them supremely employable no matter what cataclysmic event occurs next. Recruiters should be prepared to see a few extra bullets on the résumé. Xers see their varied career experiences as giving them both freedom and power, and they aren't afraid to admit to having made a few job changes along the way. But because they know their career paths are sometimes seen as nontraditional, they can be intimidated by Boomers and Traditionalists who appear to judge them. Recruiters need to ask Xers about where they've been in an open way that encourages them to express themselves. If an Xer says, "Yeah, I only stayed at that job three months because of bad management," a judgmental response like "Didn't you feel any *loyalty* to the company?" is bound to bring the conversation to a standstill. Instead, stick with open-ended questions that allow Xers to express their independent point of view. For example, "Why didn't that management style work for you?" will keep the conversation on track and will reveal plenty about the candidate's values.

With Millennials . . . focusing on the future is a sure thing, considering they haven't had time to develop much of a past. Part of the job is getting Millennials to visualize a future with an organization whose day-to-day business probably seems less tangible than Willy Wonka's Chocolate Factory. Questions that help Millennials understand specifically what they will be doing in a company go a long way toward helping them make a commitment. Use detail in questioning; for example: "At our design firm, you'd have your own cubicle in a bullpen with other Millennials, all of whom would be developing and sharing design ideas on a big project over a period of several months. How would you handle that style of working?" By crafting a picture of a situation they've never experienced before, you can help Millennials focus on a future that's tangible.

Of all the generations, the Millennials might be the most fun to interview because of their optimism and can-do attitude. But their confident ways can also come off as cocky, so be prepared to muffle your annoyance when a seventeen-year-old appears to have his entire career planned even though he could barely figure out the directions to the interview. Millennials in conversation tend to achieve a jumbled mix of big dreams and practical realities. Boomers and Xers find themselves wondering if they were *ever* that self-assured. Don't be surprised if asking a Millennial about her future means learning that she intends to take over your company one day and that she calculates she can do it by age thirty!

To Traditionalists, Millennials' attitudes can seem egotistical and even a tad disrespectful. To get over this, you might try finding out what experiences Millennials have had that convince them they really can realize their goals. To Boomers, even though they've raised many of them, confident Millennials can be challenging. Boomers had the wide-eyed optimism to believe they could change the world, and they accomplished some amazing things. The trouble is that the Millennials don't seem to know or care much about those. Perpetually youthful Boomers need to be prepared to feel like fossils interviewing Millennials and to resist the temptation to lecture or reminisce. To hardened Xers, who tend to look at the business world as a tough nut to crack before it cracks you, the buoyancy of the Millennials can seem downright annoying. Xer interviewers wonder sometimes if Millennials are operating in the real world, and if they are, how come Xers never got a taste of it? Because the task of managing Millennials is going to fall most heavily on Generation X, asking good questions is one of the best ways to get to know their values as a precursor to managing them.

GO WHERE THEY GO

A fisherman stood for hours by the side of the river without ever getting a nibble. Finally his neighbor wandered over to commiserate.

"They sure aren't biting here," he observed.

"I know," said the fisherman, "all the fish are over there under the bridge in the shade."

"Then what in the heck are you fishing here for?" queried the incredulous neighbor.

"Because I like it so much better in the sun!"

When it comes to recruiting, the ones who only stand in the sun will get burned. Too many companies never realize that to get the recruits you want, you have to go where they go. Often organizations will recruit and recruit without ever stopping to think about whether or not they are really fishing in the spots where the candidates are likely to bite. Even the most ideal fishing hole dries up eventually. That's the time to stop going after four generations of candidates in the same old ways.

You may not have realized it at the time, but Bill Clinton's appearance playing the saxophone on *The Arsenio Hall Show* during the 1992 presidential campaign was an earth-shattering event. He was the first presidential candidate to stray from *Meet the Press* so he could get out there and meet the rest. Bill Clinton found a forum where Generation Xers were likely to listen. And listen they did. Because Clinton went where the Xers went and spoke directly to them, Generation X has been credited with pushing Clinton over the top and into the White House.

When it comes to recruiting, failing to pinpoint where the generations can be found is like producing the world's greatest TV commercial but playing it at the wrong times and on the wrong channels.

An obvious new channel has been the World Wide Web. Companies have made huge strides in posting jobs on employment Web sites as well as building their destinations on the information superhighway. But don't think for a minute that just being there is enough. As younger generations of job candidates cruise by, they are deciding whether or not to enter based on what your home page looks like. In fact, a recent poll by MonsterTRAK.com, a job search Web site for college students and young people, found that 79 percent of college students said that the quality of an employer's Web site is important in deciding whether or not to apply for a job. "If you build it, [they] will come" might work in movies like *Field of Dreams*, but it doesn't hold up when it comes to Web sites. Going where the generations go on the Web means creating recruiting sites that your target generations of employees will love using. And it mean listing them in all the places those generations are likely to look.

- ■ Does your Web site talk about innovation, not just tradition?
- ■ Do you have an area that talks about careers in your industry in general, as a way of letting younger prospective employees consider you?

- Do you show images of more than one generation on the site?
- Do you talk about what it's like to work there, including career paths, training, rewards, and balance?
- Can applicants apply for jobs or get more information via the Web?

The World Wide Web is one area in which you do have a lot more flexibility with value propositions. Aside from being able to delete concepts when you need to with the push of a button, the beauty of the Web is that unlike a printed brochure, recruits visiting a Web page can actually specify the information they want to receive rather than having all of it thrust upon them. The problem is that many companies use the Web like printed brochures. They start out with a section titled "Employment" that presents a long page of text expected to appeal to everyone from a Millennial to a Traditionalist. First of all, no one likes to read a lot of text in brochures, let alone on the Web. Second, the reason people like Web sites is that they can interact with a site to grab the information they want. Unfortunately, too many companies think they are using the Internet to the fullest just because they can actually accept a résumé on-line. While this can help make the process faster and more efficient, it's still not enough. Recruiting Web sites need to offer choices, opportunities for visitors to the site to select the information they are most interested in, and opportunities to interact. Those three features make the World Wide Web the best tool to get a company's value proposition heard by the right generation and disseminated in a consistent manner. Therefore, why not have a Web page that features *all* the different value propositions you have to offer, then allow recruits to click on those they want to learn about? That way, the recruiting messages can truly be about what is most important to the candidate, not the company.

Some companies are pushing the "go where they go" philosophy past their own Web sites and into cyberspace. One national clothing store chain took the attitude "Why bother inviting people to your house when you can crash someone else's party?" Their challenge was how to make themselves the employer of choice for hip high schoolers. So they asked some of their most satisfied teen employees to visit on-line chat rooms to talk to peers about the company and what a cool place it is to work. If a fellow chatter seemed interested, the employee referred him or her to the company's Web site. It worked like a charm. As every parent knows, a teenager will listen to what a peer has to say about a job long before he or she will listen to an adult. As a result, this outfit's applications soared as soon as the chats began.

Sometimes we get so caught up trying to play catch-up with the cyberworld, we forget there's a real face-to-face world out there. Going where job candidates go sometimes means forgetting the fancy stuff and just showing up. One employer we spoke with wanted to recruit Traditionalists with great people skills to work as part-time customer service representatives. He found them by going to churches, community centers, and senior organizations, posting signs, and then following up with a personal pitch. He got the employees he wanted without ever placing a single newspaper ad or posting anything on-line. What he did was think about where outgoing, active Traditionalists might go and then showed up to find them.

Other times, "go where they go" requires hitting the road. *Newsweek* reported on a Web design firm, Interactive Communications & Entertainment (ICE if you're an insider), that was frozen out of a huge convention of the digital in-crowd when all the exhibitor spaces were sold out. Still hoping to gain access to Silicon Valley's tight supply of talent, they hired a Mister Softee ice-cream truck, plastered it with their logos, and parked themselves in front of the building. Handing out free cones and coffee to those entering and leaving the meeting generated enormous goodwill and created buzz inside the hall. Ultimately the truck drove a 30 percent increase in hot prospects to ICE's cool job page.

From a specific magazine to a community center's bulletin board, from job fairs in shopping malls to a booth at the state fair, companies need to wake up to the notion that if you want the generations to pay attention, your best bet is to go where they are likely to be.

WATCH YOUR RATINGS

Why would companies spend so much time developing value propositions and strategies to recruit the generations but spend so little time tracking the results? Producers don't pull TV shows off the air or change their time slots just because they feel like it; they look at the ratings and then react.

Sometimes the best approach to improve your recruiting hit rate with the generations is to take your own pulse. Invent your own form of the Nielsen rating system. Ask yourself, Which generations reject your offers most frequently, and why? Is your hiring percentage where you want it to be for each generation? When candidates turn down a job offer, how good are you at ferreting out the real reason why?

Often, generational influences show up in turndowns that can't be explained until you really dig in. Learning from a Traditionalist that a particular Generation X recruiter created an unprofessional image by using sloppy grammar allows a company to avoid turning off Traditionalist candidates in the future. Or finding out that Millennials hate your Web site might be just the ammo you need to convince the powers-that-be it's time to invest in an upgrade. At the very least, interviewing successful new hires will give you an idea as to where you stand in the ratings. Do you ask new hires what you could have done differently or better during the interview process? Do you find out what it was that made them say yes? Odds are, yours wasn't the *only* job interview they went on, and they most likely can offer a competitive perspective and insight you don't have.

A few months after his initial eye-opening conversation, a pumped-up Gen X recruiter burst into the office of his Baby Boomer colleague. "I just closed another one!" he crowed. "I am so pumped."

"Who'd you hire this time?" she asked, grinning at his enthusiasm.

"A Boomer rep for our new sales district. She's a stellar performer, and she's totally excited about the job. You know," he continued, "ever since you talked me into having that focus group of Boomer women employees and asking them what it's like for them to work here, it's like a light bulb went on. I finally understand what's important to them. Now when I interview Boomers it's completely different. And they are totally shocked that a Gen X guy understands them so well."

"That's just awesome," she said, laughing. "Too bad you didn't know all this stuff when you were dating!"

13

DIAMONDS IN THE ROUGH

Not long ago, we decided BridgeWorks needed a new bookkeeper. Because our business was growing rapidly and the accounting questions were becoming more complex, we wanted a high-energy person with fanatical attention to detail, the ability to relate to both an Xer and a Boomer, and an ambitious commitment to helping our company grow. We bet you're picturing a hard-hitting young go-getter with energy to burn. We doubt you're picturing Alice, the demure gray-haired woman in her seventies whom we actually hired.

While we didn't set out to recruit a card-carrying member of the AARP to handle the books, we ended up with exactly what we were looking for. She just wasn't what we expected.

Now we ask you, if a company that specializes in generational diversity has preconceived notions about hiring, can you imagine what other companies are doing when it comes to recruiting the generations?

The overheated economy and low unemployment rate kicked off a very positive trend for American business. Companies desperate to staff everything from law firms to pet stores have been forced to look in new places for the best employees. In fact, our survey found that in just the past eighteen months, over 60 percent of respondents' companies had had to look in new places. Even as the economy cools, this strategy will continue to be a sound one, because hiring in new ways shakes up old assumptions and uncovers opportunities. Too often, however, when we set out in good faith to look, we are blinded by generational biases. Face it: we all make the mistake of searching for employees who are like the ones we've always hired. Or we hire people who are generationally "just like us." That kind of boxed-in thinking limits diversity, whether we're talking about race, gender, color, creed, or generation. And it severely limits the size of the labor pool we have to draw from.

It also puts companies behind the eight ball when it comes to beating the competition. When asked how their companies were coping with the tight labor market, over a third of our survey respondents told us that their companies had already started to "go after different types of recruits." Businesses that are slow to start searching out new sources of talent will lag behind in the race to recruit. Mining for new sources means either tapping into new generations that haven't been considered before or scouring the landscape to unearth generational niches where the ideal potential employees might be lurking, just waiting to be discovered. The bulk of the U.S. workforce is currently made up of Generation Xers and Baby Boomers, because they are the prime ages to be in the workplace. Smart organizations can find hidden treasure by uncovering the deep veins of talent running through the Traditionalist and Millennial generations as well.

MINING FOR SILVER: THE TRADITIONALIST WORKFORCE

Meet Sam. He's an excellent manager—smart, dedicated, and passionate about his work. Lately he has felt underappreciated and disengaged and has started thinking about moving on to a more challenging opportunity. While that would be a terrible loss to his company, no one seems to have noticed that he's losing interest. Nor have they made a concerted effort to retain him. Why? Does he have halitosis? Did he offend the boss? Not at all. But you see, Sam is sixty-eight years old.

Companies today are so focused on attracting young people that they are ignoring one of their most valuable resources—Traditionalist employees. Traditionalists have the skills, qualifications, experience, and maturity organizations need to retain, and they're right under our noses. Rather than losing them, companies need to springboard them back into the labor pool long before they all end up poolside in Miami. Unfortunately, in our survey, a surprising 40 percent of Traditionalists disagreed with the statement "My company does a good job making me want to stay."

Traditionalists are feeling overlooked or taken for granted, and we think that's a big mistake on the part of companies. Being proactive about retaining your best people is almost always more cost- and time-effective than having to go out and find someone else.

As employers continue to fight the war for talent, they complain constantly about the quality of applicants. Yet applicants of quality are right under their noses. Traditionalists are ready, willing, and able to work if only we can look past a few gray hairs and see the characteristics that truly made them the greatest generation.

"I think I've acquired some wisdom over the years, but there doesn't seem to be much demand for it."

Loyalty

Traditionalists are the generation that invented the one-page résumé. Job-hopping was almost unheard of, and many stayed with the same company their whole career. Ralph Thorp, a seventy-one-year-old district representative for Lutheran Brotherhood, has been with that company forty-four years. "When I do retire," he commented, "I want to be sure my customers are taken care of. The company relies on me for that." How many would kill to have Ralph's attitude to rub off on their employees?

Experience

Many Traditionalists have formed incredible relationships not only within the companies they work for, but with vendors, suppliers, and customers as well. They've experienced virtually every type of economy, and they've seen all that competitors have to throw at them. With high turnover in so many industries today, experience is in short supply. Tapping into Traditionalists to share the wealth of their knowledge often means ramping up the learning curve for the younger generations.

Consistency

In times of rapid change, these seasoned workers can provide much-needed continuity for a corporate culture. They've lived a company's legacy, and they need to be around to share it so that customers are served, mistakes get made only once, and golden opportunities are not missed. Ralph Thorp is busy training younger salespeople. "I have a history to share," he says, "and best of all, they are interested in listening. We can learn a lot from each other."

The good news is that most Traditionalists have bigger and better plans than sitting on a porch swing all day drinking ice tea. The bad news is that most managers aren't so good at identifying the high-potential Traditionalist candidates. They might be great at singling out the twenty-five-to-thirty-five-year-old with spunk, but few are taking time to spot the sixty-two-year-old with the energy and imagination to morph into new roles. According to the Bureau of Labor Statistics, in 1998 only about 12 percent of those over the age of sixty-five participated in the labor force nationwide. That means there's a rich vein of potential labor out there just waiting to be mined. In our survey, when asked what they are most likely to do when they "formally retire," 45 percent of Traditionalist respondents said they would like to "continue working in a different capacity" with their same company. Another 28 percent said they were likely to "enter a new field of paid employment." The question is, are you prepared to identify those highly motivated and qualified Traditionalists and snap them up?

Many Traditionalists in previous studies who said they did not plan on working after formal retirement might have been discouraged by Social Security regulations that penalized older workers financially if they chose to work while collecting payments. Now retirees have even more impetus to continue working if they choose to do so. Congress recently passed a bill aimed at helping companies fill labor shortages by not penalizing seniors who go back to work. Previously, they were penalized $1 for every $3 they earned over $17,000. Now workers ages sixty-four to seventy can earn as much as they want without having it affect their Social Security benefits. With that disincentive lifted, more Traditionalists will be willing to take on extra hours and get paid for them. But can you attract them?

It's no surprise that if you want to recruit Generation Xers, you have to explore every option from work-at-home policies to job sharing. But companies are forgetting how appealing alternative work options might be to the generation that has earned a little flexibility. Traditionalists have lived and breathed the nine-to-five concept all their working lives. Companies that can find ways to break this mold and offer schedules this generation never dreamed of are uncovering a wonderful retention strategy. Many Traditionalists can't imagine going straight from full-time work to full-time retirement. Assisting in the transition creates a win-win recruiting strategy for everybody. "Time off became more important to me," commented one Traditionalist. "So when I decided to stay on the job and not retire, I negotiated to have more time off instead of a pay increase. This gave me a chance to slow down a little, but still keep my eye on the job." Many Traditionalist employees have accrued huge amounts of compensatory time owing to their stellar attendance records and strong work ethic. Rather than just letting them take all those days and retire six months earlier, why not use them to build a dream schedule that will keep a valuable Traditionalist on the job and loving it?

Jess Bell, the Traditionalist son of the founder of the $100 million cosmetics company Bonne Bell, had his own epiphany about hiring Traditionalists. After fifty-two years in the cosmetics industry (Mr. Bell is seventy-six), he noticed how he felt when he had to work side by side with people who were younger and faster than he was. "He didn't like it," reports Sue Shellenbarger of *The Wall Street Journal*. "He felt self-conscious about his own ability to keep up." That realization, combined with an expanding business and a shrinking labor pool, helped him conceive the idea of forming a Traditionalists-only production department.

While Mr. Bell was concerned that he might lose the benefits of cross-pollination that a multigenerational team provides, he gambled that the pluses of grouping seniors together would be worth it. The call went out via churches and senior centers, and retirees now make up close to 20 percent of Bonne Bell's five-hundred-person workforce. Turnover among the Traditionalists is exceedingly low, and production goals are met. This is in part due to the camaraderie and comfort level established by the company and the employees themselves. "It's my turn to be with people my own age group. We can talk to each other. We don't have to compete," explained one satisfied Traditionalist employee.

Other organizations, like Travelers Insurance and Target Stores, utilize Traditionalist retirees on a regular basis. Days Inn recruits retirees for 10 percent of its reservation department, and a company spokesperson said they "show up, they are on time, they care, and they are fine role models for the work ethic sometimes lacking in younger workers."

In some areas, Traditionalists are being tapped to take over where historically much younger bodies were preferred, like at the beach. Owing to the booming economy and a high employment rate among teens, the summer of 2000 saw one of the greatest labor shortages ever in the seasonal tourist industry. One result of this was a nationwide shortage of lifeguards so severe that some municipalities were forced to delay pool openings and close beaches. In the national surfing capital of Huntington Beach, California, several of the candidates who finally did show up to apply for lifeguard jobs were so woefully unqualified they had to be rescued from the surf during tryouts! (And it looked so easy on *Baywatch*.) Enter the Traditionalists, who by May of 2000 were being recruited up and down

California's coast. As one manager put it, "Hey, they're great swimmers, they're in great shape, they have great judgment, and we need them." Traditionalists may never make it to the cover of *Shape* magazine, but if you ever have to be pulled from the surf, we guarantee they're the ones you want carrying you to safety.

We cannot be so focused on recruiting the younger generations that we forget the past. Traditionalists have accomplished amazing feats that have served as our launching pad into the new century. It took an unprecedented work ethic to get the job done. We can't afford to lose them now.

MINING FOR GOLD: THE MILLENNIAL WORKFORCE

If you sell blue jeans or Barbie dolls, you are probably already well acquainted with the Millennial generation. But if you're a hiring manager, you might not be. That's because Millennials have just started entering the workforce. With the numerical peak of this huge population currently around age ten, millions of Millennials are being trained right now to become part of a workforce the rest of us will soon have to learn to recruit and manage. The time to get to know them—and to let them get to know you—is now. Yet few organizations have a real handle on who the Millennials are and how to attract them.

For many companies, summer is a time when the halls are suddenly flooded with the bright, shining faces of individuals with titles ranging from "intern" to "gofer." They are standing at the bottom of the corporate ladder, looking skyward. You watch them smile at every corporate bigwig, and you listen as they make suggestions that couldn't possibly be implemented unless hell froze over. You think, *Wow, look at them, they're so young and so naive.*

Well, guess what? If you haven't already gotten ready to recruit the Millennials, you might just be the naive one. The Millennials are on the move with more energy than the Energizer Bunny and are emerging into the workforce with plans to just keep going and going and going.

Unfortunately, when it comes to Millennials, organizations are making two costly assumptions:

Some assume that the Millennials will be just like those who have gone before them. Nothing could be further from the truth. If there's one thing we've learned about the generations, it's that each one has its own generational personality. Organizations will have to get to know the Millennials without making the same mistake so many made with Generation X. When Xers entered the workforce, most of us assumed they'd view the world of work the same way the Baby Boomers had and that our tried-and-true management methods would work just fine. That turned out to be painfully wrong. Generation Xers behaved differently from their predecessors, and the organizations that didn't take the time to get to know them are still paying the price in high turnover, low hiring rates, and poor morale. Millennials, too, will have a unique set of values and expectations about work, and unless their viewpoints are clearly understood, history is bound to repeat itself.

Others assume there's no hurry to get to know the Millennials—after all, most companies are still struggling to figure out Generation X! The fact is, the time to recruit them is *now*. Not all Millennials are hanging out in shopping malls, drooling over Britney Spears and the Backstreet Boys. One-third of Millennials already work twenty hours or more per week, and if they aren't already working for you, watch out! You might soon be working for *them!*

In many industries such as high tech, Millennials are being recruited while they're still in trade school, high school, or college. At Vir2L, one of the hottest Web design firms, the average age of a top designer isn't twenty-five to forty-five; it's seventeen to twenty-four! In fact, one employee at Vir2L told us he was starting to feel too old for the game at age twenty-three!

Smart industries are forming connections with schools through internship programs and mentoring opportunities that can introduce Millennials to their companies in positive ways—long before they're ready to hit the workforce full-time. The Fibre Box Association, for one, isn't waiting around until the Millennials have all decided where they want to work. It can't afford to. The Fibre Box people know that not many Millennial designers are sitting around computer screens pondering the future of the litho label. So Fibre Box has gone on the offensive and formed relationships with trade schools to introduce Millennials in computer-aided design programs to the industry. It's a real eye-opener for young designers who might never have thought about where that colorful Cap'n Crunch box came from. By providing job placement opportunities with the manufacturers who are their members, this old world industry is carving out a brave new world by opening Millennials' eyes to an exciting career option.

Cisco ran a recruiting ad recently, but it wasn't to attract an existing workforce to fill open positions. Instead it was a plea to attract partners to *create* a workforce to fill positions that are going to exist in the future. The ad pictures three Millennials standing under the Golden Gate Bridge. The copy reads:

> *Imagine having your pick of jobs. These kids can. With your help they'll have careers in computers and networking. There are more than 346,000 IT jobs open right now. You can help our local youth prepare for these openings through the Cisco Networking Academy Program. This 280-hour program helps high school and college students develop computer-networking skills that will carry them either to higher education or to their first job. Donate equipment, fund teacher training, or offer internships in your community. . . .*

Was Cisco out to do a good deed when they designed this program? Maybe. But they were also out to fill a recruiting need. Companies that participate reap the goodwill of the communities they are helping, but they also get the chance to train the labor pool they are going to need over the next few years. And they get first crack at hiring the newly graduated trainees. The result is a partnership that joins schools, teachers, companies, and communities to help kids get ahead and to help move them into job categories that need them desperately.

The ad goes on to quote Shanti, age eighteen: "Recently we configured Cisco Series 2501 routers enabling AppleTalk and IPX!"

If we had asked Shanti a year ago what she wanted to be when she grew up, we doubt she would have said, "Oh, I plan to configure Cisco Series 2501 routers to enable AppleTalk and IPX."

Instead she might have said she wanted to be the first female Tiger Woods or the next Madonna. After all, how many inner-city, or even suburban, teens have ever been exposed to a really heroic router guy? Millennials win through programs like these by being exposed to careers they might never have dreamed of otherwise.

It's so important that organizations engage Millennials *now* in conversations about their options for their future, while there's still time for them to consider your industry and get the education they need. By the time they've committed to a career in aerospace, it's a little late for you to come along babbling about box factories. Ask yourself what you can do to help a Millennial get to know your industry or company so when it comes time to choose, you'll find yourself mining pure gold.

DIGGING INTO NICHES AND GOING PLATINUM

If you always go where you always went, you'll always get what you always got. To find new employees to fill new niches, you're going to have to step outside the status quo.

As we've already discussed, sometimes this means tapping into a generation you've never hired before. Other times that's not enough. But once you understand who the generations are and what makes them tick, you can use that knowledge to discover generational niches that are the equivalent of buried treasure. These niches are valuable not just because they can provide a ready source of labor to fill your needs, but also because they might provide employees who are so ripe and so right for what you're doing that they bring with them a whole new, unexpected level of commitment. Here are just a few examples of organizations that understood how a particular generation might be evolving and used that insight to uncover a valuable generational niche they could mine with platinum results:

Wherever there's a glitch, there's a niche. We recently consulted with a San Francisco–based recruiting firm that specialized in the high-tech industry. When the dot.com bubble burst, leading many locals to refer to those companies as "dot.bombs," the technical recruiting field took a bit of a nosedive. The challenge was how to reframe the needs and goals of the Gen Xers who suddenly found themselves ex-techies as their companies downsized and reroute that talent pool into areas where they were sorely needed.

We saw this as the opportunity of a lifetime for traditional companies to finally be able to compete against Silicon Valley by snatching up the Xers who tired of swimming against the tide and looking for someone to throw them a life preserver. Sure, some of the techno-literati were itching to get back into the shark tank as soon as they could catch their breath. But others were searching for more stability with a company that had been around for a while. As one senior recruiting executive of a Fortune 500 company put it, "We've seen a shift now where Xers are tired of moving around all the time and wondering if their company is going to make it. They want stability. I think so many of them came from broken homes and a series of jobs that didn't stick that they now find a stable workplace very attractive. That's something we can offer them."

As Xers are starting families, buying homes, and making big emotional commitments to their careers, they will increasingly look for companies that are willing to commit to them in return. That, combined with the decline of the dot.coms, should cause recruiters in old-line companies to take a second look at a group they formerly thought they couldn't attract.

To fill a niche, create an itch. Some of the toughest recruiting battles in the country are being waged in the field of education. As the Millennial boom has exploded into schools, the battle to fill teaching positions has reached crisis proportions. In California alone, two hundred thousand teachers will be needed in the next ten years, and twenty thousand of the state's existing teachers are operating on emergency credentials. In Minneapolis, Minnesota, districts have had to hire so rapidly that 65 percent of the city's teachers have less than five years' experience. When it comes to recruiting, necessity is certainly the mother of invention. The teacher shortage has forced districts to think in radically new ways about how to find niches for mining recruits and how to go after *all* the generations of teachers, not just the Cuspers and Millennials coming right out of college.

To tap *Traditionalists, Newsweek* reported that administrators in Chicago are recruiting retirees as a way of boosting the rolls of available substitute teachers. "Creating an itch" means first finding the retired teachers, letting them know how much they are needed as subs, and then providing transportation to and from school via van shuttles. It seems senior subs tend to turn down assignments located too far from public transportation, but they'll fill a niche for the district if they have a built-in way of getting to and from work.

To bring in the *Boomers,* Las Vegas's Clark County School District has developed a new program called E-March, aimed at snatching up retiring military officers. That means getting out to military bases and targeting those forty- and fifty-somethings who have put in the twenty years necessary to be eligible for a full pension and enticing them with the idea of a new career. They know that retiring military Boomers who have spent half their lives in the armed forces form a niche of highly qualified recruits who are looking for a way to transition to civilian life with a built-in support system and an instant role in their new communities. They also know that these candidates are schooled in the skills teachers need, like discipline, leadership, and self-confidence.

Vegas isn't just targeting *external* niches as a way to locate Boomers who might be able to teach. They've been smart enough to seek out *internal* niches as well. One new program is aimed at recruiting Boomers who are already employed by the school district in other capacities and who would like to enter the classroom as teachers. Already, the first class consisting of bus drivers, teachers' aides, and office workers has been enrolled in a one-year certification program.

But the Las Vegas district doesn't stop there.

To extend a hand to *Xers,* Dr. George Ann Rice, the Las Vegas district's assistant superintendent in charge of human resources, is enlisting technology. "Creating an itch" means finding them in somebody else's school and enticing them with promises of year-round sunshine, sans blizzards and state income tax. For candidates who can't afford to fly to Vegas for an interview, the district provides high-tech videophones to interview them remotely. Techno-flexibility has convinced Gen X teachers from forty-two states to pack their bags and relocate.

To mine the *Millennials,* Las Vegas has created its own niche by developing a program for high schoolers that starts preparing them now for careers in education. It makes loads of sense to connect with Millennials while they're right under the noses of administrators and while the impact that teachers can make is still foremost in their minds. "My [parents] told me teachers don't make much money," commented fourteen-year-old George Redlin. "But I told them it's not the money that counts. Schools need more guys as teachers."

Suddenly teachers aren't saying the Pledge of Allegiance anymore, but "Viva Las Vegas!" We suggest you think twice about letting any of your staff visit Vegas—they might never come back!

As these examples demonstrate, targeting the generations in

new ways requires more effort spent in uncovering niches and more creativity expended in mining them. The reward is opening up rich veins of previously undiscovered talent.

Find somebody else's niche and steal it. Farmers Insurance, which has been experiencing a dearth of qualified candidates to become insurance agents, is doing its part to make the teacher shortage even worse. (Not that this is any crime—we think it's a rather ingenious example of what Harvey Mackay calls "niche picking.") The company created a profile of who makes the best agents and then opened their minds to search the universe for where that new niche of candidates might exist. Boomers and Xers who are established, successful teachers sprang to mind and onto the pages of a new recruiting campaign. While it's probably not too popular with school principals, the Farmers strategy makes sense. Schoolteachers are well-organized, people-oriented self-starters with vast numbers of contacts within their communities to help them get launched in sales. Plus, they possess the ability to explain complex topics in ways people can understand that is absolutely vital to a successful insurance agent. It's a natural fit and should help Farmers harvest a record crop of candidates.

Create a new identity entity. If all else fails in the effort to identify creative new generational niches where your best workers can be found, you might have to create your own. The CIA did just that in Silicon Valley. Unable to compete for the brightest Generation X workers and the hottest new technology against the glitz, glamour, and cold hard capital of Silicon Valley, the CIA decided to become a player. Think about it. You're a bleeding-edge twenty-something who's invented the latest and greatest in spy toys. Odds are you'll get a lot more money selling it to private industry than turning it over to a government agency. So, reports *Newsweek* magazine, the CIA decided to get out from under the image of the slow-moving government bureaucracy that prevents the hippest knowledge workers from showing up for recruiting fairs at the Pentagon. The result is a newly formed venture capital company called In-Q-Tel, a private nonprofit funded with $28 million authorized by Congress. Its mission is to "invest in high-tech start-ups that will help the spy agency regain the edge in gizmos and gadgets that it once held over the private sector."

Forming a new entity with a hipper style enables the CIA to get the best of both—access to the Gen Xers they want and acquisition of the technologies they need to thrive in an increasingly competitive global environment. Even In-Q-Tel's style is a sharp departure from the buttoned-down recruiting approach you might expect. Their Web site promises freewheeling techies the opportunity to work on "cool s——!"

We doubt that's a value proposition you're going to see being adopted by too many other government agencies.

14

HERE'S YOUR BOSS AND BENEFITS; THERE'S THE BATHROOM

It's Dan's first day on the job. He is eager to hit the ground running and show what he can do. His day begins with a stop at the human resources department, where he's given a lengthy lecture about his employee benefits. Not to worry, though, just in case he doesn't remember the details, he also receives a manual the size of the Yellow Pages that he's asked to read carefully.

Dan's grand welcome continues with a quick tour of the building, during which he is introduced to whoever happens to pass by. The tour concludes at his new cubicle, where he is told to get acclimated to his computer and call if he has any questions. Except, oops, his phone doesn't work yet, but he can borrow his neighbor's phone until Technical Services shows up to activate his. The good news is that Dan can look forward to meeting his supervisor after lunch. He has the rest of the morning to do . . . uh . . . well . . . ummm . . .

That night, Dan is at dinner with a bunch of friends:

"So . . . how's the new job?" they all ask with excitement. Dan looks cautious. "Well . . . it was okay."

"Just okay?" they all respond. "But it's such a great company."

"Well," Dan exclaims, "I don't have a clue what I'm supposed to be doing yet, I couldn't tell you one person's name, I didn't do anything constructive, I felt like a total loser, and I ate lunch by myself! How was your day?"

The table falls silent.

Too many companies are making a critical mistake by overlooking orientation as a crucial recruitment and retention tool for the generations. Organizations spend boatloads of money getting candidates in the door, only to squander their investment by doing nothing when the new employees walk through it.

With turnover rates on the rise, organizations can't afford to blow this opportunity to make new hires from every generation feel great about the choices they've made and reconfirm their commitment to stick around. With the war for talent so fierce, orientation can be a recruiter's most underutilized public relations tool. New hires are often a company's best source for referring talent and can be light-years more effective than the classifieds. "Hey . . . you have got to check out this great company I just joined!" goes a whole lot further than "Help Wanted."

Unfortunately, too often a new employee's sales pitch for the firm reads more like an obituary. After spending days, weeks, or months zeroing in on an organization they are really excited about joining, they show up on the first day only to be let down.

Call us crazy, but "Here's your benefits, there's the bathroom, make yourself at home" is a lousy first go at gaining an employee's commitment. Orientation needs to be more than just a quick tiptoe through the take-home and a sashay through the sick leave. It should make employees feel both challenged and comfortable and convince them that making this their new home was a very good choice. Like an unforgettable first date, orientation at the new company ought to be something employees will tell their grandchildren about twenty-five years from now. More often than not, the sparks die and that first date doesn't make it past dinner.

The situation is serious enough that in our recent BridgeWorks Generation's Survey, over *one-third* of Generation Xers said they would rather go to the dentist than attend their company's orientation program! And dentists have an advantage: they can opt to give the patient nitrous oxide. If only nitrous were available to help people through orientation!

Some companies are stepping up to the plate. From scavenger hunts to bungee jumps, companies are gradually dumping the quickie tour and slide lecture and opting for a more experiential approach. Purina Pet Products recently rolled out a new orientation program called Ambassadors Making a Difference.

"Our goal is to instill ownership into our employees and to let them know that they are the ambassadors to our products and services and that they made the right choice in choosing to work at Ralston Purina," explained Tina Salazar, director of organizational learning. And they do just that. The orientation experience kicks off with a speech from the CEO, then continues with a variety of presentations, activities, and field trips that allows participants to do everything from visiting retail stores to developing long-term personal and career goals. You know you're off on the right foot when new hires comment, as one Ralston Purina employee did, "The program made me even more excited to become a productive, contributing member of the organization."

This is a great start . . . but it's not enough. The brave souls in charge of designing orientation programs face an audience that can vary widely in age, experience, sophistication, pay level, education, learning style, and so on. It's a daunting task!

But as daunting as it is, it does no good to look at all these factors if you continue to ignore the most crucial factor of all: generational differences. By examining the generational perspective of participants, companies can gain a much better understanding of what employees are looking for when they arrive at orientation, what can be done to create the ideal experience, and how to gain a distinct competitive advantage in recruiting and retaining much-needed staff.

TRADITIONALISTS

If you're surprised to see Traditionalists leading the generational lineup in a chapter on orientation, you're not alone. Most people don't immediately picture an orientation class stocked with bright-eyed, bushy-tailed sixty- and seventy-somethings. But if you're leaving Traditionalists out of the orientation picture, you're making a big mistake. Although they tend to be extremely loyal to their employers, Traditionalists *are* making job changes and entering new, unfamiliar work environments. As we mentioned earlier, the recent tight labor market has convinced many companies to go "mining for silver" as they rediscover the value of workers age sixty and over.

Companies are examining how they can attract skilled veterans away from the competition, lure retirees back into the workforce, and keep their own talent from walking out the door as soon as they are eligible to retire. Clearly, Traditionalists have a place in the orientation scheme as they continue down a career track many assumed had reached the finish line.

What do Traditionalists need from an orientation program? No, not a set of reading glasses handed out with the workbooks. With their strong sense of legacy, Traditionalists are prime candidates for orientation programs that focus on the history, culture, and mission of the organization. These are the parts that trainers often blow by at top speed because they've heard it so many times before. Well, for this generation tradition has meaning. Traditionalists actually *care* that you've been around since 1876, and they won't be stifling yawns during your video on the founding fathers (unless you dim the lights and your chairs are *really* comfy!). Orientation should showcase the past accomplishments of your organization with pride.

Because Traditionalists believe in the power of working together toward the common good, it is crucial to discuss how their role will contribute to the larger picture. Orientation programs should highlight why the organization needs Traditionalists and should demonstrate the special value they bring to the workplace. This requires more than just lip service. Visuals should show Traditionalists performing important tasks, whether that means being out front with customers in a Wal-Mart store or troubleshooting the assembly line in a plant. Assess your orientation materials to make sure older workers are pictured. Showing images of hip young Ashleys and Zacharies at the computer is fine, but leaving out images of Traditionalist Rogers and Mildreds makes them feel both disrespected and disconnected.

In this youth-oriented culture, Traditionalists, regardless of how competent they are, often worry that they are "behind the times" or that they won't be able to keep up. Orientation programs for older workers should highlight the training opportunities that will be available to them. Some may lack computer skills; others might need to be brought up-to-date on how to operate new types of machinery. Orientation programs should cover when, where, and how they will get that training and when they are expected to have it completed. At Liberty Diversified, a privately owned marketing and manufacturing company in Minneapolis, Minnesota, the orientation program includes a half day spent in the training department. Participants receive an overview of all the courses that are offered, meet with trainers and learn specifics about classes, and find out how to register. The goal is to reduce fears and make people feel comfortable and supported.

Traditionalist learners tend to be respectful of the presenter, hesitant to interrupt, and eager not to look foolish in front of the younger set. That makes for a polite, appreciative audience, but facilitators need to find ways to get Traditionalist learners to speak up, ask questions, and express their concerns. The Coca-Cola Enterprises Operations University is a highly respected training and orientation program for midlevel bottling plant employees from around the country. The participants are seasoned workers who have been out of the classroom for a long time and don't know one another well. To counteract the natural nervousness about being back in "school" with a room full of strangers, the trainers often kick off with a problem-solving activity: Think about a time when you had to solve a complex problem at work. What was the challenge? What roadblocks did you have to overcome? How did you solve it? And what was the result? One by one, the participants tell their stories. Gradually, an amazing thing happens. The seasoned veterans stop thinking about what they don't know and start focusing on how much expertise they have amassed over the years. Heads nod, laughs are shared, the teasing begins. Grounded in respect for where they've been, the Traditionalists can move forward.

Once you've become sensitized to the gray-haired new hires just walking through the door, hold on . . . you're not finished yet. What about the ones who are right down the hall—and have been for twenty years? Granted, it's a huge mistake to overlook the orientation needs of older *new* hires, but it is an even bigger mistake to forget current employees who could benefit from the opportunity for "reorientation." Okay, we know that sounds a little like those "reeducation" camps that were used to brainwash people in Communist countries, but we don't mean it that way. What we do mean is that reorientation is a chance to take members of this loyal, hard-working generation who might already have one foot out the door and get them recommitted to jumping in with both feet for a few more years.

Whenever Ralston Purina starts up an orientation class, they invite a few long-term employees to join in. The old-timers can hobnob with the new hires and offer plenty of perspective about how the company works. But they can also sink their teeth into an exciting overview of what their company is up to. That builds pride and knowledge of the organization. It also gives older employees the option to consider new careers in areas they might not have thought about. If done right, orientation programs can become extraordinary tools for getting veteran employees back in touch with why they joined the organization in the first place—and what they might want to do next.

Liberty Diversified gets their current employees involved not as "orientees," but as "orientors." Ann Miller, a training and development specialist who led the employee task force that designed the new orientation program, commented, "We felt it was important that the orientation be owned not solely by HR, but by the entire company." The theme they built the orientation around is "Path to Growth," where current employees serve the role of pathfinders for new hires setting off on their career paths.

"Pathfinders play an integral role in a new hire's orientation," explains Miller. "They answer questions that the new hire might not be comfortable asking a direct supervisor. This could be something as simple as 'Where do I eat lunch?' or 'What do I wear on Fridays?' The point is that we know new hires have a lot of questions that are less about policies and more about fitting in with our culture." Anyone who remembers what it felt like the first day at a new school can appreciate how nice it is to have this support. Pathfinders also serve the role of company historians. They spend time with new hires talking about the company's eighty-year history and what the plans are for the future. The company believes that having this come directly from an employee's mouth and not a PowerPoint presentation adds a sense of personal connection and instills excitement.

The smart move behind Liberty's use of current employees as pathfinders was that they didn't post a sign-up sheet and beg people to participate. Instead they rolled it out companywide as an honor. To be selected, prospective pathfinders must meet certain criteria and be nominated by peers or supervisors who feel they are a fit. The chosen pathfinders go through extensive training and are provided with tools to help them, such as a checklist that covers everything from taking time out for a coffee break with the new hires to helping them set up their computer and voice mail. As a result, not only do the new hires start off on the right foot, but, as Miller put it, "this has also become a key retention strategy, as it gives us a chance to honor certain employees and let them know that they are appreciated."

BABY BOOMERS

While they may be the largest group ever to hit the workforce, when it comes to orientation, Baby Boomers have been ripped off. That's not something this success-oriented generation likes to dwell on, but it's true nonetheless. Boomers, who had literally millions of competitors for scarce jobs when they entered the work world, often suffered lackluster or even nonexistent orientation programs and had no recourse but to put up with it and get on with the job at hand. They relied on what we call "black-market orientation" from co-workers who filled them in on how things *really* worked.

It's not too late to offer Boomers the orientation experience they never had. Baby Boomers are still entering and reentering the workforce at all levels. If there's one generalization you *can* make about Baby Boomers today, it's that they are all over the map. They might be running a company, reentering the work world after years spent raising a family, recareering in an entirely new direction, scaling back to cope with increasing family demands, or preparing to retire. This generation will be surprised and delighted to be part of a well-thought-out, smoothly run orientation program that takes their needs into consideration and eases the transition.

What do they need? Like Traditionalists, Boomers can be intrigued by a well-produced opening video. How the company got started back in 1806 is important to Boomers. But the video can't end with a montage of black-and-white photos fading in and out to strains of "America the Beautiful." Patriotism and organizational loyalty are fine, but they aren't enough. Boomers have experienced major corporate upheavals during their careers. They want to know how the company has evolved since 1806 and where it's going!

General Mills's orientation video features clips from vintage Betty Crocker commercials that date back to the 1950s. But rather than end with a smiling Betty pulling a cake out of the oven, they bring the video up-to-date by interspersing key messages from the CEO explaining how Betty has gotten them to where they are today and how she will continue to evolve into tomorrow. That's just the right approach for Baby Boomers.

In general, Boomers are politically savvy and keenly aware of subtle nuances of corporate culture. Ever conscious of the next strategic career move, Boomers in orientation need to know who's in charge, who reports to whom, and who has the power within the organization. They also expect to hear about corporate strategy. Explain who your major competitors are today, who they have been in the past, and who might emerge as competitors in the future. Discuss how your products and services have evolved over the years and what innovations lie ahead. Include an overview of the financial picture. Talk about how new strategic directions might create future career opportunities. Highlight how the participants' specific positions contribute to the big picture. Boomers want to know where they fit, what the assignment entails, and how they will make a difference. In fact, in our BridgeWorks Generations Survey, the number one complaint Baby Boomers had about orientation was that they didn't learn enough about their actual job.

When talking about the future, keep in mind that Baby Boomers have seen so many corporate initiatives come and go that they are somewhat jaded by the latest buzzwords and organizational development fads. At the same time, they are idealists looking for something they can believe in. Orientation is a prime chance to put them in touch with your company's mission and tap into the Boomers' natural desire to put their stamp on something.

Too often a company's vision is nothing more than a poster hanging next to a few "Successories" plaques over the Xerox machine. It's a sad fact that in our BridgeWorks Survey, more Boomers said it would be easier for them to recite the ingredients in a Big Mac than their company's mission statement! Because they are the supervisors, managers, mentors, and leaders in many organizations, Baby Boomers need your company's mission to flow off the tongue more easily than "two all-beef patties, special sauce, lettuce, cheese, pickles, onions on a sesame-seed bun." Orientation is the place to start.

As with Traditionalists, keep format in mind when designing orientation for Boomers. They did not scratch and claw their way up through the hierarchy just to find themselves watching a slide show next to someone the age of their baby-sitter who is wearing ripped jeans and Skechers. Many companies are realizing the importance of a multitiered orientation approach. Sure, the opening address and video are important for all levels on the organizational chart, but beyond that, one size does not fit all. Different rungs on the ladder require different levels of orientation. A recent college grad, no matter how sharp or well paid, is going to require different information than someone who's been around the block a few times.

That said, even experienced Boomers should not be omitted

from orientation classes altogether. If your plant tour is a really good one, or your company video extraordinary, *all* new hires should participate. Cross-pollinating the generations can be valuable. In fact, upper-level new hires *should* participate in orientation, at the very least so they know what their own employees are learning. The key for the higher-level folks is to divide the orientation into components—one part where different ages/levels can rub elbows, another part designed specifically for their peer group, and other portions, such as the financial piece, to be conducted privately.

General Mills divides its orientation program into three distinct phases. On the first day, the formal three-hour program includes signing paperwork, watching the corporate video, and hearing from key managers. That's over by midmorning, and then trainees are off to meet with their new bosses. This lets people roll up their sleeves right away and prevents information overload.

Within the first six months, new hires go through a week of advanced orientation in which they are introduced to the various job functions and all of the key leaders within the company. The thought is that after the employees have been on the job a while, they are ready to take a step back and see the company as a whole.

Phase three occurs twelve to eighteen months after starting at General Mills. This is the introspective phase and focuses on self-awareness. The program uses Myers-Briggs and other tools to home in on strengths and weaknesses and assess how each individual might grow within the company. The belief here is that after a year on the job, people have the main skills down and are ready to dig deeper and learn how they can effectively influence change within the organization.

This three-tiered approach is ideal for new Baby Boomer hires because it enables them to focus first on learning the job and then adds the strategic and personal development pieces within a reasonable amount of time.

Unfortunately, because companies are short-handed, and because many Boomer bosses bypassed orientation themselves, there's a tendency to allow new hires to skip the up-front stuff and get right to work. That's a shame. Many company orientation programs, like the one at General Mills, have a lot to offer a Boomer coming in from another corporate culture. But if skipping orientation is unavoidable, it's a great idea to offer a "CliffsNotes" version that can be studied independently. This can be done via written manual, video, CD-ROM, or even a company's internal Web site.

It's also important to acknowledge Boomers' desire to roll up their sleeves and dive in. Managers should be trained to incorporate new Boomer hires into daily business activities right from the get-go so they feel productive immediately. Orientation programs that assimilate Boomers ASAP will get a great bang for the buck.

Liberty Diversified includes new hires in departmental meetings around the company starting on day one of their employment. And recruits aren't allowed to just sit passively and observe. That's too easy. Liberty has trained staff members in how to welcome, include, and engage new hires so that they are able to participate immediately.

General Mills has another, more tactical approach to helping Boomers hit the ground running. They've made it standard operating procedure to have the new employee's desk ready, telephone turned on, and business cards already printed for the employee's first day on the job. Not bad ideas, considering the employee is actually there to start working!

GENERATION XERS

Generation Xers are hardly unfamiliar with the concept of an orientation program. In fact, because they have been willing to change jobs more often than other generations, they may have been through more orientations already than their predecessors experienced in their entire careers! This puts pressure on instructional designers to make a stellar first impression.

Adding to that pressure are the sophisticated expectations of this media-savvy generation. When Gen Xers are involved, it's not okay to be boring. They are accustomed to superior production values and highly visual presentations. They are born innovators, and they want orientation programs to demonstrate that they've chosen a cutting-edge place to work. Unfortunately, they are often disappointed.

So how *do* you plan orientation programs for Xers? First and foremost, accept that more often than not, you are the enemy. That doesn't mean you get to play out your childhood fantasy of being Darth Vader, even though you might be tempted to put a little fear into this cocky group. It means that you need to be aware of the innate skepticism that has haunted Generation X throughout their formative years. Xers need to be convinced that they've made the right choice when they start a new job, because as far as they are concerned, the jury is still out. Orientation programs are a great place to derail the doubts and distrust that could poison their attitude and attitudes around them.

As you proudly present the same big picture that the Traditionalists and Baby Boomers ate up, it is crucial to know that for Generation X, if you say you do it, you've got to prove it. Rah-rah platitudes are guaranteed to fall flat. Talk about the innovative, exciting things your company does while being factual and straightforward. The Xers' sensitive BS-O-Meters are turned all the way up all the time, ready to tune you out the minute you fail to tell the truth.

"Proving it" to an Xer means talking about the bad with the good. While Boomers might accept your need to frame your recent downsizing/toxic spill/federal indictment in the best possible light, Xers will be disgusted by what they see as glossing over a serious issue.

Some thought Weyerhaeuser's chief executive officer, Steven R. Rogel, was crazy when he opened the 1999 "state of the company" video with a long shot of a single warehouse employee speaking directly to the camera about what it felt like to watch a colleague die in a plant accident. Yet nothing could have proven more forcefully how seriously this leader takes employee safety. Talk straight about the negatives and you'll be rewarded with respect by Generation X.

Like the other generations, Xers have their own needs in terms of format. Remember, this is a generation raised on sound bites and accustomed to instant access to information. Break down the orientation process for Xers into smaller chunks that can be spread out over a longer time. Bill Walsh, former coach of the San Francisco 49ers, said it best when he advised coaches and managers never to teach anything in a module longer than twenty minutes! Present these info bites through a variety of media. For example, include PowerPoint, video, and CD-ROM as well as discussion and interaction. If your company video is really outdated, consider tossing it and replacing it with a hands-on activity like a visit to the plant floor or to a retail outlet where your products are sold.

Use experiential learning to give Generation Xers a real-time feel for what it's going to be like to work in your company and, ideally, to inspire their commitment. The number one complaint of Xers in our BridgeWorks Survey was that training sessions did not include enough interaction. Xers want hands-on exposure to their new company, and they prefer active participation. One worker who was hired to help open a brand-new vegetable packing plant said it best: "We took our first tour when they were just starting to test the assembly line. At this one turn, the conveyor belt malfunctioned. Boxes were flying off the line, crashing into the opposite wall. I just couldn't wait to get my hands on that equipment and make it run right." While malfunctioning equipment might not have been what the orientation designer had planned on, it demonstrated a real need that connected with that employee.

When configuring orientation groups, make sure Xers have access to some of their peers. Because of their much smaller population size, and because Xers have been in the shadow of the Baby Boomers all their lives, they can't stand feeling like the only Xer around. This group will feel much less isolated if even a few of their peers are present.

Also, it may seem strange to talk about an employee's career path when he's barely located his parking space, but addressing the topic can make orientation all the more effective. We are not suggesting it be like a trip to the high school guidance counselor; we are simply saying that talking about career pathing as soon as possible sends out the message that the company is planning on a long-term relationship and foresees a lot of opportunity.

As with Baby Boomers, Xers' orientation programs must allow them to hit the ground running as soon as possible—but for different reasons. The red-hot economy of the late 1990s, combined with the explosion of jobs in technology, has convinced Gen Xers that if they aren't happy where they are, they can always get hired someplace else. Even in a down economy, Generation X is the most likely to leave if they are dissatisfied. Because of this, Xers abhor the concept of dues paying. Orientation should focus on dos, not dues. It's crucial that companies get Xers involved and turned on to what they will be doing as quickly as possible, because studies have shown that Xers make the decision whether or not to stay on long-term within the first six months of employment. Traditional companies must be prepared to make Generation Xers part of a high-performance team starting on day one, or they're likely to lose them by the end of the first quarter.

MILLENNIALS

The Millennial generation will not only be flooding the front rows of orientation programs, they might be filling up *all* the rows as the next big boom rolls into corporate America. And considering the courtship this generation will likely receive to get them to accept the job, a lame orientation program will be like serving a gourmet meal and then offering Twinkies for dessert.

Millennials are a smart, practical generation that has already amassed a fair amount of work experience. And some Millennials have already held jobs that might normally fall to a much older person. For instance, Manpower, the country's largest employment service for temporary and part-time workers, recently instituted a successful placement program that put high school students into summer jobs developing corporate Web sites at hourly rates of up to $35! For Traditionalists who mowed lawns, Boomers who baby-sat, and Xers who made espresso, that's pretty enviable work experience. Call us crazy, but a get-acquainted name game and simple slide show won't cut it at orientation.

Millennials may have punched a few time clocks in their day, but that doesn't mean they know it all when it comes to work. Because they've filled in the worker shortage created by Gen Xers, they've never had to search very hard to find jobs. And because the economy has been so strong as they've come of age, Millennials have had the luxury of working when they need to and not working when they don't. As a result, organizations are looking at a highly capable generation that needs to be educated not just about the job and the company, but about how to work and what's expected of them.

It won't be enough to present them with a one-page job description drafted by the human resources department. This is a generation that questions everything! They've had instant access to information throughout their lives, and they'll find it insulting to be told, as one Millennial was told on his first day at the mall, "There are the piles of clothes; your job is to fold them." Understanding merchandising strategy may not make folding any more fun, but it will make the Millennial a more engaged and committed employee.

Cardiff, the Southern California firm, encourages employees to visit all the departments in the company during orientation and to keep on visiting throughout their tenure. They've sacked the old belief that employees should stick to a single function throughout their careers. They believe it's perfectly logical for a technical support rep to eventually make a move to sales, marketing, or public relations. They encourage employees to look around the company and search out the next place they'd like to work. As a result, the next place is usually Cardiff—not a competitor.

At Galactic Marketing, CEO Daniel Mohorc not only encourages employees to seek out other opportunities, but supports career pathing even if it means with a different company. He has a policy that if employees want to interview with another company, they get two days off, no questions asked. If they come back and turn in their resignation, Galactic throws a going-away party. If they come back and want to stay, then they are welcomed with open arms. Imagine the goodwill Galactic engenders by supporting Millennials in pursuing the career paths that are best for them!

Millennials are a pragmatic generation with a highly developed ability to sort through information. All their lives, they've had data spewed at them from every direction at warp speed, and guess what? They can handle it! They'll respond best to an orientation program that is hands-on and moves at a rapid pace. Incorporating some computer-based instruction is a good idea for Millennials, as it allows them to go at their own speed and acknowledges their ability to manage information.

Because they have been such active participants in the running of their own households, Millennials tend to respect authority without being awed by it. It's tough to tell a Millennial not to approach a senior vice president directly with a question when he or she has had the ability to e-mail the president of the United States since first grade!

Millennials tend to see leadership as a participative process and will learn best from managers who engage participants in orientation rather than just lecturing. The only top-down management model this generation will respond to is in game mode, through playing Mach IV on Sega and getting to be the commander. They won't be satisfied with the old command-and-control motif that said, "We'll give you the amount of information you need to do the job and no more." For this reason, they are also likely to question rules and procedures, so facilitators should be prepared to handle objections easily and comfortably without sounding too officious.

Millennials will expect to learn what to do, but they'll also want to learn "why." A valuable component of the orientation process might include personal career planning to help them see the connection between what they are doing now and where they are going. Many Millennials don't understand how their current jobs have any bearing on where they'll be ten years from now. They also have trouble relating to industries they haven't been exposed to through television or through their parents. It's a great idea to speak directly with Millennials about where their current position might lead them and how the skills they are learning now will relate to future careers. This is an early and effective way of getting them to think about staying with your company long-term.

SEND OUT THE WELCOME WAGON

Regardless of the content of the formal orientation program, organizations are missing a huge opportunity if they fail to recognize that the impression made by orientation begins *before* a new employee shows up on the first day. The true orientation wizards see this as a chance to really engage a new hire and reassure him or her about the decision to come to work at their place of business. Imagine a Traditionalist receiving a handwritten note from the CEO containing a simple but heartfelt welcome. Or a Boomer's family receiving an invitation to attend a plant tour on family day. Or a new Generation X assembly-line worker opening a package containing the company's sweatshirt and baseball cap—and an invitation to join the softball team.

General Mills was hoping to recruit a high-potential Millennial right out of college. Knowing he would have numerous job offers and that he would consult his mom and dad for help in decision making, the company focused on convincing the whole family that General Mills would be the ideal choice for their boy. The week before Thanksgiving, a frozen turkey arrived at the student's house, accompanied by the famous *Betty Crocker's Cookbook*. Betty's recipe for success was proven a winner when the graduate accepted the offer a few weeks later. Whatever way you choose to do it, it is possible to create momentum before a new person even pulls up in the parking lot.

Designing orientation programs is plenty challenging in this day and age. But to get the most benefit possible from the orientation experience, organizations need to stop and think about how each generation arrives at the first day on a new job and what can be done to take advantage of that once-in-a-lifetime opportunity. Almost 40 percent of respondents to our survey agreed with the statement "If orientation had been better, I could have been more effective in my job from day one." Understanding the subtle nuances of what makes each generation tick can make a tremendous difference in the success of orientation programs and the experiences of employees. Ultimately, that will translate to higher employee satisfaction, greater levels of commitment to organizations, decreased turnover, and a cohesive workforce made up of all generations.

Think back to how this chapter began, and imagine Dan's story if only it could have gone like this:

"So . . . how's the new job?" his friends ask with interest.

Dan smiles with pride. "I love it! My first week flew by, and we are doing amazing things. I think I could be happy working there for a long time. I like the values, too. No BS, but

we plan to be number one in our marketplace within the next
five years. And we have the highest customer satisfaction of
anyone in our industry. In fact, you should check this place out,
Amy. They have a great training department. . . ."

Suddenly, the table is buzzing.

RETAINING AND MANAGING THE GENERATIONS

15

THE SOLID OAK DOOR HAS BECOME A REVOLVING ONE

Carolyn, a Generation Xer, went over her speech one last time before going into her Baby Boomer boss's office. She had practiced her resignation in bed, in the shower, and in the car, but she was still quite nervous. She closed her eyes and mumbled, "Roger, I can't thank you enough for the opportunities you have given me over the past fourteen months. I have learned so much. But recently I have found a different opportunity that I really—"

Knock, knock, knock. There, standing in the doorway, was her Boomer boss. There was no time like the present to just go for it.

"Uh, Roger, I have something I need to talk to you about."

"Good," he replied as he came in and shut the door behind him. "I have something I need to discuss with you as well."

RETAINING THE GENERATIONS

Carolyn didn't want to drop the bomb that she was quitting right away, so she invited her Boomer boss to go first.

"Well, Carolyn," he began as he sat down, "you know how much this company means to me, and how well our sales are going. While I truly believe there are opportunities here, I personally have reached a point in my career where I need a change. I wanted you to be the first to know that I turned in my letter of resignation early this morning."

Carolyn was stunned. Her generation wasn't the only one dropping a bomb.

Our turnover rate has always been around 6 percent. Now it's moved up to 9 percent, and frankly, we're concerned.

—Division president, Fortune 500 packaged goods company

We've never had to deal with associate turnover like this—it's close to 40 percent by the third year, and it's killing us.

—Managing partner, one of the largest U.S. law firms

We can work with turnover at 50 percent. But when it's getting close to 100 percent we have to pay attention.

—Senior HR vice president, national service franchise

It doesn't matter what type of organization you're in or whether your turnover rate is 5 percent a year or 500 percent. What does matter is that turnover everywhere is on the rise. Suddenly, everyone from AT&T to Zycad is struggling with attrition.

Our survey findings are telling us that a larger number of employees are thinking about taking a walk than you might think.

When asked to fill in the statement "For me to stay another two years in my job . . . ," about one-third of all Baby Boomers and Gen Xers chose either "hell would have to freeze over" or "there would have to be major changes made in my job or in the company." That's not good news for organizations hoping the employees they've hired are going to be around for a while.

But as companies from A to Z are recognizing that turnover is a problem, many are still sitting back hoping that all it will take is a drop in the Dow to correct the *employees'* problem of keeping their eyes on somebody else's prize. When you ask managers about their troubles with retention, the finger immediately gets pointed at the employees (yes, we include that infamous middle one as well). Too often the excuse is, "Nobody's loyal these days," or, "Everybody thinks they can get rich quick somewhere else," or, "Nobody wants to work at a traditional company anymore."

But as any successful employer will tell you, a company's greatest asset is its employees. If this is true, then the finger-pointing needs to stop. Retaining the generations rests at least 50 percent in the employer's court. After all, when employees leave, the employers are the ones left to fill the void and cover the cost.

Employee turnover eats up management hours and dollars spent advertising and conducting searches for, interviewing, hiring, and training new recruits. It takes up employees' time covering open positions. It damages productivity when inexperienced workers perform important jobs. It damages morale among those who stay behind. It frustrates customers who receive substandard or inconsistent service.

Companies usually calculate the costs involved in turnover by analyzing the amount of time and money invested in the employee. But they need to look deeper and think about the level of competence that is also walking out the door. You'd better believe the grand total is a lot more grandiose—especially if that competence ends up with the competition.

Mark Bailey, director of staffing and recruitment for General Mills, explained it best when he said, "When we calculate the cost of replacing an employee, we factor in way more than the direct recruiting costs and lost production while the job is vacant. Some people are just much more painful to lose than others. Take, for example, our marketing managers. People who are hired on this track take five to six years to get to the top of their game. If they leave, we lose everything they have learned about our consumers and how to effectively market products to them. If we lose one, we estimate it actually costs the company millions of dollars!"

Companies will always be faced with the reality that employees are not handcuffed to their desks. But retaining employees today is harder than ever before. The reality is that compared to the past, today a host of cultural factors are turning the solid oak door into a revolving one.

DIAGNOSIS R.D.D. (Retention Deficit Disorder)

Major cultural values like loyalty don't just pack up and move out overnight. It takes some pretty profound changes to get people to throw off fear and inertia and to abandon their commitments to projects, co-workers, and even organizations to make a major change. Employers only have to put themselves in the shoes of an employee today to see why leaving is not only more attractive, but more accepted.

A booming economy during the 1990s allowed employees to find new jobs with more pay relatively easily. When everyone's hiring, pounding the pavement doesn't seem half as hard. Why wouldn't you look around if the whole question of whether or not you could find a job was answered with an emphatic *Yes!* Even as the economy softens, employers need to realize that Pandora's box has already been opened. Employees have seen the light and realized they *do* have choices.

Better communication through the Web and e-mail as to what's available has made finding the perfect job a lot easier. Top that off with increased mobility of Americans and you have an ease of access never seen before. Imagine living in Podunk prior to the advent of the Internet and wanting a job in Philadelphia. You'd have to go to your local library and look at back issues of employment journals. Perhaps you'd subscribe to the *Philadelphia Tribune* for a few months or sign on with an employment service in that city. The search was long, drawn out, and daunting. Now you can log on, search, correspond, and even *apply* for the job via the Web. The only thing you have to actually show up for is the interview, and with videoconferencing becoming more viable via the conference room or the computer, that might soon be a thing of the past as well. The Web has made it easier to job hunt right in your own backyard. Suddenly, sneaking onto the Web for a few minutes during the day is a lot easier than sneaking out for an informational interview that you'd have to lie about. Not to mention the endless excuses you'd have to dream up to explain why you are so dolled up for work that day.

Reduced level of corporate loyalty among Generation Xers is setting the tone for others. "When I lost my fifth Xer to one of our competitors," explained a Boomer boss, "I started wondering why I was riding around in circles watching everyone else grab the brass ring." The sense of decreased faith and trust in institutions is felt not just among Xers. Increasingly, the older generations are feeling more empowered to leave when they're unhappy. Mergers, acquisitions, layoffs, and restructuring have hit employees hard, and as a result, employees have become less concerned about the organization and more focused on making career moves that suit them. Many are tired of riding out endless corporate upheavals. If it's that disruptive where you work now, how bad could it possibly be somewhere else?

JOB CHANGING AND THE GENERATIONS

These three reasons have made it easier and more acceptable for all generations of employees to leave. But that doesn't mean they view job changing in the same ways. In fact, they see things very differently.

CLASHPOINT AROUND JOB CHANGING

Traditionalists . . .	*"Job changing carries a stigma."*
Baby Boomers . . .	*"Job changing puts you behind."*
Generation Xers . . .	*"Job changing is necessary."*
Millennials . . .	*"Job changing is part of my daily routine."*

Traditionalists

For Traditionalists, job changing was something you did only if you couldn't make a go of it where you were—often a sign of failure. Traditionalists put the value of loyalty and security above personal happiness, and many stayed in one place for decades because they felt loyal to the company or were supporting families. Leaving a job raised a lot of questions. Couldn't you fit in? Was your performance subpar? Was something (gasp!) wrong with you? We all know Traditionalists who can boast twenty-five-, thirty-, and even forty-year careers with one company. In fact, we know one employee, Ruth Byrone, secretary to Bill Reid, president of Mechanics Bank in Richmond, California, who has been in the same job for *fifty-seven years.* Yes, she started there when Franklin Delano Roosevelt was president! She says she has no intention of retiring any time soon. As long as she "still enjoys helping the public, why stay home?" was how she put it.

But be careful: many Traditionalists have reached the place where they are financially secure enough to consider making a move if they are unhappy. As a result, turnover among Traditionalists can be a barometer as to how bad retention problems really are. If members of the most loyal generation are willing to leave, the internal issues might be very serious indeed.

Baby Boomers

For Baby Boomers, who needed eyes in the backs of their heads to keep tabs on who was nipping at their heels, job changing was okay as long as you didn't lose any ground. Taking a lesser title or lower salary was something you did only out of desperation or because you were making a stellar move that would turn others green with envy. And job changes didn't come fast. Most Boomers would agree it was a smart idea to put in a few years at a job before you made a move so it would look good on your résumé.

If your turnover is high among this generation, it's time to reexamine your value proposition or the number of high-profile opportunities you are offering. You might also want to take a look at the opportunities for mentoring you're providing your high-potential Boomers. In our survey, 43 percent of Boomers disagreed with the statement "There are good opportunities to be mentored where I work," and 30 percent of Boomers said that not having a mentor "contributes to their job dissatisfaction." Those are very high numbers, especially when competitors are out there convincing your Boomers that changing jobs won't put them behind and may even get them ahead.

Generation Xers

For Gen Xers, who were labeled "job-hoppers" even before many of them could drive, job changing is a strategic imperative. The goal is to get as many skills and experiences on the résumé as possible, without looking like a complete flake. To Xers, job changing means making the calculated moves needed to make to feel that you will be hirable and desirable in the open market. Maybe that's one reason Generation X seems to be the most challenging generation for the other generations to manage. When our survey asked respondents which generation they felt most comfortable managing, only about 14 percent chose Generation X, *and this included the Xers themselves!* What can seem like a form of disloyalty to the Boomers and Traditionalists who are trying to manage them is just common sense to Xers. "Who knows where this company will be a year from now? I just need to be prepared in case anything should happen," said one satisfied employee taking business classes on weekends to prepare for his next career *just in case.*

The problem is that too many employers are using this as an excuse and comforting themselves with the belief that the Xers would have left anyway. That's a mistake, because many Xers are looking for organizations they can be loyal to. Employers can meet Xers' need to scavenge for that next skill set by helping them get their needs met *internally.* Xers don't necessarily have to leave to feel alive. They just need to be shown they're on a path that's going somewhere they want to go.

Millennials

For Millennials, who have mastered multitasking, "changing jobs" is something they will actually see as part of their daily schedule. They believe they can handle more than one job at a time. That might even mean that a Millennial will work in accounting three days a week and marketing the other two. The good news is that we're predicting they will be more loyal than Xers. The challenge in keeping them, however, will be providing direction, learning, stimulation, and the ability to take part and speak up early on. Strauss and Howe call this need for genuine participation the "loyalty/disloyalty paradox." That means a state in which an employee cares passionately about the work at hand and feels strong loyalty to see a project through to its successful conclusion, but at the same time retains just enough disloyalty to be willing to question the status quo. Is this product as good as it should be? Is our process or technology becoming obsolete? Are we really going in the right direction to outrun our competitors? If you thought Xers loathed the concept of dues paying, unless you ban it for the Millennials, you'll be the one paying the dues as you continually have to replace them.

DEADBOLTING THE REVOLVING DOOR

With all these forces making it more difficult to stop the revolving employment door from spinning faster and faster, you'd expect that organizations would be actively examining potential solutions to their retention problems. Not so, says a 2001 Watson Wyatt study entitled "Playing to Win: Strategic Rewards in the War for Talent": "Fewer than one in five organizations has a formal retention strategy despite the retention difficulties already discussed and the fact that firms with retention strategies generate significantly higher share-holder returns than those without."

Money makes the world go around, but not necessarily the door. When you ask about retention, employers tend to focus on compensation as the key, convinced that if they could wave more dollars at their employees, they wouldn't be waving good-bye. But in study after study, it's not the money that persuades generations of employees to stay: it's creating the right mix of financial, personal, and cultural factors that produce a sense of fit, loyalty, and opportunity. Not surprisingly, many of these factors have a generational component. After all, we've heard that generational differences are often part of what *attracts* individuals to a place of work. Why shouldn't the decision to *leave* also be generationally motivated?

As part of our BridgeWorks Survey, we asked the generations whether or not they knew if they could make more money elsewhere if they left their current job. We then asked those who said "Yes" why they stayed. The answers were intriguing from a generational perspective. The Traditionalists' top two reasons for staying had to do with loyalty to clients/customers and the amount of time off they had. That fits with our profile of Traditionalists as being extremely loyal but also beginning to find ways to downscale their work hours. Boomers' number one reason for staying was "making a difference," which we equate to their idealism and their strong desire to put their own stamp on things. Boomers selected all the other choices equally, leading us to believe that it's incredibly important to talk with Boomers about which parts of your value proposition are keeping them around and to pay attention when those things start to slip.

Among Xers, the overwhelming number one reason to stay was "autonomy." A perfect example is Generation Xer Jim Casey, a midlevel associate with the law firm of Alston & Bird. Traditionally in law firms, work is distributed via layers. A senior partner generates work and hands it off to a junior partner, who filters the project to a midlevel associate, who then might filter it even further down to an entry-level attorney. The problem is that this top-down distribution of work can make it really difficult for those lower on the totem pole to understand their role in the bigger picture.

In Jim's experience at Alston & Bird and in his area of practice (technology transactions), the firm's lawyers do a good job of eliminating the unnecessary fat in the middle. Junior associates work directly with senior lawyers and gain valuable experience. Since the day Jim got there, he's been given the opportunity to work on sophisticated projects. Because of this, midlevel and junior lawyers know how their work fits in with the bigger picture. As Jim put it, "I see the nature of the whole project and not a narrow perspective or snapshot. I truly understand how my work fits in . . . whether it's a small or large transaction. This really allows me to feel I am making a difference."

Lawyers at the firm use the word *own* a lot. The senior lawyers encourage the newer lawyers to "own" their work and their relationships with clients. For this to work, the senior lawyers must have a lot of trust that the junior lawyers will use their best judgment and ask for help when they need it. When senior attorneys have that kind of confidence in younger lawyers, it emboldens the junior lawyers and gives them a much greater stake in the work of the firm. The benefit is an energized, turned-on junior staff who appreciate the opportunities they've been given and do everything in their power to succeed. As Jim put it, "We have to learn on the job, and our culture truly allows us to do that successfully."

By eliminating the unnecessary filtering of work and fostering camaraderie among all generations of attorneys, a natural form of mentoring takes place. Jim mentioned Jay Krutulis, a new attorney fresh out of law school, who recently joined the firm. When Jim asked Jay why he liked Alston & Bird so much, the first words out of Jay's mouth were about the high level of responsibility he was given right away. In fact, during Jay's first months at the firm, he went to London and played an integral role in a high-profile project. Jay was impressed and empowered by the confidence the firm showed in him. Jim Casey explained, "We really focus on what it takes to have a 'special culture.' We all feel this is a special place to work." At Alston & Bird, senior lawyers often ask, "Are you happy here?" or, "What makes this a special place?" Just by having senior lawyers ask the question, they communicate they care about junior associates. It's no wonder *Fortune* magazine named Alston & Bird one of the one hundred best places to work in the country.

Among Xers' reasons to stay at a job, second place went to "good schedule" and in third place was "time off." Clearly, Xers value freedom and control over their schedules above all other things. Xers also scored high on "making a difference." We think that's because they so want to hit the ground running and do work that has an impact, as opposed to just paying dues. When we asked Xers the question "Besides myself, my strongest loyalty at work is to . . . ," "co-workers" came first, followed by their boss or their projects (which were tied for second place). Xers overwhelmingly put "my company" in last place.

Executives of an old-line national insurance company bragged

to us about the star Gen Xer who had made it into the top management ranks at their corporate headquarters. This was a talented individual in whom they saw tremendous potential. There was just one
catch—he was the *only* Generation Xer. When we spoke with him
privately, he confided he felt not only lonely, but very isolated in a
Traditionalist-dominated organization. He questioned whether he'd
be able to stay committed to such a slow-moving culture. The Traditionalist leaders, all good and caring people, seemed to feel he was
"one of them"—that once in the door, he would adapt to the way
they had always done business and buckle down to working his way
up the same ladder *they* had all climbed up on. He, on the other
hand, felt that his perspective as a Generation Xer was valuable. He
had no intention of doing things the way they had always been
done. Unless management wakes up to his uniqueness and begins to
value the strengths he brings to the table, they're going to lose one
of their most precious assets.

One of the most common starting points for companies trying to understand why they are losing people is the exit interview.
But too often this is nothing more than a fake exchange in which
the employee says he's leaving because of a "better opportunity,"
followed by, "Thanks for everything you've done, we'll miss you,
blah, blah, blah." Some firms have realized just how useless this is
and have looked outside to companies, such as Right Management
Consultants, who do the exit interviews for them in order to up
the value of the exit interview. A third-party objective resource,
they reason, is more likely to find out what's behind an employee
exodus.

Whether internal or external, if you are going to perform exit
interviews, make sure you do something with them. Don't treat
them as a meaningless formality; treat them as an educational opportunity. Make sure your exit interviewers are turned on to generational issues and aren't paralyzed by their own generational biases. A
Gen X human resources person in an advertising agency, for example, might hear an exiting Traditionalist say, "Everything here is too

automated and too fast paced. There's no pride in the quality of the work anymore." If the Xers write the Traditionalist off as someone who is too old to cut it anymore, then big issues may go unnoticed. The firm might have genuine problems with issues like training or work quality but fail to learn about them owing to generational blindness.

Likewise, we've heard Boomer exit interviewers declare, "All the people we're losing are Xers, because they have no work ethic and aren't willing to try to fit in." Is that *really* why? Again, a generational question is begging to be asked. Why aren't the Xers fitting in? Why aren't they more willing to be loyal? Is it a problem with the work ethic or the work? Paying attention to factors that directly impact a Generation Xer's loyalty can make a huge difference in retention. We know, for example, that while Xers might not feel strong loyalty to an organization, they can be incredibly loyal to peers, managers, and co-workers. We call this "indirect loyalty," and by understanding it, companies can influence an Xer's decision to stick around. In fact, in our survey, over 40 percent of Xers said that having a mentor directly influenced their decision to stay at their current company.

Obviously, these aren't the easiest problems to unearth. But unearth them we must, because they are often repairable. One accounting firm we spoke with reported that their Gen X accountants were leaving in droves. When we dug deeper, we found it was only the ones who were being "mentored" by *one* particular senior partner. The other Xers there were doing just fine. When the firm shifted responsibilities for managing new recruits to some of the other, more flexible partners, the bleeding stopped.

In other cases, examining turnover can help organizations realize blinding truths about their business strategies as well. One workshop we led for a huge national department store chain turned ugly when several Xers stood up and announced how frustrated they were with the direction of the chain's marketing focus. "I mean, here I am a buyer, supposedly stocking the latest trends, and I can't even shop here!" exclaimed one ticked-off Xer. "We aren't going after the Generation X customer at *all!*"

We were dazzled. This was priceless information for the company. And for free! They didn't even have to commission a month-long, million-dollar marketing study. Here was their own internal group of Gen Xers stirring up a mutiny because they felt the company was wrong about its fashion direction when it came to Generation X. That should have been a call to arms for any company trying to get its arms around the consumer. Not to mention that they clearly had some pretty angry employees they needed to get their arms around as well. To us, that exchange was nothing short of a gift.

But guess what happened? On the break, we headed for the snack table to buttonhole a couple of bigwigs to see how they were handling the morning's dust-up. Lynne cornered the senior vice president of marketing, a smooth, immaculately besuited Boomer, and asked him what he thought.

"Oh, the Xers," he said with a slight curl of his lip. "They're such an insignificant population. We've made billions by never marketing to them at all, and since the Boomers are going to be around for a long time to come, why change?"

He then sauntered back to his top-floor office, skipping out on the rest of the session and leaving us to mop up the excess of emotion around the strategic road not taken. Talk about disappointed. Here he had a prime opportunity to talk with his own Generation Xers who were dying to give their perspective on the company's marketing direction, *and he didn't want to hear it.* Since then, the company has continued to lose retail market share and seen streams of Xers jump ship for savvier companies that are more predisposed to listen.

There's obviously more to be learned from the generational retention story than meets the eye, especially when it comes to connecting turnover with company strategy. This isn't something you hear about a lot, but just as frost on the pumpkin indicates fall is coming, a downturn in the retention rate can be a harbinger of bad things to come from a strategic point of view.

We know that we said the exit interview is the first step, but in our opinion, the exit interview is only a last-ditch effort to gain insight into what went wrong. In fact, as a retention strategy, the exit interview may be just about the stupidest invention since the Pet Rock, since it institutionalizes the idea that you should find out what went wrong once it's too late to do anything about it.

The total quality movement told American industry to quit spending billions on inspectors to locate all the faulty products when they come off the line and instead institute processes that result in no faulty products coming off the line at all. In the same vein, organizations should ultimately spend their dollars not on interviewing employees who've already got both feet and their head out the door, but on interviewing the ones who still have their heads in their work and their butts in their chairs.

The bottom line is that if a certain generation isn't willing to stick around, perhaps there's something you need to learn *now* that could prevent major problems in the future. Companies that can diagnose whether they are losing Millennial new hires or Traditionalist supervisors can make a concerted effort to get a handle on why and then do something about it.

When we left off, Gen Xer Carolyn had just learned that her Boomer boss, Roger, had beaten her to the punch and was leaving. As a result, Carolyn now had to give her resignation to her Traditionalist supervisor, Donna. Carolyn didn't want to drop a bomb the same day Roger had quit, so she waited a few days. She feared that Donna would be shocked by what appeared to be Carolyn's lack of loyalty. As she stepped off the elevator, there stood Donna, holding a brown cardboard box. Carolyn peered inside and saw the entire contents of Donna's desk.

"Oh, dear, you look so surprised!" Donna exclaimed. "I have been with this company for twenty-two years and have decided it's time to go off on my own. I really agonized over this, but I feel in my heart it's the right thing to do. Please don't worry, I'll still be working with the company as a consultant and will make sure that all of your projects get a green light so you don't get held up during the transition. Plus, I put in a good word for you to get Roger's job. Good-bye!"

Carolyn stood under the fluorescent lights, blinking. Since when had Boomers and Traditionalists been so willing to leave? And who was going to get all the work done now?

16

IS NO NEWS REALLY GOOD NEWS?

When we give speeches together, we usually take a few minutes afterward to give each other feedback on how it went, what worked, and how we can make things even better the next time around. When we first started doing this, we immediately noticed something odd. Our feedback styles were completely different—Kaboom! Another generational collision in the making.

Lynne: David would jump in while we were still walking away from the podium: "Awesome, except for your one joke on page three that wasn't remotely funny. And I don't really think anyone understands that other part toward the end, except maybe Alan Greenspan. But otherwise, you were stellar."

David: Okay, but at least my feedback was clear and didn't feel like a Pentagon briefing! When Lynne would give me feedback, we had to be sitting down and of course facing each other, because of Boomer rule number one: Look the person in the eye when you're giving feedback.

So she'd start in: "Let's talk about page six. Great job," she would say with gusto. "Good eye contact, loved your gestures, timing was excellent. . . ." And all I could think about was Boomer rule number two: Always begin on a positive note!

Then she'd get all serious. "Now, before we discuss page twelve, let's first talk about page eleven." And I'd think to myself, *Oooh, don't tell me, Boomer rule number three: Ease into negative feedback!*

Then she would start to talk about page twelve and I'd be thinking, *Finally she's getting around to something I need to hear.* But she would go on and on: "On page twelve, it wasn't the tone, exactly, maybe it was more the timing, or possibly it could be that the phrasing was just the teeniest bit off, then again it could have been . . ."

Lynne: At some point he would lean across the table, look me square in the eye, and say in this tense, irritated voice, "Lynne! Is there any reason you can't just tell me that on page twelve, I sucked?!"

We didn't admit for a long time that we were bugging each other. David was popping off with feedback on the fly when Lynne couldn't even hear it because the audience was still clapping or she didn't have a pen or a place to write anything down. And Lynne was being so political and was taking so long to get around to the point that David would forget what speech she was even referring to.

Surprise, surprise . . . when it comes to feedback, the generations have different styles and expectations that are causing collisions at work.

THE COLLISION AROUND FEEDBACK

CLASHPOINT AROUND FEEDBACK

Traditionalists . . . *"No news is good news."*

Baby Boomers . . . *"Feedback once a year, with lots of documentation!"*

Generation Xers . . . *"Sorry to interrupt, but how am I doing?"*

Millennials . . . *"Feedback whenever I want it at the push of a button."*

Traditionalists

Ask a Traditionalist about feedback and you're likely to hear, *"Well, no news is good news. If I'm not yelling at you, you're probably doing fine."* The top-down, "boot camp" style of coaching made sense to a generation of veterans who valued authority and discipline. The strong, silent types who made up a generation of Traditionalist leaders weren't long on praise (they weren't even long on words), but when they said something about your performance, they meant it. And you'd better listen up.

Baby Boomers

That worked fine, until along came a generation of Boomers raised with the pop psychology of the sixties that said people should open up. Suddenly, "letting it all hang out" was good, being "uptight" was bad. Boomers were in touch with their feelings and in love with communication. In contrast with the silent stoicism of the Traditionalists, Boomers believed the truth would "set you free."

Boomers' motivation for exchanging tons of information wasn't as pure as it sounds. They were highly competitive. You don't enter the work world with eighty million cohorts competing with you for the same jobs without being obsessed with knowing how you're doing. The fact that the Traditionalists weren't exactly forthcoming made the need to know even more intense. So what did Boomers do? They adopted the *once-a-year performance appraisal, with lots of documentation in the file.* It forced Traditionalist role models, bosses, and mentors to sit down with Boomers on a regular basis and let them know where they stood. To make the Traditionalists more comfortable, there were forms to be filled out in advance with numerical rating systems that made feedback less subjective and so scientific that you would have thought they were trying to calculate the next solar eclipse.

Generation Xers

Everything went fine, for a while. Boomers knew the rules and played by them. Then along came Generation X. Suddenly you're a Boomer manager in a meeting with your Gen X direct reports. You sign off on the project and head back to your office to try to nab five minutes to get caught up on your paperwork. Two seconds later, there's one of the Xers knocking at your door: "Uh, can we talk about how I'm doing on the project?" They want instantaneous, immediate feedback! And how annoying is that to a Boomer who is dying to say, "Can't we just talk about it next week at the project review?" In fact, we've asked numerous overstretched Boomer bosses the best way for managers to handle that situation, and you know what they tell us? "Keep your door locked!"

All we know is that differences in expectations about feedback can create major generational collisions wherever you work. Xers want to know how they're doing *now.* In fact, when asked in our survey how frequently they would like to receive feedback after completing a project, 90 percent of Xers said they want feedback immediately or within a few days. But many aren't getting it. In fact, almost 30 percent of the BridgeWorks Generations Survey respondents said they receive their phone bill more often than they get relevant feedback! Boomers are comfortable waiting for feedback until the next scheduled meeting, and Traditionalists might be willing to wait until the next performance appraisal. We can only imagine what the Millennials will expect!

The best way we've found to explain the clash around feedback expectations is to take a look at the ways the generations have historically interacted with technology. After all, technology defines how much and how fast we communicate with each other. Consider this:

For most Traditionalists growing up, "on-line" was where the clean laundry was hung out to dry! Interoffice communication was conducted in meetings or sent via memo. Correspondence with clients went regular mail. If you received bad news, you usually had a few days to compose your thoughts before you had to respond in writing. Books of form letters were popular guides for helping people master polite, formal business communication. Lead times for planning and executing formal communications were much longer than they are today.

Think how the pace of communication has changed for ensuing generations.

Boomers saw the U.S. mail abandoned in favor of FedEx. Messages that had taken days to arrive now appeared overnight. Combine that with the downsizing that occurred in the 1980s and companies were suddenly running leaner and meaner, with fewer staffers to perform all the complicated functions formerly regarded as routine. With flatter organizations and the advent of the personal computer, Boomer executives had to become fluent at writing and sending their own messages.

For Generation Xers, the level of immediacy was even more intense. Xers never had to merge onto the information superhighway; they were born in the fast lane. And they've been raised in a culture of instant results. Whether it's instant meals from the microwave, instant cash from the ATM, instant news from CNN, or instant information from the Web, whenever they've wanted something, they've been able to get it. Is it any wonder they expect instant feedback at work?

Karen Ritchie, author of *Marketing to Generation X,* said it best when she noted, "Xers want to monitor their performance at work the way they monitor their bank accounts with ATMs—instantly, exactly, and often."

Millennials

If that's true for Xers, imagine what we can expect from the Millennial generation. With bandwidth widening the lanes of the information superhighway, this generation will be kicking into overdrive while most of us are still back at the wayside rest.

Soon after the Columbine shootings, an audience member approached us to say she had a story to share. She lived near the tragedy and heard about the shootings almost as soon as they happened. "It was so interesting how the generations plugged in to get their information," she explained. "The Traditionalists tuned in to the CBS affiliate on their radios. The Boomers turned on the major television networks, and the Xers were all glued to CNN. But the Millennials got on-line and within an hour had put up their *own* Web sites so they could exchange up-to-the-minute information. It scared me how different we all were, and how different the Millennials will always be because of the Internet."

Think Xers are agitating for the most up-to-date feedback? Well, Millennials will want it up-to-the minute! It's no wonder that when it comes to expectations about feedback, the generations have four very different notions of the word *timely*.

FORMAL VS. FRANK

The generations also collide around feedback when it comes to style. "The older generations are so cautious and political in the way they phrase everything that half the time I don't know what they mean," complained one Xer. "It's like, 'This feedback was edited for content and reformatted to fit your screen.' "

Lynne learned this lesson early on when communicating with Dan and Bradley, her Generation X stepsons. She once tried to explain to them why she found their table manners so questionable. "You see, when you're part of a family system, in which all the parties have mutual respect and caring, it's important to recognize the cultural norms and behave appropriately in a setting of mutual respect. . . ."

After a few moments of this, both boys turned to their Traditionalist dad in unison to have him explain what she was talking about. Allan, as their father, knew exactly what to do; he turned to the boys and barked, "Dammit! You both need to use a fork!" Problem solved. It took a while for Lynne to realize that carefully phrased input wasn't what her two Gen Xers wanted to hear. They wanted straight talk.

When it comes to feedback, Traditionalists learned from the military model to button it up and listen hard to the voice of authority. Obedience was paramount, and talking back was out of the question. They knew enough to stand up straight and listen hard when they were being reprimanded, and they went out of their way to show that they heard the message loud and clear.

Boomers, on the other hand, made doublespeak a part of their style at an early age. Traditionalist parents taught them that there were certain things you didn't talk about, like money, sex, and getting ahead. They rebelled against this in their personal lives by starting support groups, therapy groups, and anger management groups to help them let it all hang out in private. But in the public world of work, Boomers learned to be much more circumspect. With too many people competing for too few jobs, and with so many Boomer subordinates reporting to so few Traditionalist bosses, it was dog-eat-dog. As much as Boomers might have liked each other, they've always known, deep down, that they were competitors for scarce corporate resources. But although Boomers had to compete, they also had to get along and get work done. Therefore, political Boomer language evolved to enable Boomers to give feedback messages without making them sting and to share information without threatening another person's power base (unless that's what they intended to do!). "Weaknesses" became "areas of opportunity." The candidate who got the promotion wasn't "better than you," it's just that "his qualifications were a tighter fit for the nuances of the position." And just to be sure they all heard the same thing, there was loads of documentation that went into the file.

For Generation Xers, the formal and political approach was too slick. Being raised on television, they saw countless ad campaigns that promised the world and delivered nothing. As a result, they didn't just watch advertising messages, they deconstructed them. They acted as if they believed the famous line from *The Godfather,* "Behind every great fortune, there is a great crime." Behind every great advertising claim, there was undoubtedly a great lie. To a Generation Xer, feedback that's not straight talk is no more reliable than the ad for the Super Slice-O-Rama that was supposed to cut through wood but barely made it through a stick of butter. As a result, when it comes to feedback, the more raw, the more real.

Put these styles together, and the feedback a Traditionalist thinks is informative and helpful can seem formal and preachy to the

Boomers and the Xers. Feedback a Boomer thinks is fair and judicious can seem uptight and overly political to a Generation Xer or a Traditionalist. Feedback a Generation Xer thinks is immediate and honest can seem hasty or even inappropriate to the other generations. Clearly, the generations have not signed off on what the feedback contract is supposed to look like.

And we don't yet know what the Millennials' preferred feedback style will be. They will definitely want communicative coaches and mentors who can model the right behavior and explain to them when something goes wrong, but technology will play a big factor in the work lives of Millennials as well. In *The One to One Future,* Don Peppers and Martha Rogers explore how information technology can allow companies to capture personal data about millions of customers, enabling them to offer personalized service in mass quantities. For example, a hotel might capture a regular client's preferences such as favorite type of pillow, preferred type of room, or desired room temperature and use that information to make sure the guest has a customized experience the next time he or she arrives.

Similarly, we believe the one-to-one future will also play out for Millennials in the form of feedback. Technology will enable companies to gather information about performance and provide instantaneous feedback to employees. For example, one of our clients, a major hair salon chain, uses software that will allow them to capture productivity information throughout the day for each employee. At the end of a shift, each Millennial stylist can receive a printout from the register that tells her how many clients she saw that day, how much she took in per customer in both services and products sold, what her total sales were for the day, and how her performance compared to that of everyone else on her shift.

Some new types of software, like Digital Dashboard, make it even easier for people to track their job performance instantly. Bill Barberg is the president and founder of Insight Formation, the Minnesota-based consulting firm that invented the performance tool called Digital Dashboard. "Because Digital Dashboard is per-

sonalized, individuals can pull up a screen to see how they are pro-
gressing in each of several key performance areas right from their
own desks." Obvious sources of information might include personal
sales results or departmental production measures, but data related to
training or customer satisfaction can also be displayed. Supervisors
and employees agree upon an individualized scorecard, and then the
software uses a combination of charts, tables, and colors to track an
employee's progress toward key goals with the push of a button.
"High visibility of performance measures dramatically increase their
power," notes Barberg. "Digital Dashboard improves both communication and motivation."

With systems like these, Millennials can expect to receive
immediate, targeted feedback at the push of a button. A company
will be able to control which factors they choose to measure and
reward. Eventually employees will be able to examine their performance over the past day, week, month, or year. While there's
nothing quite like a boss you respect telling you what a great job you
did or how to improve, technology can provide personalized and
factual feedback on an employee's performance. As such, it stands to
become an increasingly important factor in disseminating feedback
in the coming years.

A TIME AND A PLACE FOR EVERYTHING

The last thing Traditionalists and Boomers need are lessons on the
ideal setting to give feedback. These generations have been coached
to death on choosing the right time and place to make the employee
feel comfortable and receptive and yet not so casual that the message
isn't taken seriously. If today's Generation X and Millennial employees could give one message to the older generations around feedback, it would be "Lighten up."

However, Generation Xers and Millennials could benefit from

some coaching in terms of time and place. While there is something to be said for a relaxed attitude, many Traditionalists and Boomers feel the younger generations are a bit too comfy. They're not imagining things.

A Boomer told us she was crossing the parking lot on the way to her car after work with a bunch of colleagues when an Xer co-worker yelled at her from about fifty yards away, "Hey, Sharon, too bad about that meeting—that had to be so embarrassing! But that project is going down the tubes anyway, so don't worry about it! We'll see you tomorrow."

The Xer was simply trying to buck up her comrade by telling her that the meeting was stupid and the project was a loser anyway, so get over it. The Boomer was mortified. How could anyone mention her embarrassment in public when she was so unprepared to talk about it? Besides, while everyone knew that project was on its way out, the powers-that-be hadn't acknowledged it yet, so it was totally inappropriate for the Xer to say it out loud!

The younger generations are so used to getting and sending information via technology, they often forget that the human hard drive does have a soft spot. They haven't been taught some of the basics about time and place. Sometimes they need to get burned to fully "get it." One Xer was furious after her Boomer boss pointed out flaws in her work in front of her peers. When she cornered her boss after the meeting, he simply responded, "If you don't want to hear negative feedback in front of your peers, then you should quit asking me how you're doing in the middle of a meeting!"

If you find yourself taken aback by Xers' lack of concern for the appropriate time and place for giving feedback, the last thing you want to do is get mad at them. Instead, use the opportunity to coach them. In our survey, we learned that 45 percent of Xers had never received training on how to *give* feedback, and almost 65 percent of Xers had never received training in how to *receive* feedback. Is it any wonder Boomers get flustered when confronted by an angry e-mail from an Xer wondering what went wrong with a project? We believe training employees on the ins and outs of appropriate feedback presents a real area of opportunity. What a great way to reduce the potential for collisions and ratchet up the information flow!

THE NUMBERS ARE THERE

The clash around feedback goes way beyond the annoying or embarrassing dust-ups you may have experienced at work. The international human resources consulting firm Watson Wyatt Worldwide found in a recent study that "71% of top performers who received regular feedback were likely to stay on the job versus just 43% who didn't receive it." That means that even among peak performers, feedback plays a vital role in an employee's decision to stay in a job. Which means, of course, that quality of feedback, or lack of it, has a direct relationship to turnover.

In another study, the National Association of Legal Practitioners found that the number one cause of turnover among third-year Generation X legal associates was lack of feedback.

Too many leaders do not realize that the collision around feedback inevitably percolates down to the bottom line. The need for more and better feedback is pressing at all levels. In our survey, the generations were amazingly consistent in this need; over half of each generation said they do not get relevant feedback on the job. When generations of workers can't talk to one another about performance, the company suffers. Workers don't know how they're doing or where they're going. Bosses can't communicate their goals or explain what they need in terms of performance. Frustrations turn to silences, which eventually, sadly, turn to severed relationships and, often, severance altogether.

CLARIFY HOW OFTEN AND THROUGH WHAT MEANS

With four generations in the workplace, each struggling to keep up with increasingly rapid demands for information from customers, boards, bosses, and each other, everyone feels pressured to master feedback.

"I'll have someone from my generation get in touch with someone from your generation."

When we started working together, we thought the best thing we had going as business partners was excellent communication. We really liked each other. We shared a common vision, and we were working together on a project we both cared about. We assumed that was enough to put us on the same communication wavelength. Think again. . . .

Ring, ring . . .

DAVID: Hi, I e-mailed you twenty minutes ago. Did you get it?

LYNNE: Uh, no, I was working on something.

DAVID: Oh . . . don't you check them?

LYNNE: (Defensively) Well, I usually check them later in the day, like around five.

DAVID: But there's a time difference, so that would be seven at night my time. Maybe I should just ask you about this while I have you on the phone and then you could read my e-mail tomorrow. Or I could always fax it to you.

LYNNE: Why did you call me anyway?

DAVID: To see if you got my e-mail.

LYNNE: But if you were calling me, why did you even send the e-mail?

DAVID: Because e-mail is usually the fastest and most pain-free way to communicate.

LYNNE: For whom?

DAVID: (Defensively) You seem kind of testy. Bad day?

LYNNE: I have to go now.

DAVID: But what about my e-mail?

LYNNE: *Click.*

Unfortunately, this conversation actually took place. More than once.

To Lynne, "being responsive" meant she'd get back to David on whatever it was in the next day or two. To David, that was an interminable length of time, during which he was aging visibly. He needed the feedback right away, so he could get on with his project.

Both of us were frustrated . . . until we talked it over. The best way to solve these challenges is to take the time to agree up front on how often to check in and what method to use. Eventually, we got really good at stating what we needed from the other person in order to move ahead with our projects. And we started feeling less frustrated. Lynne could get the uninterrupted time she needed, and David could be reassured he'd get the feedback or input he required. Phew! If it's that much work in a firm with just a few people, we can only imagine what it feels like to be at General Motors.

While we're constantly learning from our clients and tweaking the system, our best advice is to decide with your team what works in terms of . . .

Format

One Xer disgustedly exclaimed that his Boomer boss wanted him to come in to his office for a "check-in" meeting. "What's wrong with that?" we asked.

"Well, I talked to her in the parking lot this morning, and I thought that *was* our check-in."

Managers cannot assume that employees innately know when, where, or how they should check in with their bosses. And employees should not assume that the way they've always done things is going to work for a boss from another generation.

Feedback can be given in person, by telephone, via e-mail or voice mail, by a written memo, or in meetings. At a recent workshop with a group of Traditionalist and Boomer sales managers from 3M, one shared that he was getting frustrated because one of his Generation X reps wasn't returning his phone calls. When they finally connected, the manager asked about the rep's lack of response. The rep explained that he checks voice mails only every couple of days, but that he receives e-mails right to his PalmPilot and responds instantaneously. Once they cleared this up, they were able to save days of frustration.

Frequency

Key questions should be answered from the get-go. Is it okay to wait until the end of the project and discuss how it went? Do the generations agree on how often they should be sharing feedback along the way? A one-size-fits-all approach usually will not work. But if you can be aware of everyone's different sizes, there will be fewer mishaps and everyone will be a lot more comfortable.

Style

You can't believe how many complaints we hear about etiquette when it comes to feedback. One Xer was taken aback when she received an angry-sounding e-mail from her Traditionalist supervisor. However, when the Xer asked her manager about it later, he was anything *but* upset. So what went wrong? The Traditionalist had typed the e-mail using all capital letters. He had no idea that he had just "flamed" his employee or that using all caps meant you were angry about something.

Ken Ritter, a training manager at Coca-Cola Enterprises in Atlanta, mentioned to us how surprised he was at the difference in feedback styles he noticed when conducting training in Great Britain. "I couldn't believe how brutally honest the British participants were with each other. They were perfectly willing to say, 'Positively awful!' when a colleague screwed up. It's the style they were used to."

Ken's example made us realize just how culturally determined feedback styles can be. If style can be dictated by nationality, then they can certainly be dictated by corporate culture. It would help a lot if the generations could talk about how feedback typically works in their corporate culture and what's expected of them.

It is vital to confirm your expectations with the team up front so that everyone knows what to expect. "Our Xers didn't want to have a lot of in-person meetings because many of them work remotely, so we do most of our updates and give each other feedback via e-mail," explained a Boomer running a research team. "But I also need some face time with my people, and I think they benefit from working out problems together, so we meet in person in the office once a week to touch base."

Clients will also appreciate this clarification. Deanna, in our office, asks all clients their preferred mode of communication. Some prefer to hear from her via e-mail because they're on the road all the time. Others are in their cars so much that cell phones are easiest. Still others want updates in writing so they have documentation of what's been accomplished or agreed upon. The point is, you can't imagine how grateful people are to be asked that simple question. In fact, Deanna often hears, "You know, you're the first vendor to ask me that. Thank you!"

FEEDBACK NEEDS TO GO BOTH WAYS . . . UP *AND* DOWN

What the chain-of-command model didn't advocate, the younger generations are insisting upon—that is, feedback needs to travel *up* the ladder as well as *down*. Where politically conscious Boomers would have thought twice (or more) before telling the boss what was wrong with the way the department was being managed, Xers and Millennials seem to have no problem being up front with their higher-ups. That can sometimes be seen as a real positive, but not always.

"I feel like the Xers are so 'in your face,' " explained one Traditionalist manager. "Not only am I sometimes shocked by how direct they are when they ask me for feedback, I'm shocked by how willing they are to give *me* feedback, whether I asked for it or not."

The problem is that organizations can be pretty good at downward feedback, but not so good when it comes to sending information back *up* the ladder. Xers tell us they want to be able to give feedback to their higher-ups, but they don't feel it's welcome. "Everyone is happy to tell me what I can be doing better, and that's fine. But there are a lot of things they could be doing to manage me better and handle our client load better, and no one seems to want to hear that," complained one frustrated Xer.

This type of honesty is a rare and valuable commodity in organizations, and it should be nurtured. Management consultant Steve Lundin calls this ability to speak the truth even when it might upset others in an organization "being up tough," and he highly recommends its value to organizations. "Up tough means being willing to tell the truth to others in your organization even when it's something they don't want to hear." Embracing the "up tough" notion will be even more critical as Millennials come to work. They are accustomed to questioning authority even while respecting it because they've been raised being asked for their opinions. How many Traditionalists or Boomers were asked when they were kids to plan the family vacation or help research which car to buy? Why wouldn't Millennials feel it is their place to pipe up on topics as large as strategic planning?

In a learning organization, information should flow in all directions, and no one should shoot the messenger when the feedback is bad news. But that's going to happen only if people of all generations feel clear on the expectations and safe in the execution. One way to create a safety net is to install individuals as "generational sounding boards." Two co-managers we interviewed at Ceridian Corporation, one an Xer, the other a Boomer, juggle a workforce that ranges in age from high schoolers to "old schoolers" in their seventies. What they've found is that the younger people always take their problems to the Xer manager, while the older employees tend to confide in the older manager. "It works for us," they explained. "As long as the employees feel comfortable, we feel comfortable."

Another senior manager in a large consulting office held weekly bag lunches in the conference room and invited everyone in the department to attend. It was a way to get to know people, to share information informally, and to let employees know what was going on in the company. The side benefit was that employees let him know a lot about what was going on with them, too, in a non-threatening setting.

Whatever the method, the most successful leaders find ways to let every generation be heard, even if that means being open to constructive criticism from someone who was born the year you got promoted to vice president! At the same time, Xers and Millennials should work at making feedback to their Traditionalist and Boomer bosses polite, respectful, nonthreatening, and nonconfrontational. Then, rather than be so impatient for an answer, give them time to reflect and prepare a response.

And the smartest leaders will do just that—show that they have listened and are willing to act on what they heard. After all, feedback that percolates up from below is useless if no one does anything about it.

TRAIN, TRAIN, TRAIN

When we conducted our BridgeWorks Generations Survey, we somewhat expected to find that the younger generations hadn't received a lot of training on feedback, but we hoped that the older generations had been more thoroughly coached. Not true. Instead, we were concerned to find that while 90 percent of Traditionalist respondents said they were managing others, over 50 percent of them said they had never received training in feedback skills. This points to the idea that management skills training isn't just for new managers. It should be offered to every generation of managers, with updates available as needed. All the generations should be trained in how to ask for feedback, how to give it, how to receive it, and what's appropriate behavior in feedback situations. Too many people receive this type of training only when they move up to management. Why not train everyone on the rudiments of who the generations are and how we should communicate with one another?

Part of training on feedback should also deal with documentation. Xers and Millennials tell us they think Boomers and Traditionalists overdo it. The older generations tell us the younger ones just don't get why it's so important. A compromise is probably in order. Traditionalists and Boomers might want to take a look at their forms and policies and see if there is room for some streamlining. At the same time, Xers and Millennials need to understand the legal reasons behind most documentation, and they need to know that not all documentation is bad.

Which brings us to our final point.

HARNESS THE POWER OF POSITIVE FEEDBACK

Norman Vincent Peale, a highly respected Traditionalist and role model for several generations, had it right when he wrote his famous book on the power of positive thinking. We want to take it one step further. When you want to reach out to someone from another generation, there's nothing quite like the power of positive feedback. We've found that however hard it is to get the tough messages out there, it's even harder to get the positive messages out. And sadly, *all* the generations, no matter how cocky or self-assured they may seem, are starved for positive feedback.

Traditionalists are often so competent and experienced, and have been around so much longer than everyone else, that we forget how much they still need to hear the occasional word of praise. While many Traditionalists perform hard tasks as a matter of course ("because it's my job, not because I'm looking for applause," as one Traditionalist put it), they still appreciate a quiet word telling them their efforts were noticed and that they made a difference.

Boomers are busy managing up to four generations of direct reports at work and at home. At this stage, they spend so much time *giving* feedback to everybody else, they don't always receive any themselves—especially the positive stuff. Before organizations became so flat, there were more layers of management and fewer direct reports for each manager. With the disappearance of these protective layers of fat, feedback in many organizations has gotten a little too thin. Boomers may be giving feedback to dozens of employees without receiving any themselves. And, as Boomers struggle to connect with an ever-younger workforce, they can be particularly touched by feedback from an Xer telling them they did something right.

Xers need positive feedback to tell them when they're on the right track. As one twenty-five-year-old magazine editor told us, "Some of us have been promoted so fast, we're afraid to admit what we don't know." Telling them what they're doing right reinforces the proper behavior and eliminates some of the guesswork for a generation struggling to fit in. But remember, Xers have a sensitive BS-O-Meter, so if you praise them, be sure you mean it and can prove it.

Millennials have been raised by Boomer parents whose belief in the "I'm okay, you're okay" style of communication taught their children to expect lots of praise. Millennials are likely to mistake silence for disapproval and can easily become discouraged if they don't receive a reasonable amount of verbal strokes. Managers should make a special effort to talk to Millennials about what they're doing right. This rewards good behavior and strengthens rapport. That doesn't mean managers need to be soft on Millennials. But lots of feedback, both positive and negative, is the best way to go.

WE SHALL OVERCOME

Having struggled through our own feedback collision, we found ourselves a few months later wrapping up a speech in Atlanta. As we walked through the convention center hall together, Lynne turned to David, zapped his PalmPilot with hers, and commented, "There's your feedback; I jotted it down during the closing remarks."

"Thanks," David said, grinning, as he pocketed his PalmPilot. "I wrote your feedback out as well, and I'll be happy to go over it with you while we're sitting down to lunch."

17

THE SCHOOL BELL IS RINGING MORE LOUDLY THAN EVER

Four learners sit staring blankly at the teacher. Computer monitors glare on each desk. In the flickering light, Benjamin, a Millennial, looks uncomfortable. He already learned this stuff in high school but doesn't want to embarrass anyone by letting on. Jenny, the Xer, stifles a yawn. She likes to learn by doing, and the instructor is into his second hour of lecturing. Dave, the Baby Boomer, keeps checking his watch. He had to cancel four meetings just to come to this training, but so far he hasn't heard a thing that applies to his current job. Traditionalist Sheldon squirms in the uncomfortable chair. He wants to learn about computers, but his back is already killing him and it is only the first day of training.

TRAINING THE GENERATIONS

Four learners, four levels, four learning styles . . . something corporate training has not been accustomed to. Not long ago, if you scanned the corporate classroom, you would have seen the younger generations grouped together with their peers, who were similar in age, job grade, and experience level. Being *new* to the workplace, *they* were the ones who needed the training. Once in a while, you would find the older generations in front of the blackboard, but that exposure was usually limited to executive retreats, where they would *not* have mixed with the elementary students.

Today, if you look out onto the training horizon, you won't see a homogeneous group of students. Instead, you will uncover a classroom more like a corporate Montessori, with four generations of students coming together to learn. With more generations than ever before attending training, it's no wonder that organizations and trainers are struggling to cope with the challenge of multigenerational groups of students, each with a wide range of experience levels and, more important, varied training needs.

IT'S WAY COOL TO BE IN SCHOOL

There are definitely reasons why, more than ever before, the generations' ears are tuned to the corporate school bell. Trends in the economy as well as the training industry itself are ringing out loud and clear.

The Strong Economy

The economic boom in the 1990s enabled companies to afford more training, which allowed more generations to hit the classroom. Companies have also had more positions to fill, which meant they have had to train and promote all generations more aggressively. As qualified employees became harder to find, some employers had to lower hiring standards, which meant doing even more training to get employees up to speed so they could successfully fill open positions.

The Rate of Change

The world is changing at such a rapid pace that training that used to be regarded as a nice "perk" has now become a necessity for managing in the business world. George Heenan, Executive Fellow at the University of St. Thomas Institute for Strategic Management in St. Paul, Minnesota, has noticed an overall increase in the demand for training, possibly due to a "higher sensitivity to the fact that the world is changing." Organizations need to keep employees on the cutting edge so they can adapt rapidly to changing business trends. A lot of Traditionalist and Boomer executives are attending classes because they fear being left behind. Generations of employees who are concerned about staying current increasingly see training as a benefit in this tight labor market.

More Accessibility

Training is no longer restricted to the four walls in which we work every day. Obviously, not every place of employment has its own training facility, let alone a designated department. As a result, we have seen many universities and management schools offer partnerships to fill this void. With these educational outlets, companies are finding it much more cost-effective to cover the price per head, rather than create their own overhead.

Accessibility is going even further—suddenly the Web is now a classroom. Computer-based training has been a hot trend for some time. Its ability to allow adult learners to go at their own pace has proven to be successful. And as bandwidth expands by the day, the World Wide Web is allowing more employees to log on and learn. Although high tech is often perceived as high priced, in the training arena it may just be the best bargain of all when you factor in some of the costs involved in traditional training, such as flying everyone in to one location, putting them up in hotels, covering meals, and so on. Wilsons Leather has been a pioneer with on-line training. Raelyn Trende, human resources representative for Wilsons Leather, put it this way: "Our business is so fast paced that it would be easy to blow off the need for training. At the same time, because it is such a fast-paced environment, that's all the more reason to continually train employees." The on-line classroom can meet this challenge by giving employees access to the learning they need, but best of all at the time and place that work best without interrupting work flow.

With trends like these putting a whole new emphasis on training, it's no wonder we're seeing today's classroom host more generations as they climb the corporate ladder. But it shouldn't be surprising that the generations view training from different perspectives.

CLASHPOINT AROUND TRAINING

Traditionalists . . .	*"I learned it the hard way; you can, too!"*
Baby Boomers . . .	*"Train 'em too much and they'll leave."*
Generation Xers . . .	*"The more they learn, the more they stay."*
Millennials . . .	*"Continuous learning is a way of life."*

Traditionalists

We recently met a Generation Xer who had joined a union and was working in the shipping industry on the San Francisco docks. As he talked about the complexities of the job and all the well-seasoned Traditionalists he worked with, we commented to him, "Wow, you must receive some intense training being around so many more experienced workers." He laughed as he replied, "Yeah, that would be nice, but the way they teach around here is they pretty much just yell at the new guys and laugh at us until we learn the system."

That summed up the way a lot of Traditionalists were trained to do their jobs. Author Harvey Mackay has often described his first experience as a trainee in the exciting world of envelope sales. An experienced "old grizzly" slammed a mammoth phone book down on Mackay's rickety desk, shoved a telephone toward him, and growled, "Here you go. Start calling." From these harsh beginnings, Traditionalists attended the school of hard knocks until they eventually mastered the game. Thus, the "I learned it the hard way; you can, too!" mentality we sometimes encounter when we talk with Traditionalists about training. Traditionalists today complain to us that the younger learners have no idea how spoiled they are. As one explained, "I have this employee who is so upset because two classes he is interested in are offered at the same time and he therefore has to choose just one. I feel like shaking him and saying, 'You have anything *but* a problem, so quit your whining!' " In a lot of ways, we have to agree. Too many of us take for granted the plethora of learning opportunities that are available in organizations. But at the same time, the school of hard knocks can be a pretty inefficient way to get an education. Why let valuable employees flounder around learning the hard way when you can save time, money, and frustration by giving them the tools they need right from the start?

Baby Boomers

Training for this massive generation was a perk and a way to show you were getting ahead of the pack. But limiting who went to class was also the result of an attitude that too much training could be a bad thing. The old mentality was, "If I teach you too much, you're more adept and therefore likely to leave." Training was like feeding a horse enough hay to stay in the race, but never enough to actually win. This approach made a lasting impression on Boomers that is still at play in today's workplace. Many Xers complain to us that their Boomer bosses are holding them back, only for the bosses to explain to us that they have a fiercely independent Xer workforce that can be tempted to walk out the door if they get a better offer. As one Boomer put it, "I feel I've gotten way too good at training a workforce for my competitors!"

Generation Xers

When it comes to retaining Xers, training can be an important tool. Xers need to feel they are constantly learning new skills that will make them more valuable within their companies and on the job market. In the BridgeWorks Generations Survey, 58 percent of Xers agreed with the statement "Training opportunities play a role in my staying at my company." Generation Xers want to feel they are constantly developing a portfolio of skills and experiences that will help them land on their feet should a crisis erupt. Given the rapid rate of change and the intense pressure for employees to be prepared in case they should find themselves out of a job, we've seen a steady shift in the willingness of employees to leave an organization if they feel they aren't receiving enough training. When asked, "Have you ever left a job because of a lack of training opportunities?" only 3 percent of Traditionalists responded, "Yes," compared with 15 percent of Boomers and *30 percent* of Xers!

Companies that have picked up on this are realizing that robust training departments can be an ace in the hole when it comes to recruitment and retention. In contrast with the Baby Boomers, who feared too much training might cause employees to leave, the Generation Xers' mantra is "The more they learn, the more they stay."

Millennials

Because this generation is engrossed in school and college right now, they are in peak learning mode. Their next natural step will be to enter the work world, where, for a time, the learning curve will remain high. Eventually, however, the learning should level off and Millennials will be expected to apply what they've spent their lives learning and create value for their employers and the U.S. economy. But this is a pattern that must change. To assume that Millennials will ever be finished with training is a huge mistake. This generation will not understand the leveling-off concept. Given their familiarity with the Internet and the rapid rate of change they've coped with throughout their lives, Millennials will constantly expect to retool themselves to fit into an ever-changing world and job market. The Millennials are poised to become our first true generation of lifetime learners, and the companies that will succeed with this generation will be the ones who just keep on teaching.

Yes, we have four different generations coming at training from unique perspectives. But whereas in other workplace environments having four generations together can be a real headache, in the classroom it can be a real pleasure—and a learning experience in itself!

THE ADVANTAGE OF A "GENERATIONAL MONTESSORI"

Creating training groups that are generationally diverse can be a true advantage for participants. As Bill Scheurer, director of the Carlson School of Management Executive Development Program, put it, "We want the diversity of older generations working with younger generations of students because it's more realistic and more reflective of the community in which they live and work."

When workers are trying to better themselves to help in the overall strategy of running the day-to-day businesses, generational mixing can be the best lesson of all as the younger generations get to tap into the years of work experience the older generations have, and the older generations can learn about the values and expectations of the younger generations.

While we would all like to think that this takes place on a daily basis, we have found that classrooms are even more effective because they level the playing field. George Heenan from the University of St. Thomas reports that he still sees a lot of Traditionalists who are not getting it. As he put it, "They are still wondering why turnover is on the rise and why they can't get things done that they used to. The classroom setting is perfect, because the Traditionalists are on an equal level with younger students. Therefore, they can hear and learn firsthand from the younger generations."

But don't think that it will happen automatically in the classroom. It still takes a little effort. When people choose their own seats in a training class, they tend to gravitate toward those who look like them. Naturally. That's whom we're comfortable with. But unless some effort is put into mixing, the generations' training experience won't be maximized.

YOU'VE MASTERED THE THREE Rs—NOW LEARN THE THREE Ss

While the different generations of students can get a real bang to the brain from mixing with one another, it can be a real drain on the brain if you are the one in charge of teaching them. This should come as no surprise, but each of the generations has different attitudes and expectations toward learning. Trainers need to educate themselves on these generational differences before they call class to order. We call these lessons "the three Ss": setting, style, and substance.

Setting

"Casual" may be "in," but it still hasn't translated to "comfortable" in many workplace training environments. It seems the belief still lingers that the more sterile the environment, the more serious the content, but it makes no sense for training rooms to be designed only for convenience and not for comfort as well. While this may be a less important issue for Generation Xers and Millennials who are still willing to camp out for days on the hard pavement for concert tickets, it has definitely become an issue for the older generations as they rage against age. Sitting on hard plastic chairs under weak lighting for hours can feel more like detention to those who are starting to wear bifocals and feel the aches and pains of arthritis.

As the generations age, companies need to make sure training facilities don't and that they are keeping up with what it takes to suit the older generations' physical needs. The University of St. Thomas, for example, recently ordered new, more comfortable chairs, in part because they saw a growing number of aging Traditionalists and Baby Boomers among their core clientele.

But it takes more than comfortable chairs with back support to make a suitable training setting. If you are going to have handouts or project images on a screen, it is important that participants' eyes don't have to strain to read them. Too often these materials are created by someone younger who can still boast of having twenty-twenty vision. It can go a long way if these materials are tested by learners whose eyesight is no longer twenty-twenty. The eyesight factor also applies to the lighting in the room. Too much glare or too much darkness can be hard on older eyes. But the wrong lighting can irritate any learner. If the room has poor controls, at least advise learners on where they might sit if they prefer more, or less, light.

It surprises us how often we have to remind trainers of the importance of taking enough breaks. Let's face it, everyone loves recess. Learners, especially older ones, get stiff when they sit too long, and the younger ones get antsy. Ideally, they should be able to get up and stretch. As with any meeting, if there is food, people are even more excited. However, in the training arena, this should be seen as more than just a perk; it should be a requirement. Learners are gradually becoming more attuned to the role of nutrition in learning. How many of us have been raised on the importance of starting the day off with a good breakfast? As you consider feeding the brain with endless amounts of information, don't forget to gas it up with enough nutrition to keep it going.

Finally, believe it or not, the lesson on dealing with setting also applies to the on-line world. No, we are not suggesting that you have to go into everyone's home and make sure they are seated in an ergonomically correct chair. But we are saying that for Web learners, the computer screen is the physical classroom. For starters, it is crucial that you address readability. Whether that pertains to font size, color palette, or layout, it is essential that you make sure the material is not only easy to read, but easy to access. When the University of St. Thomas started to market their courses on-line and introduced a new Web site, they were smart in addressing this very issue. According to Shauna Dodge-Oakley, marketing manager for the University of St. Thomas Management Center, "When we recently launched our new Web site, it seemed easy to design a site for Xers, but we really had to keep the older generations of students in mind. We specifically talked to Boomers and Traditionalists to get their feedback. Obvious changes such as a larger font size were important, as well as more complex modifications like making it possible to accommodate different styles of Web surfing."

A final point in addressing an on-line setting is to acknowledge expectations around speed. Nothing is more annoying than waiting minutes for course content to download, only to be greeted by some corny cartoon or piece of clip art. As a society, we are still limited by bandwidth, and too often companies dive into the on-line world and design a program that is so robust, it operates like an elephant trying to squeeze through the phone wires. Our suggestion is to design for the lowest common denominator of end user or make sure users can fulfill the system requirements to take full advantage.

Style

Most Traditionalists and Baby Boomers reminiscing about their earlier days of training will describe sitting through lengthy lectures while staring at overheads on a screen where the image got wider and more distorted the higher up they looked. Things did pick up with the invention of the color copier, as suddenly color was added to the funnel-shaped image on the screen. If you were lucky, the training was enhanced with a bit of role-playing and perhaps even a filmstrip. By the late 1970s, classrooms were blessed with VCRs, which in some companies were embraced so wholeheartedly that the only role for the instructor was figuring out how to hit the play button and then pause when it was time for a discussion or a bathroom break. At last, the infamous PowerPoint and the Internet hit the scene and instructors could play a role once again, incorporating all the elements of slides, graphics, pictures, video, sound, and more. The options now are endless. However, that has created its own set of problems.

With so many different styles available to disseminate the content, it is hard to know which ones are not only the most effective, but preferred. This probably comes as no surprise, but many among the younger generations assume that if the overhead is being plugged in, then the content about to be shown is as old as the machine projecting it. At the same time, we hear the older generations complain that trainees are spending less time on content and more on watching a headline swipe, wipe, dissolve, or flash onto the screen, accompanied by an annoying *swoosh* or *ding*. Just because programs like PowerPoint provide the most flexibility doesn't mean they are the most effective. So what's the best approach? Sorry to say, there isn't an answer other than that the trainer shouldn't be making that decision, it should be the students' call. The problem is that this goes against the experience most of us had in school. We were always told to buck up and fit into the standard learning system; but companies today are finding that one size does not fit all when it comes to learning, and the more they can fit training to the needs and styles of the individuals involved, the stronger the bond they can build with employees.

The focus needs to shift away from the teacher and toward the students. We have found something as simple as a survey asking, "How do you learn best?" has not only opened the eyes of those conducting training, but has opened the minds of the students to be more interested and willing to participate.

As Bill Scheurer of the Carlson School of Management Executive Development Program put it, "How we present materials is changing significantly because we are recognizing differences in learning styles. Teachers have had to change the way they teach. The standard lecture component of twenty years ago has transitioned to a more active, participative, learning environment. Therefore, trainers have to be willing to find innovative ways of getting their material across."

To aid in this process, trendsetting training departments are identifying learning styles as a way to make the training experience more useful and the results more lasting.

Lifetouch National School Studio's training groups now regularly encompass four generations of learners. In a recent class, members ranged in age from nineteen to sixty-three. Training manager Becky Gowan commented, "Our biggest lesson has been that it's okay for individuals to learn the way they want to learn, so we're adapting by doing a lot of hands-on and self-discovery so the students can be in the driver's seat as to how they best assimilate information." As a result of their change in focus, their attendees first use an assessment tool provided by Carlson Learning to identify their own learning preferences so they can proceed with the rest of the training in the way that's best for them.

This customized learning approach also applies to the world of computers. You have to be ready to serve the geek *and* the meek. Since it's obvious that technology will be a growing presence in the classroom, it's important to establish participants' level of computer capability before training begins. Assessment tools are becoming invaluable guides for helping learners approach technology from their own comfort level. This way, techno-savvy learners can move forward rapidly, while learners with less technical knowledge can receive the basics they need to succeed without feeling inadequate. At Wilsons Leather, on-line computer courses include an assessment tool that analyzes how comfortable students are with specific applications and then recommends the course level that best matches their skills. Test results are private so no one needs to be embarrassed.

It is also important to assess which delivery approach works best for your content and your learners because there are a variety of styles to choose from. For example, you can offer self-study courses, where students can take a class any time and from any place that has a computer. Or you can offer instructor-led courses that are presented via the computer and are led by a live person. As you explore using the Web as a learning tool, don't assume it will replace the instructor. Many trainers we meet are threatened by computer-based or on-line training because they feel it will diminish their role. The point to realize is that the magic isn't in the bells and whistles, but in whoever is making music with them. To have ultimate success, computer-based training should always be followed up with discussions at the office or on-line chats. In other words, the computer is just a tool to make it easier to reach people, and the transformation occurs when the information is put to use.

So the one-size-fits-all training approach cannot work now that we have so many different personal learning styles in the classroom and so many vehicles available for presenting training. Understanding generational characteristics can help trainers tailor the learning process even more:

Traditionalists. Older participants tend to be polite, dutiful listeners, but they don't always volunteer. It is very important that trainers get them involved as early as possible to set the tone and comfort level for the class. The sooner you can get them talking, the more willing they will be to open up throughout the session. Also, this generation is probably the least interested in playing games. That is not to say they would rather sit and listen to a talking head the whole time, but it is important to differentiate between interaction and games. Older learners enjoy participating but don't like to be put in situations where they might look stupid.

Boomers. Boomers are particularly concerned about how they will look in front of Mr. Big. If senior executives are planning to sit in on training, they should be coached in advance on how to put trainees at ease so their presence doesn't become a hindrance. Also, when it comes to training, Boomers are a political breed that learned to watch their backs before they learned to watch TV. Therefore, trainers need to work hard at creating an environment where it's okay to disagree. This will require really tuning in to what sounds more like a "safe" response and less like an honest one.

Generation X. If any generation headed up the movement to ban the overhead, it was this one—the first to play with video games. While lectures are often critical for disseminating information, too much lecturing will only disintegrate it. This generation will appreciate and respond to a potpourri of exercises, activities, interactions, games, and more. The more interactive they are, the more involved they are and therefore the more effective the training. But be careful that the smorgasbord of approaches doesn't water down the overall content. It is so important to take the time to talk about how the learning fits in with the bigger picture and, if possible, explain what it will do for their careers.

Millennials. If you thought Generation Xers like to keep training moving right along, then double that for Millennials. Their multitasking skills and playful attitudes make it crucial that training push the speed-o-meter as well as the fun-o-meter on training to the limit. Bradley Richardson, founder of JobSmarts, a Dallas-based management consulting firm, reminds us that "on television, you have a change of scenery every twenty seconds." Trainers need to keep this in mind so that the newest students in class don't tune out. Having been raised with the notion that virtual is reality, Millennials respond well to any training that is experiential, especially if it allows them to come up with their own solutions.

Substance

You may have the ideal setting nailed down and even the appropriate style, but unless you have substance, you don't have training. No longer can course catalogs limit themselves to the same standard classes that are as deeply embedded in the corporate calendar as a major holiday. It's time to shake things up and use training as a way to give employees a real challenge. Wilsons Leather, for example, has responded to the growing demand for training by creating over five hundred on-line courses on topics ranging from communicating effectively to creating Excel spreadsheets. Employees may take as many classes as they want, on any topic they choose. Because they have so many different offerings, over 40 percent of the Wilsons corporate staff is currently enrolled, and participation occurs at all levels of the organization chart, from the distribution center to the executive team.

But figuring out what you are going to offer is only half of the challenge. Managers who feel pressured to help their employees develop are often handed a list of classes the company offers. Then they sit down with employees, and say, "Well, Bob, you know we believe in training around here, so why don't you look over some of these classes and I'll be happy to sign off on any one you choose." That's great if the manager is willing to give up the employee to a day of training, but not so great if she hasn't taken the time to explain how the learning goals actually connect to career goals. This does not come naturally to many managers who are dealing with more than one generation. Trainers need to arm managers with knowledge of how to tie learning goals to career goals, so that the training is not only more effective, but appreciated by their employees.

Becky Gowan from Lifetouch comments, "This is more critical with Xers and Millennials because their career paths are not as clear to them. There are so many opportunities for them, and they're growing so fast. As they tell us, 'Here's where I want to go,' we need to be able to identify the best way for us to get them there . . . especially if we want to keep them."

Tried-and-true training courses that have stood the test of time are fine. But the goal is to consider how to keep every generation challenged long after they've achieved competency in their current jobs. This will be especially critical as the economy continues to shift over time; companies will need to be even more adept at training employees on the skills they'll need *next,* not just the ones they lack *now.* The training you offer communicates a lot about what you value most and how aggressively you expect people to keep up. What might employees from each generation require to help them fill gaps in their learning and develop the skills they need? Finally, when designing training substance, be sure you are keeping an eye on the generations as they evolve. For an example, BridgeWorks developed five topics that might be particularly beneficial to Generation Xers as they move into management roles. You can do the same mental exercise for each of the generations in your workplace.

Managing upward. Increasingly, Generation Xers will find themselves managing Boomers and Traditionalists who are not just older, but in many cases more experienced than they are. Understanding what makes those generations tick will be an ace in the hole for new Xer managers and may help prevent frustration and resentment among their older direct reports.

Management 101. This may not seem like a new course, but we want to point out that many Gen Xers have been promoted so rapidly or have had so little mentoring that they never learned management basics along the way. They may find themselves suddenly faced with managing teams of other people and being poorly equipped for the job. Xers are interested in learning basic procedures and rules and regulations that govern how to manage. Since most Boomers and Traditionalists learned this just by being in the workforce longer before making it to management, they often don't think to include it in training.

Consensus building. For a generation that has prided itself on operating individually, these skills can seem foreign. But they must be learned if Xer employees are to succeed in the management ranks. Independent Xers realize that they will have to learn the ins and outs of team building, corporate politics, and getting things done through others if they hope to survive in complex organizational systems.

Business strategy. The economic boom of the 1990s created fast tracks for Xers in many industries. In some cases they've been so busy learning their jobs that they haven't had the time or the opportunity to learn the big picture. Even the top business schools report they can hardly keep students around long enough to graduate before they are hired away by companies corralling the top talent. Xers know that millions of Traditionalists and Boomers will be retiring over the next decade, and they worry whether Xers will have enough education and experience to take over the reins. They are looking for a strategic spin on their education to provide them with the business acumen they will need to lead.

Managing Millennials. As seventy-six million Millennials emerge into our workforce, guess who will handle the brunt of the responsibility for them? That's right, it's the Xers who are going to be on the front lines, whipping those Millennial recruits into shape. Just as the Boomers were shocked to find out that Xers didn't see things exactly the way they did and would have killed for a "heads-up," Gen Xers are in for their own set of surprises as they have to suddenly sort out a whole new generation of workers. The more Millennial research that can be put into the hands of

Gen X managers now, the sooner they'll figure out how to gain the upper hand.

If there is an area of training that we are not seeing enough of in the workplace yet, it is courses that promote a richer life as well as a richer career. Courses that involve life enrichment are something *all* the generations are crying out for. Smart companies are now offering everything from financial management to stress management, from adoption support to heart-healthy living. Both Boomers and Xers in our survey said that the number one type of training they desired was life skills training (stress management, balancing work/family, and so forth). The key is to consider the generations when planning these courses. One company made the mistake of offering extensive classes on retirement planning for those nearing sixty-five. Fine, but they didn't consider what they might offer for Generation Xers who may not be retiring but are interested in saving and investing now.

In a highly successful effort, Marriott Corporation introduced a training program called the Fatherhood Initiative, which offers two courses to professional dads—"Effective Fathering," and "Daddy's Stress—Daddy's Success"—as a way to ease the burden on traveling fathers. According to Marriott, these are two of the most highly sub-scribed training programs they've ever offered! For smart companies like Marriott, the goal is to help Boomers balance not only their own lives, but the lives of those who are dependent on them as well. Boomers are the generation most crunched for time, and even small timesaving advantages can be worth a lot to them. And with Gen Xers becoming parents, this course will undoubtedly appeal to them as well. Getting to know the concerns of your generations of work-ers will make it easier to plan courses that spread the educational riches around. The payoff will be happier, more balanced employees with a longer, more productive tenure with the company.

EXTRA CREDIT

Once you've mastered the three Ss—setting, style, and substance—here are a few things to embrace if you really want to get some extra credit.

Set ground rules early. Younger generations with shorter attention spans are more inclined to socialize, so setting ground rules will keep them under better control. Older generations tend to worry more about following the rules. The clearer you can be up front, the more you put all the generations at ease.

Explain your credentials. Many of the older generations assume that if you're up there in the first place, you must have some worth. But the younger generations are less likely to give authority figures instant credibility. Be willing to talk about your credentials and experience. Then be willing to prove it to Xers and Millennials who aren't necessarily impressed by your claims of fame. Getting testy is a sure way to lose your audience. Handling challenges with confidence, even humor, is the best way to defuse them.

Remember, every generation has a success story to tell. Members of any generation can show up for training worried that they'll be seen as too old to be useful or too young to know anything. You can level the playing field and build their confidence by inviting *everyone* to share success stories. It's a surefire way to help you earn the group's respect.

Remember that age can be misleading. As Generation Xers move into upper-level positions, they are showing up more often in management-level training classes. It used to be that when we addressed management conferences and asked how many Xers were in the room, you would have thought we'd asked how many knew how to speak Czech. No hands were in the air because no Xers were in the room. Now Xers have emerged into management ranks and are taking on huge responsibilities. Don't ever assume that younger participants are automatically the least experienced people in attendance. They may surprise you.

This also applies to the trainers themselves. At a recent corporate breakfast event where David had been retained as the keynote speaker, he spotted the company's chief executive making a beeline toward him through the crowd. Although they had never met, David assumed the man might have recognized him from the posters outside.

How classy, thought David, *he's coming over to greet me.*

The CEO approached briskly, pinned David with a look, and demanded, "Young man, those coffee urns are empty. Will you please take care of it?"

Here David had gotten up at five A.M. to be a courteous professional, only to find himself a victim of stereotyping as he was demoted from keynoter to waiter! He was obviously the youngest keynoter this gentleman had ever met. Just because a trainer might be the age of your daughter doesn't mean she can't teach you a thing or two.

Be who you are. It doesn't do any good to try to pretend you know what it's like to be seventeen or seventy if you're not that age. Even the hippest Boomer is bound to look ancient to a Millennial. And the most mature Xer is still going to look like a kid to a Traditionalist. The best thing you can do to connect with the generations is be who you are and show that you respect them for who they are.

IMPLEMENT "LIFETIME LEARNING"

The rapid rate of change in most American companies is assuring that training will continue to be vital for every generation of employees. The sad and costly part is that many make the assumption that when you get older you probably know enough already. Many Traditionalists and Boomers opt out of training because they are too "busy"; in some cases, they don't even get invited anymore.

Companies owe it to themselves and employees to understand the importance of lifetime learning. Retired Traditionalists are returning to school after they leave the workplace. In fact, the Bureau of the Census found that 28 percent of fifty-five-to-sixty-four-year-olds are in school now. Fifty-two percent of them cited "personal desire" as the reason; 54 percent cited "advance on the job." Why wait until they've left your organization to merge onto the learning fast track? Why not take advantage of that motivation and curiosity now, while they're still on the payroll?

Learning has proven to be a very affordable perk that actually can be used as a retention tool. We mentioned earlier that 58 percent of Xers agreed with the statement "Training opportunities play a role in my staying at my company." It's important to note that 45 percent of Boomers and *48 percent* of Traditionalists also agreed with the statement. While training is almost always seen as a necessary *management* tool, we see it as an important *retention* tool for all the generations, especially for Generation X. But we were surprised by how important it is for Traditionalists, a generation many of us think of as being so experienced that the need for training is not as strong as with the other generations. And by the way, when we asked the generations which type of training was most important to them, Traditionalists ranked computer training number one, above life skills, job skills, business skills, and management skills, in descending order. This says to us that Traditionalists' desire to stay current and become part of the "wired" world is a lot stronger than the other generations might think.

When Lawrence Perlman was the chairman and CEO of Ceridian, he was quoted as saying, "In a rapidly changing world, the key to continued employability and personal growth is the ability of each of us to reeducate ourselves continuously. Lifelong learning isn't just a nice-sounding phrase. It needs to be very much a part of who we are."

Imagine the same computer course offered a couple of years from now. Millennial Benjamin, now a supervisor in the IT department, is teaching the class. Xer Jenny has opted to learn the new software on-line from home, at her own lightning-fast pace. Baby Boomer Dave has chosen to work with one of his company's technical tutors over his lunch hour so he doesn't miss so many meetings. And Traditionalist Sheldon is taking an advanced-level course arranged through the local university system. Four different settings and styles; four generations of satisfied students.

18

"I ONCE DIAPERED SOMEBODY WHO'S NOW MY BOSS'S AGE"

Baby Boomer Ellen Abbot had been working for a large bank in Boston as the administrative assistant for three executives. Her job was to keep the executives organized and to make them more efficient. Ellen decided she needed a change of pace, and boy, did she find one. She went to work for a telecommunications company called Nobelcom.com. What was her *new* job? She was the assistant to the CEO, now in charge of keeping him organized and making him more efficient.

You're probably thinking, *Wait a minute. I thought you said she made a change?*

Oh, she did all right. At fifty-one years old, Ellen suddenly found herself working in a company where 90 percent of the workforce was under twenty-five and her CEO was the ripe old age of twenty-three.

We often talk about how Traditionalists and Baby Boomers manage—or at least try to manage—Generation Xers, but over the last few years, we've been finding ourselves getting e-mails and phone calls about what happens when it is the other way around. What about when the Xer is the boss managing the older generations?

Don't think for one minute that Xers see this as a big power trip or an opportunity to fight back. In fact, Xers can be downright uncomfortable with the situation. When BridgeWorks hired Deanna, a Traditionalist, David made it clear from day one that she was not to call him her boss. It makes him uncomfortable. To him the title insinuated too much power and authority. Ellen's boss, Thomas, felt the same way and instead prefers to be called the team leader. Why would David and Thomas feel uncomfortable? Not from anything Deanna or Ellen is doing, but because they know it is not the norm for someone younger to manage someone older.

Many members of the older generations would rather collect an unemployment check than be managed by someone younger. They loathe the thought of reporting to someone the age of their son or daughter, especially since they can't exactly give their boss a time-out.

But what about when you don't have a choice? And what does it take for people like Deanna and Ellen to feel the move was one of the best decisions they ever made?

X MARKS THE BOSS

How can someone with a lack of experience effectively manage a wealth of it? Here's what it takes:

Respect experience and incorporate it. It's an age-old rule, but if you want to get respect, you have to show it first. If there is one thing that demotivates an older employee with a younger boss, it is when the employee feels his or her experience isn't valued. Ellen Abbott's twenty-three-year-old boss is Thomas Knobel. As he put it, "The reason my company thrives is that I have people like Ellen. She has experience that I simply don't have, and I'd be foolish not to tap into that. I work hard at showing that I respect this experience." But what really makes the relationship work is that Thomas actually *incorporates* the experiences of his older workers. "By showing I am willing to act on their advice, what ends up happening is they respect me right back." Xers in management positions need to know it is okay to ask for help from older employees. Just because they may be a rung down from you on the ladder doesn't mean they don't have a leg up on you when it comes to know-how. You may not have to be older to be entrepreneurial or have vision and drive, but you do have to be older to have experience.

Don't worry about being talked down to . . . you're still the boss. When the other half of a Boomer's or Traditionalist's job is to go home every night and be a parent, it is hard not to come into the office every morning and treat an Xer boss like one of the kids. Xers often complain to us that they feel they are being talked down to. Sometimes they are right. As Ellen said, "My son is only two years younger than my team leader. I find myself wanting to treat him like my son. I have to work hard at avoiding this." While Xers' first instincts might be to avoid someone who makes them feel like a child, be gracious. Often the older generations have your best interests in mind and can save you from pitfalls you could only discover on your own the hard way.

Prove you can learn. Everyone knows you're going to make mistakes. If you're inexperienced, you're apt to make more of them. The problem isn't the mistakes, it's when Xer managers don't show they can learn from them. If you can admit your mistakes, you'll show your older employees that you have learned from stubbing your toe and they will gain confidence in you and be more willing to help you succeed.

Don't try too hard or try to know it all. The last thing you are going to be able to do is convince someone older than you that you can do it all or that you know it all. Yet too often that's our vision of the ideal manager. Bruce Tulgan, author of *Winning the Talent Wars,* advises Xers not to be so intent on using every project as your proving ground that you steamroll people. "Look around at those who are a little older and more experienced than you are, who are comfortable with change but have some of the wisdom you need. They'll be good people to make your allies and to learn from." Bruce also advises, "Don't be so disdainful of the way things have always been done that you throw out the baby with the bathwater. Those might be really good ways of doing things. People might be resisting your ideas not because they're afraid of change, but because that was tried ten years ago when you were in junior high school and it didn't work." At the same time, don't let Traditionalist and Boomer input get to the point where you find yourself losing your nerve. Your intuition is probably what got you where you are in the first place. Don't ever stop trusting it.

Don't assume their way is like yours. Throughout this book we have urged Traditionalists and Boomers to stop looking at the world of work only through their own glasses. They have had to change the way work gets done if they expect their Xer employees to do it at all. Well, now that many Xers find themselves in management positions, they have to remember that the same rule applies. Xer managers must adapt to their older employees' styles if they expect the work to get done. A classic example is feedback. Boomers and Traditionalists are used to a more formal setting when it comes to feedback. Xers must understand that just because they might be comfortable receiving feedback while standing at the urinal, their older employees will not share that comfort level. Thomas Knobel explains, "I had to learn that the older generations really like to have rules and procedures. In fact, they ask for it, whether it be fixed times for meetings or rules for who changes the toilet paper in the bathroom. My generation has always been a bit looser about these things. Yet I know what we would do if they didn't adapt to us. Therefore, it is my job to also adapt to them."

Use them. David has been known to take offense once in a while when Lynne gets taken more seriously in business settings because of their age difference. In one supremely aggravating incident, a Traditionalist client waited until Lynne showed up for a meeting a half hour late and handed her the check for BridgeWorks's services instead of giving it to David, who had been there all along. But rather than whine about it, David got over it. He turns these deep-seated generational perceptions to our advantage. When Schwab invited us to speak at an estate planning conference on bridging the financial generation gap, where the average age of conference participants was sixty-five, David knew that it would be better if Lynne returned the call. He's no dummy; the last person a bunch of older individuals trying to protect their wealth wants to hear from is someone the age of those who are hoping to get their hands on it. Often, experience sells. If an Xer manager is trying to push through a new initiative and needs a sign-off from the CEO, sometimes having the backing of an older employee might be just what it takes to get Mr. Big's name on the dotted line. Thomas found this to be the case at trade shows: "Here I was, the chief executive of the company, and potential customers who I knew would be signing on for deals worth millions of dollars would come into our booth; I realized that I had to stand back and let my vice president of sales, who is twice my age, be the front line. Once the potential client was comfortable with our offering, I could be introduced." Rather than be sour about it, Thomas was strategic and turned the generation gap into an advantage.

XERS MANAGING THE BOSS

For Generation Xers, it's all part of learning to be the boss. But there's another variable in the organizational equation. We hear a constant stream of complaints from Traditionalists and Boomers about Xers who don't have a clue how to manage those above them on the food chain—*their own bosses!* You can be moving steadily up through the organization, but if those above you don't appreciate your style or your attitude, they can make sure your rise comes to a pretty dramatic halt. And why shouldn't they? If you don't have a clue how to please those in charge, why should they trust your judgment about anything else? So for Xers on the way up, this section is about *managing upward.*

"Any more questions?" David asked the audience of 250 at a corporate retreat for an investment firm.

A Baby Boomer raised her hand. "Hi. I was wondering if you could give us some advice as to how we can get your generation to appreciate the importance of making the boss look good?"

David was stunned. "Ummm . . . could you repeat the question?" he asked.

"I was wondering if you could give us some advice as to how we can do a better job of making your generation appreciate the importance of making their boss look good?"

Sure enough . . . he had heard correctly.

You would have thought she'd asked him to strip. As far as David was concerned, this question was up there with the time someone from a hotel chain had asked him why all Xers liked to trash hotel rooms.

Inasmuch as the only other Xers in the room were the waiters clearing the plates, David was alone on this one. All he could say was, "Why?"

The Boomer responded, "Well, we all have learned that if you are willing and able to make your boss look good, then he or she will be all the more willing to help you along. The old 'You scratch my back and I'll scratch yours.' We Boomers had to do this to get ahead, and now that we find ourselves in management positions, we also find that your generation is not so willing to go along."

David was not just in the dark, he was totally blind. "Can you give me an example?" he asked, recovering.

"Every time I turn in a report, the Xers in my department demand that their names go on it as well."

David was thinking, *And the problem would be . . . ?* He stood there waiting for her to finish her example. But she was done. Luckily, so was the speech. David gave the best answer he could and exited stage left!

On the way to the airport, David called Lynne to tell her about the experience.

"Hey, you have got to hear what this Baby Boomer asked me," he said, still in disbelief.

"What?" Lynne asked.

"She asked me if I had any advice as to how to teach Xers how they can do a better job of making their boss look good."

"Wow. What a great question," Lynne responded.

"Very funny," David said.

She wasn't kidding.

To Lynne, the question made sense. When eighty million Baby Boomers hit the workplace, one of the unwritten rules was to study your Traditionalist bosses so you could help them get ahead. There's very little Baby Boomers don't know today about managing their Traditionalist bosses. It was good for management as it made the top rungs shine bright, and it was good for your career as you aspired to get there.

Since Xers' smaller demographic size makes them the largest beneficiary of the job insurance policy, it's no wonder the question from the audience seemed ludicrous to David. As he saw it, if an Xer put effort into the report, you better believe his name should be on the cover.

Kaboom! Another generational collision rears its ugly head.

We've talked so much about how Boomers and Traditionalists need to unlock the mysteries of Generation X, but how about the other way around? Just because Xers have a numerical advantage does not give them a pass to be excused from Boss Management 101. Managing the boss is older than Brutus and Cassius managing Caesar, and done wrong it can be as dangerous as Sonny and Fredo crossing the Godfather.

The problem is that to Xers it often looks like nothing more than trying to, as David puts it poetically, "kiss your boss's ass." But as even he would admit, Xers can learn some valuable skills for managing up that go way beyond just sucking up.

Show some loyalty. While Xers can appreciate being held accountable for their work, they need to appreciate what their bosses are being held accountable for—in particular, retention of employees. One Xer we know was dumbfounded that his boss was so angry when he told her he "might be leaving the company if I get this one job offer." He felt he was just being honest. She felt betrayed. It can ruin the relationship if your manager perpetually thinks you have one foot out the door. Going the extra mile to show you are willing to be around for a while can be very motivating and, in fact, free up the manager to focus on other issues. A Boomer account supervisor at a large advertising agency told us how she has to factor in the loyalty equation when she divvies up new clients. As she explained, "If I am skeptical as to whether or not someone is going to be around in six months, I have to take that into consideration. After all, our job is to service the client, and if they constantly have to get to know new people, they start to question the consistency of the work." Xers need to relax a bit. We're not suggesting they make a lifetime commitment to corporate America, but we are saying that trying to show your boss a little loyalty can give you a lot of leverage.

Have some patience. Traditionalist and Boomer managers often feel the Xers' morning cups of coffee are laced with speed. The Xers' constant need for information and results, coupled with their attitude that they could leave at any time, can be very unsettling to their managers. Xers should manage their bosses by differentiating between what they *need* and what they *want*. They should be willing to let go of the things that are "nice" to have and fight for the things they "must have." Then clarify the timeline and do not assume that every time frame is too short. If Xers want to challenge the boss, rather than just push for more or faster, which only implies you think the boss is incompetent, Xers first need to learn why things work the way they do. Often, Xers share with us that the best thing they did was to familiarize themselves with how the pieces fit into the greater whole. Asking this of the boss feels less like a confrontation and more like an education into the reasons for the pace of things. In some cases, this type of boss management might actually end up providing an opportunity to be collaborative. The end result? The pace gets bumped up, which was the ultimate goal in the first place.

Be a team player. One of the biggest complaints bosses share about their Generation X employees is their lack of enthusiasm to work on a team. On the flip side, however, many Xers tell us they have no problem with teams, but hate when it results in a slew of extra meetings and memos. Rather than roll your eyes at the potential pitfalls, put your concerns to work. You can help rather than hinder the team by offering input on how team members will check in or how decisions will get made. Ultimately, there is a lot to be gained by strengthening the team and its efficiency, not only for the work that needs to be done, but also for your career. Let's face it—many of those people are where your next job, promotion, or assignment might come from. It can't hurt to communicate that you are indeed a valuable team player.

As Miss Betty said on Romper Room, *"Do be a 'do' bee."* In other words, don't be a doomsayer. If you have valid objections, that's great. Every boss can appreciate the role of devil's advocate, as this can save people a lot of time and heartbreak by keeping them on the straight-and-narrow. But if you're habitually the one to say the sky is falling, then your days as Chicken Little may be numbered. Can-do Boomer bosses don't relate well to those who think negatively *all* the time. And the morale of the team can suffer if you can't find at least a few reasons why your boss's vision might actually work. At least be willing to give it a try.

Make your boss look good. The bottom line is that Boomers worry about how they look in front of their bosses. Xers might not care, but Boomers do. Many Xers think this is ridiculous; why should they knuckle under to some artificial rules? The same reason you use artificial sweetener—it makes the coffee taste better. Sometimes we need to stop overanalyzing and just do something because it works. This doesn't mean you have to be a "sellout" and drop by the chairman's office to boast about your boss. Making your boss look good can be as simple as letting him teach you something and then giving him some credit when you are able to put what you've learned into action. Sure, this is the boss's job, but it is amazing how far a little credit can go.

Each of these tips represents a small investment Generation Xers can make to reap big returns in intergenerational goodwill. They should enjoy these happy times while they last. It won't be long before Xers find themselves in the same position as their bosses, facing a generation of Millennials that will test and challenge them every step of the way. That's when they'll find themselves praying that the

Millennials will be just as good at learning how to "manage the boss" as they were.

The phone rings in our San Francisco office. Traditionalist Deanna and Boomer Lynne pick it up at the same time. On the other end of the line is our Xer, David, in a complete tizzy. "What is the deal with this new graphic designer? I knew she was young, but I assumed that a nineteen-year-old would at least listen! I have told her a million times not to call the client before letting me see the graphics for the presentation. I just got a phone call from our client saying they loved the designs, but I have no clue what they are talking about because I haven't seen them! I sounded like an idiot."

While David was expecting a little sympathy from Deanna and Lynne, all they could do was smile.

19

MINDING YOUR GENERATIONAL PS AND QS

It's 1980, and Bob, a Baby Boomer, has just landed his first client. He dictates formal thank-you notes for his secretary to type on letterhead. "Classy move, Bob," says his Traditionalist boss approvingly.

It's 1990, and Bob is selling up a storm. He still sends out thank-you notes on letterhead whenever he makes a sale, but the new boss isn't so happy. "You know, Bob," she explains, "we're trying to 'partner' with our customers to achieve 'customer intimacy.' Typed letters are too formal. Let's go with handwritten notes!"

It's 2000, and Bob is supersuccessful. At the end of the day, he labors over a pile of handwritten thank-you notes. His latest boss enters. "Bob, it's time for the handwritten notes to stop. When you use snail mail, it makes us look like something

> out of the Jurassic period. Our younger salespeople are using e-mail, and I like how they're going for 'instantaneous interactivity.' I think you should get with the program!"

What's a person to do? Etiquette in the workplace used to revolve around one set of standard behaviors any up-and-comers would make it their business to learn during the first few days on the job. Not sure how to pen an impressive business letter? Copy from the company's manual on standard letter formats. Unsure about hosting clients in the office? Sign up for the in-house charm school course and learn the company way.

In today's work environment, it feels as though everything's changed. What used to be reliable rules for behavior now seem like shaky guidelines. Not long ago, we interviewed Perrin Cunningham, coauthor of *Business Etiquette for Dummies* and founder of Denver-based Ethologie, Inc. As she pointed out, the problem isn't around these reliable rules, it's that there is now more than one version. As she explained, "The reason the etiquette issue has gotten so out of hand is that every generation brings its own set of rules and behaviors with them into the business world and nobody seems to know what's standard anymore."

THE GENERATIONAL CLASH OVER ETIQUETTE

Even though we're ostensibly playing the same game, every generation has its own playbook when it comes to proper etiquette. When multigenerations of workers are sitting around the same conference table, whose edition are you supposed to go by?

We assumed that since we were both experienced consultants and had done a lot of research into the ways different work cultures operate, we'd surely agree on the right edition and how etiquette should work for the generations.

Well, we were wrong. In fact, we couldn't get past a ten-minute conversation.

Lynne: I think we should begin by explaining to Xers and Millennials the importance of "respecting their elders." This is something Traditionalists and Boomers were raised to do, and it helped us get ahead in our careers. Etiquette behaviors like calling the boss "Mr. So-and-so" or using "sir" acknowledges someone's status and is a way of showing respect. Even my dog honors me by hanging back until I go through the door first. That's his way of acknowledging my place in the pecking order.

David: Okay . . . first of all, I'm not a dog. Second, the whole "respect your elders" thing puts the Xers and Millennials in a bad position. How are they supposed to challenge a Traditionalist in a meeting? How can they experience the power of teamwork and working on equal ground when they have to start each sentence with "Mr. So-and-so"?

This brief dialogue showed just how far apart the generations can be in their beliefs about etiquette. Clearly, two schools of thought prevail when it comes to etiquette conundrums. One says the younger generations owe it to the older ones to figure out the rules of the game and play by them. The other says it's the job of the older ones to bend because the younger ones don't know the rules. In ensuing dialogues, we figured out that both are bogus. We can't write a chapter with advice on how to behave at a meeting or suggestions on how to write a thank-you note because we would never want to imply that there is one way to be and that each generation might have to compromise its own style.

What the older generations believe in and establish as the norm at work will inevitably be questioned by younger generations as they try to establish their own identities. We've all experienced this on the home front with our parents' shock over our music, clothing, hairstyles, and language. The shock is an end in itself, but the pleasure of creating one's unique style and language is also a reward. It affirms a person's individuality. And there is something to be said for each generation inventing distinctive etiquette rules: what's wrong with differentiating? Haven't we all learned by now from the diversity movement that different isn't necessarily bad?

However, we can't be so entrenched in our own styles that we offend or confuse someone else. Expressing yourself is one thing, but making someone else feel bad is another. When we have up to four definitions as to what is appropriate and what is not, the potential to offend someone at work is quite high. In fact, our survey showed that a third of respondents from all generations agreed with the statement "Someone from another generation at work offends me with something they say or do often or a lot." As a result, intergenerational etiquette gaps are buzzing around the periphery of the business world and stinging the generations.

A Traditionalist manager hosted an expensive retirement dinner for his boss. At the dinner, he was appalled to note that not a single Xer had bothered to dress up. Although the office dress code was casual, he had assumed that anyone would know enough to dress up for this after-work occasion, if only as a sign of respect for their leader.

A Boomer manager was annoyed when she received an electronic thank-you card from an Xer employee whom she had spent a great deal of time with helping with a project. "I get a card that basically costs nothing and required no effort to send, after I gave so much," she exclaimed. "Am I supposed to be flattered by that?"

And it's not just the drones stinging the queen bee. Not every etiquette-challenged individual is under forty. The younger generations are often victims of etiquette mishaps as well.

A marketing team was presenting a new plan to the Traditionalist CEO. The youngest member on the team was a Generation Xer who was very excited about the innovative spin that was being put on their retail strategy. But during the entire meeting, the Traditionalist failed to make eye contact with her even once, almost as if she were invisible. By the time the meeting ended, she'd lost her enthusiasm for the project.

Often, it doesn't take much for a person to get stung. And sometimes the smallest bites can hurt the most. In our survey, participants said the biggest etiquette offenses occurred in three areas: phone manners, forms of address, and dress code, with Traditionalists lodging the most complaints. The sad thing about these etiquette challenges is that usually people's intentions are good. As Perrin Cunningham put it, "The whole point of etiquette in the first place is to make people feel more comfortable in their surroundings, not less."

So while this chapter won't ask that you memorize an established set of dos and don'ts, it does ask that all the generations adopt a "big picture" strategy. Everyone who shows up at work (in person or electronically) needs to be ready to stop, look, and listen to see where they can be more considerate of others. We have to be willing to "read" the etiquette rules of each generation to learn what makes others feel comfortable and respected.

Sound a little too much like a round of "Kumbaya"? Perhaps. But if nothing else, if everyone knows that the others are at least trying, we'll all feel a bit more accepting the next time we get stung.

THE NEW RULEBOOK ON ETIQUETTE

Flexibility is in. No question, when it comes to sloppy grammar or profanity, freedom of speech needs to be monitored. But there's a lot to be said for freedom of style, as long as the intent is mutual respect. Freedom of expression can be hard to manage, however. One Boomer hospital administrator was tearing her hair out over developing a company dress code.

"I was sitting in an executive committee meeting the other

day," she explained, "and the Traditionalist head of our foundation said he can't hire anyone if they aren't willing to wear a suit. Then the Xer head of our IT department jumps in and says he can't hire anyone if they *have* to wear a suit. We simply aren't going to be able to have one rigid standard for everyone."

Clearly, flexibility is the key. Employees of different generations thrive in cultures where they can be who they are and express themselves, where they are encouraged to learn from one another, not become another.

Give people the benefit of the doubt. Lots of etiquette mistakes happen because people don't know any better. The employee sending her boss an electronic thank-you card had her heart in the right place. She just didn't realize how much her boss valued the handwritten word. Too often, the generations just assume that someone from a different generation is playing by the same etiquette rules, and when one is broken, they are offended.

The problem is that many times the etiquette rules of one generation are being broken because the other generation didn't even know there *was* a rule. Assumptions lead to inadequate judgments and, ultimately, to missed opportunities. Riding up in the company elevator, one besuited CEO ran into a new temporary employee working in IT. The employee was sporting cutoffs and a ripped T-shirt. "Where are *you* going?" thundered the CEO. "Band practice?" Three weeks later, at the end of the project, the temporary employee was not hired on permanently. The CEO had expressed concern over the employee's ability to set the right example. This was a potentially heavy loss to the IT department, and it might have been avoided if the CEO hadn't made an assumption, but rather had taken the time to talk with the temporary employee about his expectations around dress code.

Don't forget the little things. Who would have thought that our most powerful advice would be the easiest of all? Interestingly, when we've interviewed employees about the biggest etiquette mistakes their bosses make, the number one pet peeve was failure to say hello and good-bye and to greet people by name! Something so simple, yet so hurtful if overlooked. This will be especially critical when the Millennials come to work. This generation has not only seen the power of treating everyone equally, but, even more devastating, has felt the pain of being forgotten. After the shooting at Santee High School in Southern California, counselors convened a large group of high school students to talk about the basic things everyone could do to make the school environment less hostile and alienating. The number one suggestion was that students should make eye contact and exchange greetings in the hallways, rather than treating one another as if they were invisible.

EVEN THE WORDS CAN GET IN THE WAY

Just when we thought our most powerful advice was easy to deploy, we learned that even greeting someone is burdened with etiquette turmoil! We received an e-mail from a Generation Xer who had taken part in a half-day workshop at a large insurance agency:

> *Dear Lynne and David,*
> *Since our workshop, I have made a conscious effort to go out of my way to greet my Boomer boss rather than avoid him. I thought this was helping until I was in a meeting with him today and he told me I should try to be more respectful when talking to people. I just don't get it.*

We were confused and contacted the boss to try to understand the situation better. When we asked about the problem, he immediately complained, "Where does this kid get off saying, 'Hey, man,' to me every morning? I am his boss, not his roommate!"

As small as some complaints might seem, they can loom large

to another person. If a collision around etiquette seems to be getting in the way, be big about it. Whether you think you're in the wrong or not, asking and adapting is a gracious way to remove relationship roadblocks and potentially make an ally for life.

A Traditionalist boss overhears his Millennial intern talking on the phone.

"Man, my boss is so fat!"

The Traditionalist is disgruntled. Sure, he put on a few pounds over the winter, but what is this punk doing insulting him?!

But what the intern actually said was that his boss was "phat"—the ultimate compliment coming from a Millennial! The boss wasn't a prime candidate for Jenny Craig; he was "Joe Cool." Or, to put it in Traditionalist terms, the intern thought his boss was, well, boss!

Members of every generation find the language gap looming larger than the *Hindenburg*. (Uh, if you were born after 1970, you may not know that Germany's *Hindenburg* was the largest hydrogen dirigible ever built for commercial transport and was used by the Nazis to spread propaganda. In 1937, it exploded in a huge fireball in the process of landing in New Jersey, while an audience looked on in horror.)

Language gaps happen all the time on a personal level, as in the case of the Boomer dad who was met with blank stares when he boasted to his son's friends how he used to "neck" in the back of the car in high school.

The loyal teen jumped in to rescue his floundering father. "Really, you guys," he insisted, "my dad was a *pimp!*"

"Well now, son, I'd hardly go that far," responded the blushing father. "Although I *was* certainly successful with the *chicks* in my day. . . ."

It used to be you could never be too rich or too thin. Nowadays, you can hardly be too phat or too pimp. Technology, popular culture, and the media are changing not just the *ways* we communicate, but the *words* we use. It's tough to know where the language is going next. And without a clear understanding, the etiquette equation only gets more complicated.

One Millennial Web designer received stellar feedback at his six-month review, only to be marked down for not using punctuation in his e-mails and for calling women "dude."

"What's wrong with 'dude'?" he wanted to know. "That means I like them!"

"Well, I don't think these young wom . . . girls . . . uh, ladies, will appreciate being likened to uh, dude, but the point is, these are your professional co-workers and need to be treated as such," came the manager's uncomfortable reply.

"Whatever."

The problem with each generation embracing its own lexicon is that it invariably leaves the others out. While on the surface slang may be one of the most prevalent offensives on the etiquette front, if you are willing to go deeper, you'll find that it can serve as the impetus to unite.

An Xer was complaining about her supervisor, and a Boomer jokingly responded, "Well, remember . . . you can't trust anyone over thirty."

The Xer couldn't relate to the famous Abbie Hoffman phrase and found the advice insulting. The gap between the two only got wider. Too bad they couldn't have talked about it, since this was a wonderful opportunity for the Boomer to share some insight into a typical Baby Boomer's formative years. The phrase really encapsulates the the beginning of the Boomers' desires to change traditional institutions, desires that are still being played out in the workplace today.

Asking the other generations what they mean by certain generational words and phrases creates an invitation to communicate. The meanings each generation assigns to words provide snapshots of the events and conditions that shaped a generation's values and attitudes, which are the foundation for how each of us behaves on the job and in our everyday lives.

But if you think etiquette is only about doing what it takes to fit in, more than likely you will end up standing out. Nothing is more annoying than a generational impostor. One thing is for sure: A Traditionalist walking into a break room full of Xers and awkwardly handing out high-fives and shouting, "What's shakin'?" is not going to bridge a generation gap. There's a huge difference between understanding another generation's language and speaking it.

"I LOVE YOU . . . DUDE"

As we said, we can't tell you what to wear or say or how to behave, but we can tell you that we hear over and over again from the generations that they feel the basic rules of etiquette are overlooked when it comes to communications among the generations.

Can you put hard-core numbers to this in terms of the effect on the bottom line? Probably not.

But we've all experienced the ways the generations dismiss each other . . . the glare of a Traditionalist toward a Generation Xer whose looks he or she disapproves of, or the roll of the eyes of a Millennial when a Boomer doesn't catch on to what is being said. How can you put a value on how much better a generation would feel when these etiquette mishaps are avoided?

Respecting each of the other generations' rule books on etiquette speaks volumes about who we are as individuals and as a society. Simple gestures like making eye contact, listening, acknowledging what people say, and acting on others' suggestions are all ways we show that we value and honor another generation at work. At the same time, disregarding these rules can be a painful and disruptive way to show we don't respect one another.

It's 2002, and Bob has left to start his own company. Guess what? For his traditional clients, he sends out correspondence on letterhead. For more casual customers, he sends handwritten notes. And for the techno-savvy types, he stays in touch via e-mail. After years of struggle, Bob's happy, the clients are happy, and etiquette doesn't seem like such a source of conflict anymore. Seems it never was about trends, it's about consideration.

20

CONNECTING OVER THE KUNG PAO

"Who's hungry for lunch?" asked the Traditionalist CEO. Everyone nodded, so he buzzed his secretary.

"Marilyn, we'd like to order some Chinese food—Oh, uhhh, well . . . I mean Asian? . . . Or is it Oriental?!"

By the time he hung up the phone, he was sputtering and those around the table were looking extremely uncomfortable. How sad that we have arrived at a point with political correctness where even ordering some kung pao and dumplings is fraught with potential pitfalls! In fact, in some cases, it's getting so bad that we are choosing to say nothing at all.

A multigenerational group of employees was meeting with the department's new director, who happened to be African American. As the employees were getting to know their new boss, the Generation Xer piped up: "I'm never sure what the right terminology is. Do you consider yourself black, African American, or a person of color?"

HOW THE GENERATIONS ARE REINVENTING DIVERSITY

The Traditionalists and Baby Boomers were stunned and uncomfortable. Their company had been mostly white up until then, and they didn't want to offend or embarrass a new co-worker. Worse, Traditionalists and Boomers felt they should know the answers to these intense questions or keep quiet. The fear of looking stupid or insensitive, coupled with concern over lawsuits, made talking about diversity something to avoid rather than learn from. Much to the Traditionalists' and Boomers' relief, the African American boss actually *thanked* the Xer and gave a thoughtful response. It seems it is time to reverse the military's "don't ask, don't tell" policy and consider one that says it's a good idea to "ask *and* tell."

It is not as though the concept of diversity in the workforce has exactly gone unnoticed. From sensitivity training to diversity committees, Traditionalists, Baby Boomers, and Generation Xers have all been forced to turn up the awareness meter when it comes to gender, race, religion, sexual orientation, the physically challenged, and more. However, as high as the meter is being turned up, it seems all of the generations have different readings, even different definitions as to what it means to be diverse in the first place.

DIVERSE DEFINITIONS OF DIVERSITY

If you had asked a Traditionalist engineer in the early 1950s about diversity in his workplace, he might have said, "Hey, we're diverse. We have two former army sergeants in our department, one navy commander, and even an air force pilot!" The diversity equation was as simple as black and white. Actually, it was even simpler: they *were* mostly all white, and they were 99.9 percent male.

As a result of the women's and civil rights movements, when the Baby Boomers entered the workforce, the definition of diversity was beginning to include equality for women and people of color.

Then came the Xers, and once again the definition was

expanded. Having watched thousands of hours of television and spent a lot of time in day care and after-school programs, Xers experienced more diversity than any of the previous generations. After all, Big Bird, Ernie, Bert, and the gang taught this generation not only how to count, but also how to do it in Spanish. As a result, during their formative years, the line between the sexes became gray and ethnicity fit neatly into four distinct categories—white, black, Asian, or Hispanic.

Although the generations have different definitions of diversity, one thing is for sure: Traditionalists, Baby Boomers, and Xers should all be proud of the way they have fought, struggled, and demanded that the definition evolve, especially at work. Even with all the progress that's been made over the years, what has been a gradual *evolution* in diversity is about to become a *revolution*. It's been brewing for several years now in our colleges, high schools, and trade schools as the seventy-six-million-member Millennial generation prepares to make its definition known to the workplace.

Millennials have spent thousands of hours watching every imaginable type of person sashay across their television screens. They have mixed with one another in day care, in classrooms, in after-school programs, and in enrichment sessions. Even their families have become more diverse than any we've seen in history.

Never mind what they see in their classrooms or on TV in their living rooms; stop and think whom they are meeting in chat rooms. This generation is traveling first class via the World Wide Web and is talking to citizens in all corners of the globe. Even Iran now boasts a thriving Internet café culture! Imagine what this does to the *Millennials'* definition of diversity.

A Generation X parent recently dropped off his Millennial daughter at preschool. There on the wall was a poster—"A to Z with Diversity." He stopped and stared at the variety of colorful letters, beginning with "A" for African American and ending with "Z" for Zimbabwean . . . not to mention Hungarian, Mongolian, Polish, Swedish, and more in between. Suddenly, the Xer felt ancient, knowing that in his day that poster would have looked like that packet of four crayons your kids get at a restaurant.

While Traditionalists, Boomers, and Xers have learned to truly accept diversity as a natural way of doing business, the problem is that Millennials are way beyond *accepting* diversity; this is a generation of future workers that will *expect* it.

Now we ask you, if the generations are getting tongue-tied even ordering lunch, how can we possibly be ready to relate to a new diversity-savvy generation of workers?

YOU MAY BE MORE DIVERSE THAN YOU THINK

David's alma mater, the University of Wisconsin, hit a major snag last September 2000 when they published their annual recruiting brochure. Let's face it, the upper Midwest is not exactly a hotbed of racial and ethnic minorities. However, the university still wanted the Millennials to know that their campus welcomes diversity. So what did they do? On the cover of the brochure they showed a bunch of people cheering at a football game. In the photo are girls, boys, white people, and one black student. Fine, so they thought—until the black student got wind of it and informed the media he had never even attended a football game. Seems the school had taken a stock crowd photo and airbrushed in an African American face to make the school look more diverse.

Millennials' BS-O-Meters were going off all over campus, and the university had to reprint 106,000 copies at a cost of $64,000—a professor's yearly salary, not to mention the embarrassment factor.

Yes, the Millennials will embrace race and ethnicity from A to Z, but they will also expand the definition. They will not limit diversity to just race, ethnicity, or even sex anymore, they will also define diversity by thinking style, educational background, geographic location, generation, avocation, lifestyle, sexual orientation, work experience, and more.

John Peterson is a white male, age fifty-three, who has been with his company for sixteen years. He started in sales and worked his way up to director. He then moved over to product design and helped engineer the company's most successful new product launch in history. From there he made the leap to director of all on-line activity.

How many would put a picture of John, a "typical" white male Boomer, on the cover of their diversity brochure? Well, probably not too many of us. But consider that in the eyes of a Millennial, John's wealth of diverse career experiences makes him a poster child. Why? Millennial workers know that they are likely to have as many as ten career changes in their lifetimes. They are going to approach the work world with the attitude that diversity of experience is highly desirable, and role models who demonstrate they've succeeded in a diverse and nontraditional career path might be just what the Millennial ordered.

DIVERSITY ISN'T SOMETHING YOU *OUGHT* TO HAVE; IT'S SOMETHING YOU *NEED* TO HAVE

One recent leading-edge Millennial who graduated in the high-tech field received seven job offers. She shocked her Boomer parents by forgoing the best financial offer to pursue the company that offered the most diverse work environment. "They're hiring designers from all over the world," she explained. "How can I pass up the chance to learn about international design and be exposed to all those cultures?"

Suddenly, diversity isn't just a smart way to do business, it's a competitive advantage in hiring and retaining the next generation.

Graduate schools are picking up on this as they begin to attract the next generation of students.

Jenny Lasser, our former intern and a brilliant UC Berkeley scholar, went on to attend the University of Michigan Business

School to get her MBA. In her first week of orientation in Ann Arbor, new arrivals were put into diverse groups consisting of different ages, genders, backgrounds, professional experiences, languages, and specialties and sent on a day-long scavenger hunt and puzzle-solving mission. "It was fantastic!" reported a glowing Jenny. "All these different people, all that knowledge, all those perspectives, turned loose to solve complex problems. It made me fall in love with my school from day one. I knew I was going to have the most incredible and diverse learning experience."

Compare that to the old Ivy League experience of the traditional junior executive—a cluster of white guys in matching school ties gathering at the local watering hole to discuss which fraternity to pledge. How things have changed.

"In the interest of cultural diversity, we've hired Jason, here, who owns a number of hip-hop CDs."

The Jenny Lassers of the world aren't going to be willing to cast off the diversity of experience they've come to value to enter organizations where everyone appears stamped from the same mold. And just think how much richer we are for it. Unlike our forebears, who, in trying to create a unified new nation, saw "differentness" as a drawback, the next generation sees it as an asset.

Smart companies are catching on and working to expand their racial and ethnic diversity, while at the same time redefining diversity to include other factors. The smartest companies are already incorporating this new emphasis on diversity into recruiting campaigns.

Boeing hit a home run with this message focusing on the eclecticism of the individual:

> "There is a person inside me who wants to watch old movies, to sing on-key, to meet my neighbors, to publish something, to take karate, to design a plane, to read the trade pubs, to row on a team."
> We realize our strength comes from the individuals with different backgrounds, different experiences, and different ways of thinking. If you're ready to work for a company that embraces those differences, we urge you to apply at Boeing.

While not all companies embrace diversity for altruistic reasons, many, like Boeing, know it's good for business. In a tight labor market, taking a more diversity-friendly approach can attract new pools of talent. And whether a company is a traditional manufacturer like Boeing, retooling to compete in a new global economy, or a "New Economy" company struggling to get its foot in the door, diversity is a survival tool. Ask Candace Carpenter, chairman and founder of iVillage.com. When asked in *Fast Company*, "What's one tough lesson you learned about doing business on the Internet?" she responded:

"It's important to have a diverse team. I'm not talking about just gender or race. I mean diversity of skills and temperament. It's hard to get your team composition right. At the beginning, you need more diversity than you can imagine. When we started iVillage, we didn't have enough technical people or really anal analytical people. Instead, we had a surplus of people who could sell our story to customers and advertisers—which is great. But you still need people to build the subways. That lack of diversity slowed us down in the beginning."

If we are going to make diversity a survival tool, then we must get realistic and ask ourselves what the goal of diversity is in the first place.

MELTING POT, SHMELTING POT

Previous generations were so focused on melting together to build one new nation that the concept of a melting pot was the be-all and end-all. Margaret Johnson was born in 1903 into a small midwestern town filled with immigrants. She shared with us recollections of her impatience with the way they spoke. "We just kept on correcting them until they spoke acceptably," she explained. "They knew their bad English was holding them back, and they were ashamed and knew they wouldn't fit in until they learned it." The offending immigrant group? The Swedes! As she told us, they had to have consistency in order to build a country. The goal was clear—fit in and become part of this nation.

However, the melting pot dish today doesn't sound as tasty to a generation that, according to the American Federation of Teachers, is growing up in schools where over seventy different languages are spoken daily. So there is a new recipe in town, and it's called diversity stew. What is it like? It contains a variety of ingredients living and working together, but . . . no one has to melt.

Shelving the melting pot idea is the ultimate goal. Rather than working toward corporate cultures where everyone is becoming more similar, it's time to search out the corners of the office for people who bring different perspectives to the table.

General Mills gets it. The cover of their diversity brochure pictures a flock of sheep over a caption that reads: "What if we were all the same? Would we be a stronger company?" The brochure goes on to state: "The differences among us—our different views, backgrounds, and experiences—are what make us strong. We need to recognize, understand, value, and leverage that diversity."

In many aspects of the world of work, the older generations have shown the way. Succeeding generations have stepped into their predecessors' shoes, even while making their own paths. But on the topic of diversity, the younger generations are navigating toward new destinations at lightning speed, and they are not looking back.

Are we ready to join them?

WHERE DO WE GO FROM HERE?

21

ARE WE THERE YET?

Our speech is over, and we're picking up assorted notes, cards, and handouts. We've already talked to a few dozen people. One came up to tell us she hates her boss, but she's going to give it another try. An Xer paused to let us know he hadn't wanted to come but had been required to by his company, and he'd actually learned something about why his generation was different, and that made him feel good. Another has come over to explain that Barbie shouldn't be considered a Millennial icon when she just turned forty and really belongs to the Boomers. A nice man with a lovely French accent gave us several compliments we didn't understand. Three people stopped by to tell us they all work in the same office, they are from three different generations, and they love working together. Two told us generational jokes, only one of which was printable. We're pooped.

Then one or the other of us hears someone clear his throat softly. We turn around and there stands a person who has waited for the room to empty out before coming up to talk to us.

THE FUTURE OF THE GENERATIONS AT WORK

In a soft, almost embarrassed voice, he says, "Uh . . . I just wanted to say thank you for your presentation. After hearing what you had to say about the generations, I think I finally understand my son."

The three of us are so somber, you would think we were attending confession at church. If only we could convince him he is not alone. If there is one thing we have learned, it is that generation gaps exist far beyond our cubicles or conference rooms. They can be poignant, painfully funny, or just plain painful.

Over a long weekend, several generations of a family found themselves discussing seventeen-year-old Hannah's decision to quit her job. It seems she and her girlfriend couldn't get time off from waitressing to attend a party, so they both resigned!

"What's the big deal?" Hannah asked casually. "There are so many jobs out there, I could be waitressing again by Monday if I wanted to."

Three generations of relatives rolled their eyes.

"You should never quit until you know where you're going next," asserted her Generation X cousin, Michael. "The work world is a scary place; you should always have a safety net."

Her Baby Boomer aunt, Carol, was disgusted. "Think how that's going to look on your résumé! You should stay at one job a decent length of time—you want a good employment record so you are always hirable."

"What's wrong with your work ethic?" demanded Uncle Bob, a Traditionalist. "You left your employer high and dry, and that stinks. What kinds of values do you have, anyway?"

Hannah may have a war on her hands, but we're not worried about her. See, looking over her shoulder are three generations who are involved in her life, who care about her, and who aren't about to let her screw up.

Whether they are our grandparents, parents, aunts, uncles, sons, daughters, nephews, nieces, cousins, co-workers, or friends, we are surrounded by the generations every day. And sometimes their per-

spectives annoy, offend, or disappoint us. Whether it's the child who
quits a job instead of sticking with it or the grandparent who
refuses to come to the wedding because the bride is marrying outside her faith, each generation believes the world should operate a
certain way.

The problem is that too many family trees are split apart or
friendship bonds are broken because we are stuck in the mind-set
that the phrase *in my day* means it's "the only way." Instead, we have
to let *in my day* become a way to connect with one another. Expos-
ing ourselves to generational diversity can offer wonderful insight
into how the world once was, how it is today, and where we all
might be in the future.

What worries us is that geographic dispersion is segregating the
generations more than ever before. Young people move to the urban
areas where there's more action, families with kids move to suburbs
where they can be with other families, child-free households relocate to trendier spots where there are no Big Wheels blocking the
driveway, and the older generations with the most wisdom and
experience to share are migrating to "retirement" communities,
usually in sunny southern climates. The Census Bureau estimates
that by 2010, over half of elderly Americans will reside in just ten
U.S. states. Increasingly, the communities in which we live provide
less and less of a rich mix of generations. Florida, for example, ranks
in last place of all the states for the number of citizens under twenty-
five, but in first place for the number sixty-five and over. Families are
more mobile than ever before, and suddenly parents, children,
grandparents, and grandchildren are hundreds of miles apart. In most
locations, we are losing our easy access to the diversity of perspective
and the wisdom we derive from other generations. "Reach out and
touch someone" may sound good, but connecting over telephone
and modem lines just isn't the same.

Sue Shellenbarger of *The Wall Street Journal* recently wrote a
stirring column about a small town called Condon, Oregon, that has
produced three Nobel Prize winners. In it she discusses how such a

tiny, nondescript place could produce individuals of such far-reaching intellect and perception. One of the primary factors she names is the sense of generational connectedness that this town has never lost.

"More than most small towns, Condon has preserved much of what made it a crucible of ingenuity. Intergenerational ties remain strong. When its top-ranked high-school basketball team hits the road, some Main Street stores close so adults can go to the game . . . teenagers engage adults here, greeting friends' parents with enthusiasm.

"Those of us raising children elsewhere might ponder . . . we can reinvest in community, taking time for scouting, sports and other groups that foster adult bonds with children. We can continue to reintegrate work and home life, reversing the commuter exodus that empties many neighborhoods at midday. And we can simply take time—time to slow down and form bonds with children, including all the children around us."

We think that goes for all ages. From technology to geography, forces will only continue to obstruct our ability to bask in and learn from generational diversity. Therefore, we have to cherish the generational bonds we already have and work harder to strengthen the ones at our fingertips. If we can make a lifetime habit of finding out what makes the generations tick, then we can spread that insight into all of our relationships—with loved ones, with clients and customers, with co-workers.

Management guru Tom Peters was quoted in *USA Today* as saying, "If your top management isn't spending at least a half day a month sitting down with someone twenty-five years old or younger, then they are blowing it!"

We agree with all our hearts. But we also believe it goes both ways.

Any Xer or Millennial who isn't sitting down on a regular basis with a Boomer or a Traditionalist is also blowing it. Why? Because on both the business and personal levels, failing to sit down together and learn from one another carries a heavy cost.

We hope this book has motivated you to get out from behind your desk and get to know the generations of employees in your workplace. Over two-thirds of our survey respondents of all ages told us they wished they had had more opportunities to be mentored in their careers. It's never too late to reach out and find that mentor you've been missing. Or to become one.

Bridging the generation gaps at work can provide huge payoffs when it comes to recruiting, retaining, managing, and motivating others. The next time you bump into someone from another generation whom you don't relate to, stop and remember that no one is right or wrong . . . we're just different. Only then will you truly know what to do *when generations collide.*

BIBLIOGRAPHY

Adler, Caryle. "Wal-Mart Pirates . . . OSHA Goes Ergo . . . A Wedding
Gift to Hold On To." *Fortune,* May 15, 2000.

American Demographics, June 1999. "Who's in the Home?"

Ansberry, Clare. "The Gray Team." *Wall Street Journal,* February 5, 2001.

Breslau, Karen. "Snooping Around the Valley." *Newsweek,* April 10, 2000.

Cunningham, Perrin, and Sue Fox. *Business Etiquette for Dummies.* Foster
City, Calif.: IDG Books Worldwide, 2001.

Del Webb Corporation. "Boomer-Zoomer Poll Nixes New Romance
After Retirement; Valentines Will Ignite Flame of Old
Relationships." www.delwebb.com, February 13, 2001.

Hager, George. "Sawmill Illustrates the Buzz About Productivity." *USA
Today,* March 21, 2000.

Holmes, Charles W. "Show Them More than Money." *San Francisco
Chronicle,* June 5, 2000.

Howe, Neil, and William Strauss. *Millennials Rising: The Next Great
Generation.* New York: Vantage Books, 2000.

JobTRAK.com. "79% of College Students Find the Quality of an
Employer's Website Important in Deciding Whether or Not to
Apply for a Job." www.jobtrak.com., June 12, 2000.

Kantrowitz, Barbara, and Pat Wingert. "Teachers Wanted." *Newsweek,*
October 2, 2000.

Lublin, Joann S. "In the Race to Fill Job Vacancies, Speed Demons Win."
Wall Street Journal, July 13, 1999.

Lundin, Stephen C., and Lynne C. Lancaster. "The Importance of
Followership." *Futurist,* May–June 1990.

Merrifield, Diane. "Could You Please Pass the Trillions?" *Bank Marketing,* January 1999.

Mills, D. Quinn. *e-Leadership: Guiding Your Business to Success in the New Economy.* Paramus, N.J.: Prentice-Hall Press, 2001.

Perlman, Lawrence. "View from the Top on Lifelong Learning." *Minneapolis Star Tribune,* July 5, 1999.

Pink, Daniel H. *Free Agent Nation: How America's New Independent Workers Are Transforming the Way We Live.* New York: Warner Books, 2001 (advance reading copy).

Ritchie, Karen. *Marketing to the Generations.* New York: Lexington Books, 1995.

Salopek, Jennifer J. "The Young and the Rest of Us." *Training & Development,* February 2000.

Sheehy, Gail. *New Passages: Mapping Your Life Across Time.* New York: Random House, 1995.

Shellenbarger, Sue. "Employees Who Care for Elders Find Help in Special Collaboration." *Wall Street Journal,* October 18, 2000.

Smith, J. Walker, and Ann Clurman. *Rocking the Ages.* New York: HarperBusiness, 1997.

Strauss, William, and Neil Howe. *Generations: The History of America's Future, 1584 to 2069.* New York: William Morrow & Co., 1991.

Tellijohn, Andrew. "Golden Years." *City Business,* Minneapolis, Minn., August 4, 2000.

Tulgan, Bruce. *Winning the Talent Wars.* New York: W. W. Norton & Company, Inc., 2001.

———. *Managing Generation X.* Santa Monica, Calif.: Merritt Publishing, 1995.

Watson Wyatt Worldwide. "Playing to Win: Strategic Rewards in the War for Talent." Fifth Annual Survey Report, 2000/2001.

Zemke, Ron, Claire Raines, and Bob Filipczak. *Generations at Work . . . Managing the Clash of Veterans, Boomers, Xers, and Nexters in Your Workplace.* New York: AMACOM, 2000.

INDEX